SUBVERTED

Sue Ellen Browder

SUBVERTED

How I Helped the Sexual Revolution
Hijack the Women's Movement

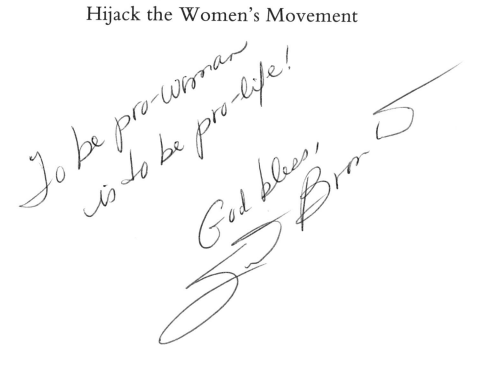

To be pro-woman
is to be pro-life!

God bless,
Sue Ellen Browder

IGNATIUS PRESS   SAN FRANCISCO

Cover image from iStockPhoto.com

Cover design by John Herreid

© 2015 by Ignatius Press, San Francisco
All rights reserved
ISBN 978-1-58617-796-6
Library of Congress Control Number 2014959912
Printed in the United States of America ∞

The chains that bind [a woman] in her trap are chains in her own mind and spirit. They are chains made up of mistaken ideas and misinterpreted facts, of incomplete truths and unreal choices.

—Betty Friedan, *The Feminine Mystique*

CONTENTS

Chapter 1

The Inside Witness

As journalists, our job is to help reshape the way one group of people thinks about another. We must dig deeper than stereotypes. . . . Sometimes we do that through immersion journalism. Sometimes we have to do it by writing about ourselves.[1]

—DeNeen L. Brown,
feature writer for the *Washington Post*,
from the book *Telling True Stories*

I can give you no justification for what I did in my former life. I will only say this in my weak defense: I was a young woman searching for truth, freedom, and meaning in the world, but I had no clue where to find them. I grew up as a small-town Iowa girl and passionately desired to escape from the prison of small-mindedness I perceived around me. My dad owned a small family shoe store, where my stay-at-home mom worked part-time. I was baptized at age nine, and we went to church every Sunday. Once a year or so, parishioners at my little white Congregational Church passed around tiny thimble-sized glasses of grape juice for what was called "communion." I didn't know what that was, and nobody told me. If New Hampton (population 3,456) had its virtues, and I'm sure it did, I couldn't see them. Something or Someone bigger was calling to my heart, but I had no idea who or what it might be.

On the magazine stands at our local Rexall Drug were promises of freedom, true love, and adventure. All the models in the glossy women's magazines were alluringly beautiful. All the big-time authors whose bylines glittered from those magazine pages spent their days (or so I imagined) basking on the Riviera, sipping champagne, and signing autographs. Surely, those writers had everything the big, wide world could possibly offer, everything my little Podunk town lacked.

And thus it was that after graduating from the University of Missouri School of Journalism, I found myself one day in New York City in the Argonaut Building at 224 West 57th Street on the eighth floor in a small office, seated across a large wooden desk from Roberta ("Bobbie") Ashley, articles editor of *Cosmopolitan* magazine. In the late 1960s and early 1970s, *Cosmopolitan* was the undisputed reigning queen of women's magazines—the hottest women's magazine in the nation.

I'd previously been offered a job on a little upstart journal called *On the Sound*, a magazine about life on Long Island Sound being launched by a handful of editors who'd lost their jobs when *Life* magazine's international edition folded. *Life* was a major journalistic enterprise: *Life* editors did what reporters considered "real" journalism. But, no, it was fluff-headed, man-crazy *Cosmopolitan* I longed to work for. *Cosmo* insiders seemed to know things I didn't know, secrets that made them successful in the world. My mind burned to know what they knew. For a small-town Iowa girl, *Cosmo*'s big-time glamour, success, and prestige were intoxicating.

The articles-department office of *Cosmopolitan* was small and cramped, with disorderly piles of manuscripts tossed helter-skelter everywhere. A scent of expensive floral perfume lingered in the air, as if Sophia Loren had left just seconds before I arrived.

Cosmo's articles editor appeared to be in her midthirties. She had big teeth, wore little makeup, and had her nondescript light-brown hair caught up in an unstylish ponytail. She seemed determined to impress upon me that *Cosmopolitan*'s editor-in-chief Helen Gurley Brown in person was not at all like the feather-brained sexpot I'd seen batting her custom-cut false eyelashes on Johnny Carson's *Tonight Show*. Helen was a shrewd businesswoman and a demanding boss who sometimes worked at the office until midnight.

"Why do you want this job?" Bobbie asked, peering keenly at me over her highly disorganized desk.

"Because I want to be sitting one day where you are," I replied. "I want to be you."

It was a cheeky answer, but Bobbie liked it. Out of eighteen applicants, I won the job. The position paid only $105 a week. But the pitifully low pay, even for those days, mattered not a twit to me. In my mind, the job—assistant to the articles editor of *Cosmopolitan!*—was a small-town girl's dream come true.

Only later would I realize how dark the dream had become. Eventually, it would lead to a cacophony of mixed, confused messages in our culture about women, work, sex, marriage, and relationships—errors that have divided our nation and continue to haunt us to this day. It would lead me to make disastrous decisions.

But when I began my journalism career in New York City in 1970, it seemed like magic.

This book was written partly in answer to requests that I tell my story about how it was in the early days of the sexual revolution when I began working at *Cosmo*. Eyewitness history, flawed as it may be, is frequently more useful and accurate than attempts to reconstruct history through secondary sources once all those who witnessed the events are long dead.*

From 1970 on, I was right there in the heart of the sexual revolution in New York City, working first on staff at *Cosmopolitan* and for the next twenty-four years as a freelance writer for the magazine, where I told lie upon lie to sell the casual-sex lifestyle to millions of single, working women. I was not one of the mighty at *Cosmo*. I was not even one of Helen Gurley Brown's favorite writers. I was just one of the ordinary foot soldiers.

Sitting daily at my little navy-blue desk in *Cosmo*'s articles department, I witnessed what seemed to me then to be a small, insignificant fact but which now, in hindsight, has assumed monumental importance. My small observation was this: In the beginning, the women's movement and the sexual revolution were *distinctly separate* cultural phenomena.

Helen Gurley Brown, author of *Sex and the Single Girl*, taught that a single girl in the big city could climb the corporate ladder and have lots of orgasms along the way by working hard and granting sexual favors to married and unmarried men—as long as she didn't have

---

*For those parts of the story I did not witness firsthand, I have, as much as possible, tracked down accounts from people who did witness events as they unfolded.

children. Feminist Betty Friedan, whose goal was to achieve equal opportunity for women in education and the workplace, understandably called *Cosmo* "quite obscene and quite horrible."[2]

So how did the women's movement (which purportedly fought for women to be free to express their full personhood) and the sexual revolution (which reduced women to ambitious sex objects) become so intertwined in the popular mind that many young women today sincerely believe that to be "liberated" is to go to college, pursue a career, and be as sexually active as possible with no strings attached? How did these two separate revolutions get blended into one in a way that has led to so much pain for women and so much division within the churches and our society?

The short answer, the part I didn't know during those sexual-revolution heydays when I was working at *Cosmo*, is that the women's movement and the sexual revolution secretly joined forces behind the scenes largely due to the influence of one man I had never even heard of—a master propagandist skilled in the manipulation of public opinion named Larry Lader. A founder of the National Association for the Repeal of Abortion Laws (later called the National Abortion Rights Action League and still later NARAL Pro-Choice America), Lader worked for years on fellow magazine writer Betty Friedan until he finally persuaded her to insert the sexual revolution's most controversial demand—abortion—into the National Organization for Women's political platform. Lader's misleading propaganda not only seduced Friedan and grafted abortion onto the women's movement but five years later became a legal pillar for the *Roe v. Wade* decision. That's right. The 1960s' women's movement was hijacked largely due to the tireless efforts of one man, whose greatest passion was to make abortion legal.

As Margaret Sanger's biographer and a fervent population planner, Lader himself said that the idea of legalizing abortion "struck at the tenets of the Roman Catholic Church and fundamentalist faiths, but even more important, at the whole system of sexual morality to which the middle class gave lip service."[3] He maintained that "to tamper with [abortion] meant that the whole system [of sexual morality] could come tumbling down"[4]—which is, of course, precisely what happened. In Chapter 3, I confess some of the many dark lies we told at *Cosmo* to soft sell the sexual revolution to single women. Chapter 4 unveils the black propaganda Lader manufactured to sell abortion under the label of "reproductive rights" to Friedan and other feminists, to me, to the American public, and ultimately to the U.S. Supreme Court.

Which brings us to the second reason this book was written. Although for many years I betrayed my calling, I am by nature and training an investigative journalist, one of those rare birds of prey known as "the propagandist's natural enemy."[5] The investigative reporter's job is to enter into those places of political or social unrest and confusion in order to pierce the deceptions and reveal the complete truth, so the public will not be misled by propaganda that dulls the mind, misdirects public policy, and harms people. If there's any aspect of modern society that needs to be scrutinized with a keen eye for partial truths and error, it's the women's movement: why what became known as "feminism" began with such high hopes in the '60s and how it became twisted into the wretched caricature of itself it has become today. Here I was, a smart cookie, an eyewitness to many behind-the-scenes events. I was there. Yet at the same time I was deceived by and blind to other events that would lead me into error and would one day cause me to suffer the greatest sorrow of my life.

It's important to understand the modern women's movement as it was packaged and distributed visibly by my colleagues in the media, but it's perhaps even more important for you to know how it was packaged behind the scenes. Because it is those often undetected individuals like Lader—people whom journalist Vance Packard called "the hidden persuaders"—who are now directing public opinion and shaping the world in which we all live.

The 1960s' women's movement, to the extent that it attempted to break the chains that prevented women from enjoying the same professional and educational opportunities as men, grew out of a genuine cry for justice. All persons, male or female, certainly do deserve to be treated with equal dignity and respect at home, at work, in school, and under the law.

The 1960s' sexual revolution was an altogether different matter. As it was conceived on the foundation of Alfred C. Kinsey's limited science[6] and promoted by lifestyle marketers like *Playboy*'s Hugh Hefner and *Cosmopolitan*'s Helen Gurley Brown, the sex revolution was based largely on "half truth, limited truth, and truth out of context."[7]

That is to say, the sex revolution was fabricated largely from propaganda. I know because I was one of the propagandists who helped sell single women on the notion that sex outside of marriage would set them free.

It is commonplace in our culture today for people to use the term *propaganda* for any opinion they happen to dislike. But the widespread misuse of this word only serves to make propaganda's menacing powers more hidden and effective. As a form of withheld truth, propaganda can be 90 percent true. It's the deceptive 10 percent that gets you. In his introduction to Jacques Ellul's classic work *Propaganda: The Formation of Men's Attitudes*, Rand Corporation political scientist Konrad Kellen explains:

> Most people are easy prey for propaganda ... because of their firm but entirely erroneous conviction that it is composed only of lies and "tall stories" and that, conversely, what is true cannot be propaganda. But modern propaganda has long disdained the ridiculous lies of past and outmoded forms of propaganda. It operates instead with many different kinds of truth—half truth, limited truth, truth out of context. Even Goebbels always insisted that Wehrmacht communiqués be as accurate as possible.[8]

Propaganda—withheld truth—cuts off democratic discourse, blocks genuine dialogue, and keeps the public from participating in reality. By the time the propagandist's deceptions are exposed for the twisted truths that they are, untold and irreversible damage has often been done to the external order of human existence. To decide which ideas from the women's movement need to be uprooted and which more tenderly cultivated, we must reexamine contemporary claims to see how they were implanted in the soil of history.

The 1960s' women's movement's demands—particularly its contraception and abortion doctrines—have led to so many vicious political and cultural battles between the right and the left that we are all weary of the war. To end this civil war between brothers and sisters and to begin anew, we must start at the beginning. The sexual revolution, with its fervent insistence upon contraception and abortion as the paths to women's freedom, was not part of the original women's movement. We must retrace our steps to see where we left the path of freedom and became enslaved to illusions.

Because what's become popularly known as "feminism" has led to so much upheaval in our society, some people want to reject the women's movement entirely. They long to return to the "good old days" when women stayed home, took sole responsibility for bringing up the children, earned no money of their own, and had little say in politics, business, arts, or the rest of the world. From a distance, the 1950s may sound idyllic and simple. But women and the world have changed far too much for us to go back again, and in any case, we must not romanticize the past. As any reasoning woman who was there will tell you, the "good old days" weren't so hot.

No, we can't go back again. But there's no moving forward, either, until we do the hard work of addressing the difficult questions my generation asked in the 1960s and '70s but failed to answer. How can a woman find her true identity? What is the connection between a woman's work and her life? What will promote her genuine freedom and happiness? What does a woman's *personhood* mean? Unless we embrace the steady, diligent work required to answer such fundamental questions, we will never be able to answer the questions so many thoughtful women are now asking: How can a modern woman successfully balance children, marriage, and work? And how can she navigate a safe course across the roiling sea of cultural confusion my generation has left in its wake?

Many people who reject the tenets of radical feminism erroneously lump Betty Friedan in with the anti-man, anti-marriage, anti-motherhood crowd. I have no great interest in defending Betty Friedan, but in all truth that's not where she belongs. As the widely proclaimed "mother of the women's movement," Betty was an ardent defender of working mothers. What's more, she fought relentlessly against what she called "the bra-burning, anti-man, politics of orgasm school" of feminism and warned younger women not to be seduced by the sex radicals' divisive rhetoric.[9] Political liberal that she was, Betty was in some ways surprisingly conservative. Since few women and fewer men under age sixty have read *The Feminine Mystique*, let me begin my reflection on the history of the women's movement and how it changed all of our lives by reviewing what Betty actually said.

Chapter 2

The Problem That Had No Name

Feminism is diverse and contentious, but, in its current manifestation, it began with the work of a single person: Friedan.

—Nicholas Lemann

The year I turned seventeen, the modern women's movement began to gain public attention in the United States. It was 1963. That was the year Betty Friedan published *The Feminine Mystique*. Awakening hundreds of thousands, if not millions, of women to a deep dissatisfaction they had felt but had been unable to put into words, Friedan reported that stay-at-home wives and mothers across America were suffering from "the problem that had no name."

"The problem lay buried, unspoken, for many years in the minds of American women," Friedan wrote. "It was a strange stirring, a sense of dissatisfaction, a yearning that women suffered in the middle of the twentieth century in the United States. Each suburban wife struggled with it alone. As she made the beds, shopped for groceries, matched slipcover material, ate peanut butter sandwiches with her children, chauffeured Cub Scouts and Brownies, lay beside her husband at night—she was afraid to ask even of herself the silent question—'Is this all?' "[1]

Middle- and upper-class women repeatedly spoke of what sounded like deep, unmet spiritual yearnings. A woman would say, "I feel empty somehow ... incomplete." Or, "I feel as if I don't exist."[2] A young Long Island homemaker confessed, "I seem to sleep so much. I don't know why I should be so tired. This house isn't nearly so hard to clean as the cold-water flat we had when I was working. The children are at school all day. It's not the work. I just don't feel alive."[3]

Women reported inexplicable crying jags, anger attacks, and "a strange feeling of desperation."[4] They were flocking to psychiatrists by the thousands and "taking tranquilizers like cough drops."[5] Some women described "great bleeding blisters" that broke out on their hands and arms.[6] One woman said, "You wake up in the morning, and you feel as if there's no point in going on another day like this. So you take a tranquilizer because it makes you not care so much that it's pointless."[7]

Much material for Friedan's book came from a survey she did of her Smith College graduating class. These affluent wives and mothers tucked away in their suburban homes, furnished with washers, dryers, televisions, dishwashers, electric floor-waxers, and every other new modern gadget, were living the post–World War II American dream. Why were women suffering what Betty called "this nameless aching dissatisfaction"?[8]

Setting out like Sherlock Holmes on the trail to solve a great mystery, Friedan uncovered clue after clue until she reached what she called "the hidden economic underside of reality." Stopping there (and many would say stopping too soon), Betty concluded all these women were suffering from the same malady. She named the problem that had no name the "feminine mystique," which she defined as the deeply engrained cultural belief that the only path to feminine fulfillment was to be a wife and mother. Time and again, a woman would complain she was "just a housewife," a phrase that echoed through *The Feminine Mystique* like a mantra.

Betty claimed the women's magazines for which she freelanced played a central role in keeping women "trapped in endless and empty housewifery." She knew that women's magazines, like the Internet and all popular media, offer more than just mindless entertainment (although they do offer that). They are also vehicles of culture. They lay out paths for us all to follow in our quests for happiness, love, and freedom. Debating *Redbook* editor Robert Stein before the Women's National Press Club in 1963, Betty declared that women's magazines in her day led a housewife to believe the only answer to her longing for fulfillment was "having another baby or dying her hair blonde."[9]

When Betty uttered these words, I was seventeen.

On one level, I thought I didn't need a women's revolution to liberate me, because my dad had already done that. Thin-faced with

twinkling gray-blue eyes and a boyish grin, Floyd Hurdle had grown
up dirt-poor on an Iowa farm during the Depression. A fugitive from
poverty, he vowed his beloved only daughter would know how to
take care of herself in the world. When I was just six, he began telling me when I grew up I'd go to college, an opportunity he himself
regretted having missed. At age eight, I started running the cash register in the family shoe store. At ten, I had my own bank account. If
a woman had to work twice as hard as a man to earn her way in the
world (as the new feminists claimed), well, then no problem: I figured I'd simply work twice as hard. Thanks to Dad, I had my wings
and I was eager to fly.

Yet on another level, the findings Betty reported in her book spoke
deeply to my heart, because she seemed to be describing my mother.

"Just a Housewife" in Iowa

Four feet eleven inches tall, Naoma Guthrie had brown eyes, porce-
lain skin, and black hair that sparkled like dark-red flames in the sunlight. As high-school homecoming queen, valedictorian, thespian,
and yearbook editor, she dreamed of becoming an actress. Instead,
she got a two-year degree at a junior college and became a first-grade
schoolteacher.

Then came World War II. Home on a three-day liberty, Naoma's
high-school sweetheart surprised her by dropping in at the boarding
house where she'd taken a room with two other young working
women. In Naoma's eyes, Floyd Hurdle in his handsome Army Air
Corps uniform resembled a young Gary Cooper. When he asked her
to marry him, of course she said yes. Two months later, she was pregnant with me and quit teaching. I was born in January 1946, making
me one of the first of the Baby Boomers.

After the war ended, Dad left the army and decided to go into the
shoe business.

"No matter how economically bad times may get," he reasoned,
"people will always need shoes."

Mother had bigger dreams. Trapped in New Hampton, she poured
her abundant energy and creative flair into parenting, keeping up
with the latest fashion trends, and home decorating. Each month,

the latest issues of Mother's magazines—*Redbook, Good Housekeeping, McCalls, Better Homes & Gardens, Glamour, Vogue,* and of course *Reader's Digest*[10]—were carefully laid out in a fanned display on our early-American maple coffee table, as if they were artistic objects for everyone to admire. When Paris designers pronounced plum "the stylish new color for autumn," Mom (an accomplished seamstress) bought yards of purple-plum wool, from which she fashioned for me a smart new suit for the season. The interior of our two-story white clapboard house on South Walnut Avenue looked like a six-page spread out of *House Beautiful.* My bedroom, with its powder-blue carpet, early-American maple furniture, and white-eyelet ruffled canopy bed, resembled a guest room in a seventeenth-century New England country inn.

I don't remember how old I was on that unforgettable day when I stood in this bedroom created by my mother's love. But sunbeams shone like specks of gold through the lacy white curtains. As I grasped a slender post of my maple canopy bed in my left hand and looked out across the grassy-green backyard lawn below, I made a solemn promise to God: "I know right from wrong," I vowed silently in my heart, "and I'm never going to do anything wrong."

As a child, I imagined God to be way *up there* in the clouds in a magical place called "heaven," while I was left way *down here* in this world alone. Further, I was taught the motto "If it's to be, it's up to me." So I believed it was up to me to distinguish right from wrong—and to do it without God's help.

Although Mom enriched us all with her intelligence and creativity, she was frequently irritable and snappish. Her frustration was only aggravated by New Hampton's social structure. New Hampton was comprised of three middle classes: upper-middle, middle-middle, and lower-middle. We were middle-middle. On a little rise at the edge of town, grandiosely known as "the hill," lived the upper-middles—the realtor, the jeweler, the contractor.... Mom resented the people on the hill, who turned up their noses at a simple shoe-seller's wife. She came home spitting mad one day after a woman on the hill snootily told her, "It's not *what* you know, Naoma, but *who* you know." No matter what she did, Mom was never going to be number one in New Hampton, because her husband ran the shoe store.

Gentle and soft-spoken, Dad was more easygoing. He tried to assuage Mom's desires for higher status by promising her the moon (the moon in this case being that he'd one day own a chain of shoe stores and become a millionaire).

Every night when I was a toddler, about the time Dad was due home from work, I'd listen intently until I heard his car pull into our driveway. Then I'd run to the front door. When he walked in, I'd grab him around the knees and giggle with delight, "What did you bring me?" Laughing, he'd lift me up, swing me around, and then hand me some small trinket or treasure he'd picked up for me during the day: a stick of Black Jack gum, a red rubber band, a Hershey's milk-chocolate kiss. I loved him immensely. Dad was the surprise in the Cracker-Jack box.

My life was all sunshine, daisies, and somersaults down green grassy hills—until 1954. That was the year my parents took me one night to see *The Glenn Miller Story*, starring Jimmy Stewart and June Allyson. The film is an inspiring rags-to-riches tale filled with music, love, noble struggles, friendship, and joy—until the tragic end, when Miller suddenly, out of nowhere, inexplicably, senselessly, dies in a plane crash. Miller found the jazzy big-band sound he was seeking. His music lives on in "Little Brown Jug" and other tunes. But he's dead, and the film leaves us with the message that, somehow, we're supposed to feel good about all this.

The film's ending brought me face-to-face with a harsh reality I had never before considered. I suddenly realized that if Glenn Miller had died, I was going to die too. The tragic news of my own death plunged my eight-year-old heart into a pit of grief and despair. Here I was having this wonderful life. Everything up until now had been sheer delight. And now I was going to *die*? It was too much to bear. I couldn't stop crying.

At home, as Dad tucked me into bed for the night, I was inconsolable. As I hiccupped, gasping for breath through my tears, he sat on the edge of my bed, trying to comfort me.

"But it was a true story," he gently reassured me, trying to make me see reason.

"I *know*!" I cried, wailing even louder. That was the point: it was *true*!

Did my father tell me that night about eternal life? I don't remember. I only recall the news of my own death being a great catastrophe.

If the end of life came to me as a shock, the beginning of life posed an even greater mystery. Children in small Midwestern towns in the '50s still had a chance to grow up innocent, and I was no doubt among the super-protected. I saw no sex on TV, no sex in the matinee movies I attended every Saturday (admission was a dime), no overt sex scenes in the *Reader's Digest* condensed books my parents read. When Alfred C. Kinsey and his Indiana University colleagues published *Sexual Behavior in the Human Male* and *Sexual Behavior in the Human Female* in 1948 and 1953, I heard nothing about the books. I didn't even know what sex was until I was in sixth grade.

My naïveté didn't end there.

One sticky-humid summer evening when I was about thirteen, Dad and I were riding along in the family's black-and-white Buick, headed up South Walnut Avenue on our way home from Hurdle's Shoes.

"I just don't know what's wrong with your mother lately," Dad confided as we drove past the schoolyard of Saint Mary's Catholic Church. Mom was becoming increasingly irritable and testy. Where was the joyful, playful girl he'd married? He was genuinely perplexed.

"Maybe she's going through menopause," I suggested.

"No...." He shook his head thoughtfully. "She's too young for that." Mom was just thirty-six.

We fell into puzzled silence and continued motoring along Walnut Avenue.

In our mutual naïveté, neither Dad nor I mentioned that Mom, in her determination to keep her 103-pound figure, was taking diet pills (amphetamines) by day and sleeping pills by night. Daily uppers and downers would make anyone testy!

Decades later, when she was in her eighties, Mom would look back on that period of our lives with alarm. "Sue," she confided on the phone to me one day in horror, "I was addicted to *drugs!*"

Yes, she was. Yet no one—least of all, I suspect, the five-dollar-per-visit doctor who prescribed the pills—thought much about dangerous side effects. Prescription drugs in those days didn't even come with package inserts.

Although Mom's problems baffled my dad and me, they didn't confuse Betty Friedan. In Betty's eyes, educated women's need for creative work could "be seen as the key" to the problem that had no name. Betty didn't want to live life halfway. She was seeking a wholeness, a completeness, a fullness of being, and she concluded

she and other women would find this fullness in work. "The only
way for a woman, as for a man, to find herself, to know herself as a
person, is by creative work of her own," Betty declared. "There is
no other way."[11] Calling on women to use their full human abili-
ties in all aspects of life, from law and politics to science, education,
and the arts, she declared: "The problem that has no name ... is simply the fact that American women are kept from growing to their full
human capacities."[12]

Much of what Betty said in the name of women regarding work
and money rang true to her readers for good reason. Women's economic status in 1963 left much to be desired. Wives' credit cards
were issued only in their husbands' names. "Help Wanted" ads were
split into "Male Wanted" positions (all the good jobs) and "Female
Wanted" jobs (waitresses, clerks, saleswomen, and cleaning ladies).
In the mid-1960s, women accounted for only 8 percent of all scientists, 6 percent of all physicians, 3 percent of lawyers, and 1 percent of engineers.[13] Women who worked for the telephone company
weren't allowed to apply for any job above operator. Airline stew-
ardesses were forced to resign if they got married, gained weight, or
turned thirty-two.

The Feminine Mystique struck a loud chord of recognition in the
minds and hearts of middle-class women across America and made
Betty the most widely known feminist in the nation. Emerging as
a major spokesperson for the women's movement, Betty gave the
media the "star image" they demanded—"the focus on an individual,
like Ralph Nader in consumer protection, who can project the aims
of a whole movement."[14] In the broadcast and print media's eyes,
Betty did not simply speak for herself: she spoke for the silent majority of women in cities and small towns across America.

My Pal Walter

It was in 1966 at the University of Missouri in Columbia, where I
was in journalism school studying to be a magazine writer, that I met
Walter. With intense brown eyes, a Roman nose, and a crooked
smile, Walter had the firm stride of a man who knew where he was
going. To earn money to put ourselves through college, we both

worked at a stylish women's shoe store called the Novus Shop. Walter sold shoes on commission. I was paid one dollar an hour to sell hosiery, run the cash register, and dust handbags. On Saturdays, Walter and I sometimes went to lunch together. It wasn't a "date." It was just a pal thing.

Walter was older than I by six years. When I turned twenty-one, he treated me to lunch at the Tiger Hotel and bought me my first cocktail, a salty dog.

Walter had grown up on a series of poor sharecropper farms around the tiny village of Tightwad, Missouri.* His dad, Monfred (nicknamed "Rosie") Browder, worked as a union carpenter in Kansas City during the week and came home only on weekends. A wiry little man with a sour disposition and a bitter set to his thin mouth, Rosie always bought food for the family on Friday nights before he bought his booze. When he got drunk, he sometimes took his shotgun off the wall and threatened to kill everyone in the house. Rosie habitually ran his sons off the farm when they turned sixteen. On the day one of Walter's older brothers, Bob, left home, Bob broke one of Rosie's ribs in a knife fight. Family legend had it that Rosie had been married and divorced numerous times before he met Ruth. The mother of five of Rosie's sons, including Walter, Ruth buried her depression and anger under layers of fat. Five feet tall, she weighed 350 pounds and measured five feet around the waist, a perfect sphere.

As a child, Walter naturally longed to escape from the brutal, ugly circumstances into which he'd been born. Determined to rise above the fear and ignorance around him, he tried to look beyond the suffering of the moment to see the bigger picture. Walter was quick at devising brainteasers and puzzles, which he used to distract Rosie when he was about to fly into one of his rages. Using his cleverness and creativity to keep his father's anger at bay, Walter managed to stay home until he could achieve his goal of becoming the first of six brothers to graduate from high school (he had no sisters). After a stint

---

*Legend had it Tightwad (population 69) got its name when a mailman offered $1.50 for a 60-pound watermelon at the general store, saying he'd be back to pick up his purchase when he finished his route. In his absence, the storeowner wangled a better deal and sold the watermelon to another customer for $2. When the postman returned, he called the merchant a tightwad, and the name stuck. Others say the dispute was over a rooster.

in the Navy, Walter enrolled at the University of Missouri with only twenty bucks in his pocket. The first semester he sold his stereo to pay his college tuition; the second semester he sold his car. When I met him, he was a junior, struggling to finish his degree in chemical engineering, but his heart wasn't in it. His secret desire was to be a novelist, and he longed to live in New York City. With a strong streak of the Irish in him, Walter was a poet, philosopher, storyteller, and dream weaver.

I lived in Johnson Hall, an all-girls' dorm, where meals were provided, except on Sunday nights, when every woman had to fend for herself. Walter had an apartment just off campus—and a stove! Delicious freedom! One wintry Sunday night after I'd cooked us a pork chop dinner at his apartment, the clock read almost 10:00 P.M.— time for me to head back to the dorm. Ever the gentleman, Walter helped me on with my coat. Suddenly, he spun me around and kissed me. I was totally surprised! That kiss set off fireworks that took my breath away.

Back in the dorm, I couldn't sleep. I lay awake in the dark in my upper bunk and gazed through the window at the moon. The kiss had really shaken me up. I needed to rethink this "buddy" relationship. Maybe I needed to look at my pal Walter in a new light.

A convert to Christianity (from no religion), Walter had become an Episcopalian in college before we met. I was a generic Protestant, an indifferentist, so the church he preferred made little difference to me. Should I become an Episcopalian? Sure. Why not? No problem. I was in love. Fifteen months after our first kiss, we were married in June 1967 in the historic Calvary Episcopal church (founded in 1855), where Walter had been baptized. Walter's story and my story differed dramatically. But on our wedding day, his story and my story became deeply interconnected. Our journey together had begun. There was no longer any way to tell my story without also telling his.

I married Walter with my heart, because he was irresistibly charming, and the heart has its reasons. But I carefully thought through where our life together might lead, and I also married him with my mind, because he dreamed of having children and a New York City writing career. A high-chroma type of guy, Walter shared my ambitions. From the moment we met, we laughed at the same jokes and finished each other's sentences. We both believed ours was a match made in heaven. We were chasing the same rainbow.

The following year, 1968, as we settled happily into married life and continued to work on our degrees, the world went mad. Martin Luther King and Bobby Kennedy were assassinated. The Tet offensive in Vietnam caught the U.S. military off guard and left Americans watching the nightly news in shock. Anti-war demonstrations erupted. Following Dr. King's murder, violent race riots raged in more than 115 American cities, notably in Baltimore, Louisville, and Washington, D.C. That same year Pope Paul VI issued his prophetic encyclical letter *Humanae Vitae*, which laid out the reasons for the Church's opposition to contraception, and ten theology professors at Catholic University of America immediately composed, published, and broadcast a six-hundred-word "Statement of Dissent." Also in 1968, Mary Daly (the first of the dissident Catholic feminists) published her hostile *Church and the Second Sex*,[15] in which she unmasked what Thomas Merton referred to as the "latent anti-feminism in so much Catholic thinking and practice."[16] That same year the radically angry National Assembly of Women Religious was formed.[17] The year 1968 marked the opening of a "new age" in the United States. "The entire country was caught up in a paroxysm of revolutionary renewal, intent on building a new culture. Far from being oriented toward tradition and the inheritance of the past, now society ran headlong toward a future deemed 'shining'—this new future that would stand in sharp contrast to the darkness of the past."[18] British historian Paul Johnson dubbed 1968 the year of "America's Suicide Attempt."[19] James Francis Cardinal Stafford observed, "By any measure, 1968 was a bitter cup."[20]

One of my former dorm roommates, a Catholic who'd recently married her college sweetheart, had always been Little Miss Righteous, trotting off to Mass every Sunday while the rest of us slept. Now she defiantly told me she was going to take the Pill, anyway, no matter what the Pope said. I thought to myself, *Oh, so this is what it means to be Catholic: Follow the rules—until you don't like them. Then do whatever you please.* I found it kind of creepy that she was so quickly deserting what her Church taught and turning to a different religion (one of her own devising).[21]

Of course, *I* took the Pill without a qualm. Although I went to church only because Walter wanted to go, *I* was Protestant. *I* was free.

Or so I thought. In reality, my freedom to enjoy sterile sex and control my own sex life was an illusion. The Pill put me on a hormone-powered emotional roller-coaster, which regularly plunged me into black pits of depression. The chemicals altering my body were far more in control of my life than I was.

One autumn day on campus during my senior year, I had been on the verge of tears all day. As I passed between classes, I could go on no longer. Struggling for composure, I took refuge in the nearest ladies' room. To my relief, it was empty. In my depression, I hid in a bathroom stall and sobbed. After a minute or two, I dried my eyes, blew my nose on some toilet tissue, and took a deep breath to pull myself back together. Then, with a heavy sigh, I trudged on to my next journalism class. Being on the Pill was supposed to make me feel empowered. In reality, it made me feel as if I were losing my mind.[22]

New York in Purple Shorts

In June 1969, even before Walter's final grades were posted, we packed everything we owned (our clothes, our typewriters, a few books, a coffee pot, an electric skillet, and our cat) into our ruby-red VW Bug and sped off to southern California. Two dreamers off to see the world, we didn't even stick around for the graduation ceremonies. Walter and I were going to find ourselves a little bit of heaven on earth. We planned to stay in the Los Angeles area for one year, basking on the beaches under the sun. Then we'd continue on our journey to New York City, to get serious about our dream of becoming writers. L.A. was more laidback then than it is now—in our eyes, a sort of party town. We were amused when we heard a *Saturday Evening Post* writer had once wittily described L.A. as "New York in purple shorts with its brains knocked out."[23]

Although Walter's degree was in English literature, he'd taken many math courses while majoring in chemical engineering, and he snagged a job as a math teacher in a private school in Pomona. I landed a job as a staff reporter on the women's section (the "pink-collar ghetto") of the South Bay *Daily Breeze*, a midsized daily newspaper in Torrance.

It was in the bedlam of the *Daily Breeze*'s newsroom, amid phones ringing and the staccato of typewriters clacking, that I first learned lying is a lot easier than telling the truth, and some journalists do it routinely. Lying means you can skip the hard legwork of tracking down reliable sources (so-called "real people") who are willing to talk and go on the record. Lying means you can meet tight deadlines with less hassle. Lying means you don't even have to try to get your facts straight, because you made most of them up.

I learned this new "insider reality" at the *Breeze* from the sardonic female reporter at the desk adjoining mine. M— had also attended the University of Missouri (one of the finest J-schools in the nation), where she too had learned a journalist's first ethical obligation is to tell the truth. In the words of Bill Kovach (founding chairman of the Committee of Concerned Journalists) and Tom Rosenstiel (founding director of the Project for Excellence in Journalism): "Journalism provides something unique to a culture—independent, reliable, accurate, and comprehensive information that citizens require to be free."[24] But now we were in the "real world," my new mentor informed me, and all that cornball ethics stuff was yesterday's news.

M— told me the best last name to choose for a fictitious news source you've invented is "Johnson." "Smith and Jones sound fake," she confided in a conspiratorial tone, peering down her sharp nose like a schoolmarm over her wire-rimmed glasses. "Johnson is the third most common last name in the United States, but it doesn't sound fake." Quote Jack or Jennifer "Johnson," and you could be quoting any of a thousand people in L.A. "Garcia" works too.

So this is how the real world works, I thought. I don't recall making up any sources myself at the *Breeze*. But looking back on it now, I believe that's when the first chink in my ethical armor as a journalist began to appear. For M—'s lies didn't hurt her career. On the contrary, she cheerfully hobnobbed with politicians and soon went on to land a job at the *Los Angeles Times*, followed by a cushy position in public relations. A part of me was appalled at M—'s chicanery. But another part of me lapped up her advice like a kitten drinking its first bowl of sweet cream.

Fired for Being Pregnant

Two months after being hired by the *Breeze*, I accidentally got pregnant. I say it was an accident, although something tells me it was part of a plan much larger than I understood. Maybe I forgot to take the Pill. Maybe I skipped a pill because I was sick of the side effects. Maybe I unconsciously longed for a baby. I don't know. I only know the surprise news we were having a baby filled me with a strange new delight, a mysterious wonder I'd never felt before.

When I told Jim, the *Breeze*'s editor in chief, I was pregnant, he scowled. As I sat like a condemned criminal before him in his cubicle, he sternly informed me I was permitted to work only through my fifth month of pregnancy. Then I'd be fired with no promise of being rehired after the baby was born.

You're pregnant? You're fired. No discussion. Case closed. Even as late as 1969, that was the corporate policy in many offices across America.

Reality had smacked me in the face. So much for my small-town belief I'd be able to get ahead in the world just by working twice as hard as a man. Suddenly, the women's movement's cries for freedom, equality, and justice struck home to me in a new way. Plainly, the women's movement was necessary, after all.

Although another woman might have angrily retaliated over the injustice of being fired, I took it with a dose of humor. After all, Walter and I had already decided we would soon pack up the Bug once again and journey cross-country to New York City. So rather than fight the *Breeze*'s sexist policy, I simply lied about how far along I was in my pregnancy. Like my mom, I'm small: only five foot two. In my eighth month of pregnancy, I was waddling about the busy newsroom like an overweight penguin, absurdly claiming to be only five months along.

To my surprise, every cynical, hard-bitten male reporter on staff went along with my charade. "My God!" a sportswriter in the cubby next to me teased one day with a wink. "You're going to have an elephant!"

Being sacked for being a mother was commonplace in those days, as it had been for decades. Betty Friedan had also been fired for being pregnant from her job as a reporter on a union newspaper in the 1940s. Bitterly feeling the injustice of it all, Betty complained to the Newspaper Guild. "I was being fired because I was pregnant, not because my work wasn't good. That wasn't fair. But Jule, our hard-boiled, chain-smoking 'Front Page' type copy editor, who was head of the Guild unit, said: 'It's your fault for getting pregnant again.' There was no word for sex discrimination then, no law against it."[25] Betty said sex discrimination wasn't just tolerated by big business. "Sex discrimination *was* big business."[26] And now I knew from personal experience she was right.

Friedan's Family Feminism

Betty was also right on target when she insisted the new women's movement must be pro-family. This is perhaps another surprise. Called "the mother of the women's movement" by hundreds of newspapers, Friedan was a fervent defender of a woman's right to be a mother. Thirty years after she published *The Feminine Mystique*, Betty said in an interview she granted to *Playboy* magazine, "Women are the people who give birth to children, and that is a necessary value in society.... Feminism was not opposed to marriage and motherhood. It wanted women to be able to define themselves as people and not just as servants to the family. You want a feminism that includes women who have children and want children because that's the majority of women."[27]

She further stated that a view of sexual "liberation" that turns woman into a sex object is a false freedom that denies a woman's personhood. "Maybe some people still haven't caught on," Betty told *Playboy* readers in 1992, "but the best sex requires a deeper, more profound knowledge of oneself and the other person. In the Bible, sexual love was to *know*. It suggests something deeper."[28]

In a 1999 interview with the *London Daily Telegraph*, Betty reiterated her defense of what I later came to think of as her "family feminism." She declared, "I'm not anti-marriage and anti-family. I always thought it was dangerous to go against the idea of family. I don't even like the phrase 'women's liberation,' because that idea of being set free from everything doesn't seem right to me. I like to think of the women's movement as a fight for equality."[29] When feminist Gloria Steinem called marriage a form of prostitution, Betty replied, "That extreme form of thinking tends to come from women who hate having to deal with the complexities of juggling a career and a family and so, almost literally, they want to throw the baby out with the bath water. It's just unrealistic to be a feminist who is anti-family."[30]

As a mother of three, Betty frequently said that her children were never a problem for her but were "a sheer delight, so beautiful, so bright, so funny, so themselves. They seemed like a *bonus* in my life, an unexpected, maybe undeserved, marvelous bonus. Well, of course, they wet the bed, and had to be toilet trained, and I had to insist that the maid spank Danny when he went out into the street, because it was dangerous. But, I have to admit, it was delicious for me being a mother."[31]

The *maid*? Well, yes. You see, Betty wasn't exactly the ordinary American housewife she portrayed herself to be on the pages of the *Mystique*. Some say she was a Marxist. One of her most influential Smith College professors, James Gibson, expressed the hope that educated people would develop what he labeled "good propaganda." Gibson even taught his students "how to develop effective propaganda for desirable goals."[32] Betty took careful notes. Was *The Feminine Mystique* not an honest investigative report, but cleverly disguised propaganda? I'll leave that question for you to think about as the story unfolds. But whatever hidden agendas Betty may or may not have harbored, she still had a soft spot in her heart for children.

In the first edition of *The Feminine Mystique*, Betty made no mention of what later became known as "reproductive rights," such as abortion or the Pill. Her goal was not to alter a woman's body with surgery or medication so she could fit more easily into a corporate slot that had been molded for the organization man who was willing to give himself 24/7 to his career. Rather, Betty wanted to see a more woman-friendly corporate culture that would give equal respect and equal pay to working mothers. When she first articulated the goals for the National Organization for Women (NOW) in June 1966, at a luncheon meeting in the Washington Hilton Hotel, Betty wrote (in words scribbled on a yellow, paper cocktail napkin): "to take the actions needed to bring women into the mainstream of American society, now, full equality for women, in fully equal partnership with men."[33] That was the original rallying cry of the modern women's movement. Betty called on women to create "a new life plan, fitting in the love and children and home that have defined femininity in the past with the work toward a greater purpose that shapes the future."[34]

Betty plainly said the 1960s women's movement was all about "the personhood of women."[35] But what did she mean by *personhood*? From the women's movement's first hour, this was the deeper question Betty implicitly posed, but failed to answer.

Had the utopian promises Betty made to women in *The Feminine Mystique* come to pass, women and their families in America today would be far happier than they were when I was growing up in the 1950s. Strong, happily married women would be serenely fulfilled by their creative, lucrative work. Men and women would freely love one another in collaboration as equals. Mothers would be respected and honored both at home and in the workforce. All children would be wanted and cherished. Today we would be living in a world far closer to an earthly paradise than Ozzie and Harriet or my mom and dad ever imagined. Or at least that's the utopia Betty promised if only I and other women would listen up and follow her lead.

But the story Betty told about a future and better world, a place where "the problem that had no name" would disappear like a ghost into the mist, was not to be—for two reasons. First, Betty misnamed "the problem that had no name" and therefore got her solution to the problem wrong. As any working woman can readily attest, more work outside the home isn't necessarily the ultimate path to complete fulfillment and wholeness of personhood. Second, this was the 1960s, an era of violent social upheaval, and powerful counterrevolutions were in the wind.

Chapter 3

Making Up a Revolution

God looked down from heaven upon the children of men to see whether any of them understand, or seek God.

—Psalm 53:2

We first set foot on the asphalt pavements of New York City and began apartment hunting on an unbearably hot and muggy Fourth of July. The baby was due August 1. Trudging around the city in the sweltering heat, the humidity hovering around 90 percent, soon wore me ragged. Respectable rentals in New York were not only hard to find but priced far above our modest means. Several apartment-building managers wanted to be bribed hundreds of dollars just to rent us a few rooms. Realizing our plan to locate a New York apartment within a few days had been naïve and foolhardy, we dug out our trusty Rand McNally road atlas and began considering what to do. Hartford, Connecticut, seemed like a promising place to investigate: it was a small city, but large enough that we figured we could find an apartment there, enlist a doctor, have the baby, and then work out a plan to swing back into New York. Leaving New York temporarily behind, we crossed the Throgs Neck Bridge, caught the New England Thruway, and headed north.

That night, as we settled into a comfortable motel, we collapsed side by side together into bed and merrily asked ourselves, "What are we doing in Hartford, Connecticut?" The frustration of the day behind us, our spirits soared. We were sojourners on the move. The small trials of a pilgrim's life were just part of the adventure. The next morning, we found and took a furnished, one-bedroom, third-floor apartment for forty dollars a week on Niles Street, a miniature slum one block wide and two blocks long. We called Hartford Hospital, received a referral to a top-notch ob-gyn, and scheduled a strategy meeting. Meanwhile, Walter signed up with a temporary employment agency and had work within a week. His first job, which amused us, was as a model in an auto-parts ad.

The Niles Street apartment was small and dingy, with only one lazy fan to provide meager relief from the steamy heat. Our neighbors down the hall frequently had loud, vulgar, angry fights. We befriended a sad little boy named Bobby, age four or five, who loved the Popsicles we gave him but who all too often sat curled on the floor in the dark hallway crying piteously until his mother unlocked the door and let him back in. In a scene out of Alfred Hitchcock's *Rear Window*, on moonlit nights after most neighbors were asleep, a thin, spindly legged old man who lived in the red-brick building across the way would crawl spiderlike down the fire escape and sneak around the courtyard naked.

The night my contractions began, Hartford was under siege. A police officer, who had shot and killed a nineteen-year-old Puerto Rican kid in an Albany Avenue alley after a high-speed car chase, had just been acquitted. Race riots erupted. Three days of looting, shooting, and arson ensued. Hartford's mayor declared the city to be in a state of emergency. Four-man SWAT teams of state police snipers, armed with automatic rifles with telescopic sights, were patrolling parts of the city in state-police station wagons. Police fired tear gas to disperse gangs of roving young men throwing rocks and bottles. Buildings were set afire. More than one hundred National Guardsmen of the 169th Infantry Regiment, armed with M-1 rifles, were holed up in the West Hartford Armory, just waiting for the word to be deployed.

To drive to Hartford Hospital at 1:15 A.M., Walter and I had to violate the 9:00 P.M. curfew (anyone on the streets after then was to be arrested). Would we encounter rioters? Sniper fire? Police barricades? If we encountered police, would they escort us to the hospital? We had no way of knowing what might happen. But my contractions were ten minutes apart. We could wait no longer. We got into our Bug and journeyed into the dark night.

As if we were sheltered by angels' wings, the city streets we drove along were deserted and silent. Hartford felt eerily like a

post-apocalyptic wasteland. It felt strangely surreal to stop at a red
light at a major intersection in the middle of the night with no other
car anywhere in sight. We continued along our way, seeing no one,
and arrived at the hospital without incident.

For the rest of the night, as tidal waves of pain and fire swept
through me, Walter stayed by my side, holding my hand. When I fell
asleep from exhaustion between contractions, he walked over to the
hospital-room window and looked out across the dark city, watching raging blood-red flames devour a paper-supply warehouse in the
distance. On that flaming night, all creation seemed to be in labor.

The next morning, the doctor joyfully proclaimed, "It's a boy!"
Everyone in the delivery room was merry, and, if I recall it right,
two doctors were present and one doctor slapped the other on the
back. The scene of cheery rejoicing in the hospital under bright-
white lights stood in stark contrast to the bitter violence the besieged
city had endured during the night. When the nurse handed me our
cuddly little bundle of love wrapped in a warm, white flannel blanket, I wept with a mix of weariness and joy. Walter smiled in awed
wonder. For unto us a child was born. We named him Dustin Scott.

Later that cloudy morning, as Walter left the hospital in a happy
daze, he passed two teenyboppers in miniskirts, standing on a street
corner, flirtatiously giggling and wiggling their hips at passersby.
One day ago, he might have enjoyed their flirtiness. After the night
of truth he'd just endured, the exhausted but wiser new father
thought, *You clueless little girls: you have no idea the kind of fire you're
playing with.*

Back at the apartment, Walter collapsed into bed in a stupor, only
to be awakened from a lethargic trance by the jangling phone. The
female principal of a private school in Darien was calling in response
to a job-application letter he'd sent her. Totally wiped out from
the previous night, Walter later recalled little of their conversation.
He only remembered groggily informing her he was certainly the
right man for the task, because he was more than willing to teach
Episcopal doctrine in his math classes.

There was a dead silence at the other end of the line.

He didn't get the job.

Two days later, however, while baby Dustin and I were still in
the hospital, Walter came bursting into my hospital room with the

good news. He had just come back from New York City, where he'd landed a teaching position at venerable Adelphi Academy in the Bay Ridge section of Brooklyn. Founded in 1863 when the Civil War was raging, the school was supported in its early years partly by renowned preacher and orator Henry Ward Beecher and newspaper publisher Horace Greeley. Oh joy! Now we were headed back again into New York, this time with a new baby in our arms and a job in our pockets.

Freedom = Sex without the Kids

The job at Adelphi turned out not to be what Walter expected. A lot of political infighting soon left him fed up. Putting our heads together, we decided he would quit teaching and stay home with the baby to write his first novel (his real dream), while I looked for work on a national magazine. I was strongly bonded with the baby. It was emotionally wrenching to leave him. But knowing Walter would be at home to care tenderly for him with a father's love helped resolve my ambivalence and allowed me to feel comfortable enough to strike out and pursue job hunting full blast.

I quickly learned if I were to land a position with any future, I would be wise to conceal the fact I was a mother. During one interview at *Baby Talk* magazine, I committed the unforgivable job-hunting *faux pas* of revealing I had a new baby at home. At this revelation, the interviewer's eyes narrowed, and I instantly realized I'd blown the interview. I could have kicked myself! After being fired from the *Breeze* for being pregnant, I should have known better than to admit to being a mother, even if the magazine was called *Baby Talk*.

During my interview at *Cosmopolitan*, I carefully omitted any reference to our baby—and, of course, I got the job. Freedom for women was in the air. But mothers were still in chains.

Whereas Betty Friedan's message to women was "Creative work of your own will set you free," Helen Gurley Brown's message to the single woman was "Hard work and sex will set you free (as long as you don't have children)."

As author of the smash best seller *Sex and the Single Girl*, published one year before *The Feminine Mystique*, Helen saw the single girl as "the newest glamour girl of our times"[1] and viewed children as "more of a nuisance than a blessing. For those who had the poor taste to want children anyway, she supplied this advice: 'Never waste time feeling guilt, never agonize too much, and have a lot of paid help at home, and never, ever, let them interfere with the long climb to the top.' "[2]

Helen saw not lack of education or economic opportunities but motherhood as "the insurmountable obstacle to real liberation for women."[3] When feminist Naomi Wolf, author of *The Beauty Myth*, criticized women's magazines like *Cosmopolitan* for keeping women focused on unrealistic standards of beauty and thereby distracted from political issues, Helen snapped back at Wolf during a TV talk-show debate: "There is a conspiracy against women, and I'd be the first to say so.... But getting us to be beautiful ain't the problem! We are encouraged to be mothers, to be pregnant."[4] Helen claimed that what held women back from success in the corporation was the "built-in mechanism in their bodies that allows them to have babies."[5]

If you entrusted yourself to Helen's lifestyle teachings (as many young women did and still do), you'd soon come to believe the way for a smart woman to be free and to succeed in her career and her life was to (1) work hard; (2) take the Pill or use some other contraceptive; and (3) if the contraceptive failed, get an abortion. In an unseen way, which eluded me at the time, the sexual revolution was both *for* unmarried sex and *against* motherhood. The two went hand in hand. To shape your lifestyle according to *Cosmo*'s sex-revolution philosophy, you almost had to take the Pill or use some other form of contraception. And since all forms of pharmaceutical contraception can fail, you "needed" abortion as a backup if you wanted to stay on the fast track. Since some contraceptives can prevent the embryo from implanting—and hence *are* abortion—the line between contraception and abortion is sometimes a wavy gray.

Marketing Fairy Tales

One of my assignments while studying magazine markets at the University of Missouri School of Journalism had been to choose a popular magazine to analyze for the class. In my small-town fascination with glamour, I chose *Cosmopolitan*. I told my fellow journalists-in-training that many of the anecdotes in *Cosmo* were so pat they appeared fabricated. They just didn't ring true.

Once on staff at *Cosmo*, I soon learned my J-school instincts had been correct. Many of the alleged "real people" we wrote about in the magazine were entirely fictitious. Helen had even written a set of writers' guidelines suggesting it was fine for us to make up "experts" to quote and to invent anecdotes about ordinary single women, whom she called "civilians."

The Cosmo Girl was not a real person but a *persona*, a mask the single girl lonely and alone in the world could put on to turn herself into the object of a man's sexual fantasies. In *Sex and the Single Girl* (the forerunner of *Sex and the City*) Helen wrote: "When a man thinks of a single woman, he pictures her alone in her apartment, smooth legs sheathed in pink silk Capri pants, lying tantalizingly among dozens of satin cushions, trying to read but not very successfully, for *he* is in that room—filling her thoughts, her dreams, her life."[6]

This was our childless Cosmo Girl, and we encouraged our reader to exchange her authentic identity for this unreality. We urged the lonely single woman to let go of her "guilt" (moral concerns) and to sleep with any man she pleased, even if he was married. Since sleeping with another woman's husband had obvious drawbacks, Helen advised: "It seems to me the solution is not to rule out married men but to keep them as pets. While they are 'using' you to varnish their egos, you 'use' *them* to add spice to your life. I say 'them' advisedly. One married man is dangerous. A potpourri can be fun."[7]

In the beginning, there was no Cosmo Girl, or at least as far as I could tell there weren't many real-life copies of her yet. She was mostly a product of Helen's clever imagination, a marketing fairy tale. Yet we wrote about this sexually "free" woman as if she really existed. Over time, readers who regarded the fantasy as real began to live out the *Cosmo* lifestyle. Within a decade or so, those of us who wrote regularly for the magazine began to find single women openly sleeping with their boyfriends everywhere, and I no longer had to make up so many anecdotes to produce an article Helen deemed publishable. Between 1970 and 1999, the percentage of unmarried couples just living together increased more than sixfold.[8] Such is the power of skillfully crafted propaganda to change people's attitudes and lives. Fiction had become reality.

Severing Sex from Love

Helen's favorite slogan, embroidered on a small pillow she kept on a floral loveseat in her office, was "Good Girls Go to Heaven, Bad Girls Go Everywhere." This slogan succinctly expressed our *Cosmo* philosophy, which turned every conventional value upside down. Bitchiness and selfishness were good, generosity and putting others first were bad. My first feature-length story, published in April 1972, was "Girls Who Have to Be Liked," based on the premise that it was "bad" (self-defeating) to be too kind, considerate, and helpful toward others. The article appeared just a few pages from a double-page spread of actor Burt Reynolds, the first near-nude male centerfold in U.S. publishing history.

At *Cosmo*, I was a dedicated follower of Planned Parenthood founder Margaret Sanger, the foremost proponent of birth control as a panacea to the world's problems. Sanger idolized sex without the kids. "Through sex," Sanger sang joyously in *The Pivot of Civilization*, "mankind may attain the great spiritual illumination which will transform the world, which will light up the only path to an earthly paradise."[9] Sanger dreamed of "that dawn" when sex would be freed from all chains, and men and women would at last realize "that here close at hand is our paradise, our everlasting abode, our Heaven and our eternity.... Not for woman only, but for all of humanity is this the field where we must seek the secret of eternal life."[10] It's hard to deny that Sanger idolized sex as her god. At *Cosmo*, I danced in Sanger's procession.

Many people accused *Cosmo* of trivializing sex. Fair enough, for so we did. But our critics failed to realize that trivialization was part of our marketing package. Written in the intimate tone of "big sister talking to little sister," our unspoken message was "Don't think about any of this too deeply, my dear, or you may spot the deception. Just relax and have fun. Leave all that serious thinking to the old fuddy-duddies."

Cosmo sounded stupid, but the breezy tone in my articles was painstakingly contrived. I rewrote and rewrote, tweaked here and tweaked there, all to perfect the product. I soon learned that if I wanted to write an article Helen would consider "good" enough to pay me for and publish, it would be advisable for me to mimic her voice and try to make my writing sound a lot like hers.

In a typical made-up anecdote, the Cosmo Girl had a glamour job, traveled a lot, and spent her hard-earned cash on pricey commodities to support her self-centered lifestyle. Here's one example of a fictional anecdote from an article I wrote entitled "When He Doesn't Want Sex." The article was about "inhibited sexual desire," a ubiquitous new malady sex therapists had only recently noticed and were attempting to "cure."[11] Note the lack of tenderness in this imaginary non-relationship. My bracketed asides highlight the unspoken messages intentionally worked into the story to encourage our young, single reader to buy, buy, buy.

> Carly, a twenty-four-year-old fashion model [so she plainly buys lots of makeup, perfume, and beautiful clothes] says of her once-fiery Italian lover Tony [perhaps they met on one of her adventure trips to Italy], "I've tried dozens of ways to seduce him. I bought a vibrator and masturbated in front of him, spent three hundred dollars on playthings from Frederick's of Hollywood, learned to belly dance. Absolutely *nothing* stirs him." [Totally absorbed in her narcissistic, consumerist "self," our imaginary Carly pays no attention to her lover nor to any struggles he might be facing. Rather, she spends hundreds of dollars on material commodities to acquire the only thing she desires and "needs" from him—sex.]

This was little more than advertising copy thinly disguised as editorial content. We had only one on-staff "fact-checker," a young, single, black woman who doubled as a file clerk and occasionally looked up a statistic or two in the *World Almanac*. But we had no legitimate fact-checkers, because we had few facts to check.

That's not to say everything I wrote for *Cosmo* was entirely untrue. Articles on subjects like "Biking in the City," "Handling the Job Interview," or "How to Buy a Used Car" were entirely factual. The anecdotes manufactured to support Helen's sex-revolution philosophy were the ones most frequently fabricated. Laced with partial truth, propaganda's bitter poison becomes more difficult to detect and sweeter to swallow. Another anecdote I invented for an article titled "Ambition: Yours and His" read:

> Mia (an ambitious, twenty-five-year-old corporate attorney) met Rob (a laid-back, thirty-eight-year-old documentary filmmaker) in Paris at a Jewish deli on the Champs-Élysées. He was struggling to order a

pastrami sandwich. Mia came to his rescue with her flawless French. He asked her out for a cup of café au lait ... and after that afternoon and a night of gentle lovemaking in a hotel on the Left Bank, Mia knew she was in love.

Make no mistake. We're not talking here about what's popularly called *spin*. This was hard-core sex-revolution propaganda masquerading as fluff. Is it any wonder that another of my articles was "What to Do about Those Ubiquitous Vaginal Infections"[12] and yet another was "Just How Neurotic Are You?"[13] As we visibly pretended to set women sexually free from their biology (via the Pill and abortion), we were invisibly catering to, and even helping to create, millions of sexually troubled, insecure, confused women, who were likely to attract equally confused, insecure men.

How ugly my career was then. Trained to be the propagandist's natural enemy, I had betrayed my true calling and had become a propagandist myself.

Our Riverdale Retreat

Yet God was showing me a better way, and at home my life with Walter and Dustin was filled with light, laughter, and love. We had run a classified ad in *The Riverdale Press*—"Writers looking for inexpensive rooms" or something to that effect—and an incredible deal had fallen into our laps. Andrea Simon (the widow of Richard Simon, cofounder of Simon & Schuster) called to offer us free rent in her Georgian mansion in Riverdale in the Bronx in exchange for walking her two Dalmatian dogs (Circe and Pandy) and watering her plants when she went out of town. Built in the '20s, the mansion was red brick with two white-frame additions at either end. Andrea, who in her early sixties resembled Katherine Hepburn, offered us several furnished rooms on the top floor. I guess our little suite was a maid's quarters. But it was cozy and well-appointed. Compared to the apartment on Niles Street, it was a palace.

Free rent in New York City!

If we had asked a realtor where we might find free rent in an exclusive neighborhood in New York, he would have rolled his eyes and said we were mad. Yet it was ours. The Simon home was hidden away in a secluded, elite neighborhood of palatial lawns with privately owned aristocratic streets, patrolled in the evenings by a congenial armed guard who knew us personally by name. Even after dark, it was safe for us to walk the Dalmatians under canopies of leaves along moonlit lanes with baby Dustin (now nearly one year old) jauntily riding on Walter's shoulders.

It was on one of these walks under the soft moonlight that Walter revealed a secret about himself, which seemed to me to help explain why he'd always been able to handle so many difficulties in his life without complaint.

Looking up in awed wonder at the stars, he said quietly, "I won just by being born."

So, on the one hand, my life at home was as cheery as a scene out of *Mary Poppins*. Yet, on the other hand, my days at *Cosmo* left my soul shackled in darkness. How, you may ask, was I able to write such unscrupulous sex-revolution propaganda and still live with myself? What had happened to my childhood promise to God that I wasn't going to do anything wrong?

I chose not to think about that prayer anymore. I still believed in the promise. But it was tucked deeply away in a corner of my mind, far from my conscious awareness. I told myself the lies I invented and the philosophy I peddled at *Cosmo* were just part of the publishing game. My mind was so filled with trivialities it was easy for me to skate over the surface of life without asking deeper questions. In some ways, I believe I had even unconsciously adopted a male-playboy mindset. If any single young woman actually believed and followed *Cosmo*'s silly advice—and got hurt in the process ... well, I chose not to think about that. I was a mercenary, a literary soldier for hire. The lies I told to peddle the wares at *Cosmo* were nothing personal, just business.

A War Within

The choices we make to betray others and violate our own integrity, of course, have consequences, whether we want to recognize them or not. Gradually, the interior war being waged deep within me took its toll, and my spirit sickened. Although I didn't understand why, anxiety gnawed at me, and my stomach was often upset. I had escaped being "just a housewife." Yet I, too, was suffering from a problem that had no name. And Betty Friedan's solution, "creative work of one's own" (at least the shabby kind of work I was doing),[14] had not set me free. A nameless fear stalked me. My weight dropped precipitously from 118 to 103 pounds.

One evening an incident occurred that was so humiliating I haven't told anyone about it until this moment.

It had been a particularly angst-provoking day at the office. As I left *Cosmo*'s offices, descended the elevator, and exited the Argonaut Building, my stomach felt exceptionally queasy. Riding the lurching, screeching Lexington Avenue Express from Manhattan toward the Bronx, I became so nauseated when the subway train jerked to a sudden stop at one station, I had to disembark to keep from throwing up.

The muggy air on the subway platform reeked with the stench of urine and sweat. The thick air only intensified my nausea. I pushed my way through tight-lipped crowds of weary commuters and rushed past winos and drug addicts who lay slumped in underground shadows against filthy, graffiti-splattered walls.

Managing to locate a public restroom, I entered a fetid latrine, stumbled into an empty stall, and vomited into a feces-splattered toilet.

I had worshipped emptiness, and this is where it had led me. Rushing from that hellhole, I made my way back to the subway platform to wait for the next train.

Hell is first and foremost of our own making. I was spiritually perishing. Yet in my folly, I ignored all warning signs that I was on the wrong path. I wanted money. I wanted fame. I wanted recognition. Blindfolded by my determination to "be me" and to "fulfill myself," I charged willfully ahead.

Whether it was before or after the subway incident, I don't recall, but I remember one day triumphantly feeling that everything was going my way. The women's movement had my back, freedom and equality were in the air, and I felt on top of the world. I had left behind my small Midwestern town, discarded its values like an old rag, and I was in the big-time glamour capitol of the world: *New York City!* Just the excitement of those three little words stirred my ambitions. As I breezed along West 57th Street on my lunch hour in my red-white-and-blue polka-dot hot pants, the lyrics of a popular tune rang sweetly in my head:

> These small town blues, are melting away.
> I'll make a brand-new start of it—in old New York.
> If I can make it there, I'll make it anywhere.
> New York, New York—it's a helluva town.

I didn't know I'd mixed up the lyrics. The first three lines were from an old Frank Sinatra tune. The last line was from the hit musical *On the Town*, which was enjoying a Broadway revival at the time.

But scrambling lyrics in my head was the least of my confusions. My deadliest error was my fantasy that if I could only learn how to "make it big" on my own in New York, I would be a "success": I would be free, and I would be happy.

It's an error that has infected the world.

Spreading the Errors

As corporate America faced intense pressures from the women's movement and the courts to hire more women in well-paid positions, the ambitious, ever-childless Cosmo Girl was a marketer's and CEO's dream come true. She worked hard, bought lavishly from the pharmaceutical, medical, beauty, fashion, and travel industries, *and* (the triple perk) she didn't push for all those pricey, bothersome extras like family tax breaks, maternity leave, shorter work weeks, and more flexible work arrangements.

Further, by inserting its "sex-without-children-will-set-you-free" agenda into men's and women's most intimate lives, the sexual revolution could sell all sorts of merchandise: the Pill and other contraceptives, lacy underwear, makeup, singles-only cruises, pornography, sexy red convertibles, STD treatments, abortions, marital counseling, divorces, and even in-vitro fertilization treatments when young women chemically neutered themselves for so long they passed their prime childbearing years and could no longer conceive naturally without help from a doctor. Splitting sex from babies spawned many lucrative new industries and would continue to do so as the decades rolled by and the sexual revolution juggernaut barreled down the tracks, crushing babies and families under its wheels and silencing anyone who dared to speak out or to stand in its path. As *Cosmo*'s circulation soared from fewer than eight hundred thousand to nearly three million copies, annual advertising revenues leaped between 1964 and 1985 by eighty times, from $601,000 to $47.7 million.[15]

In 2009, long after Helen was relieved of her duties as editor-in-chief, *Cosmopolitan* marched on with sixty editions published in thirty-six languages, distributed in more than one hundred countries, and reaching more than one hundred million female readers. As one biographer put it, these international editions "are a long arm for Helen Gurley Brown's continuing philosophy." Their editors, "described by one journalist as 'lifestyle evangelists,' follow their mentor closely, for like 'all good evangelists,' their work will not be completed until the Cosmo Girl confidently struts the boardrooms and bedrooms of the whole civilized world."[16]

The world is in a bad way, for the fantasy of womanhood we created at *Cosmo*—the fantasy of a woman as a radical individualist who belongs only to herself and is disconnected from others—betrays the truth of women's lives.

"We are what we pretend to be, so we must be careful about what we pretend to be," observed novelist Kurt Vonnegut Jr.[17] Embracing sex without genuine love—the vision of woman as an isolated being who belongs to no one but herself—left many single young women ambivalent, confused, and in situations of regret. C—, a writer friend of mine, lived the Cosmo Girl lifestyle to the hilt, to the point that years later when dining in a crowded Greenwich Village restaurant, she would see a man across the room whose face looked vaguely familiar, and ask herself, "I wonder if I had sex with him?" As she became increasingly caught up in a pattern of using men and being used by them merely as an object for sexual gratification, her relationships became blunted, superficial, and twisted. She became so phobic about being touched that even a girlfriend's hug in greeting could cause her to pull back in cold fear. Imprisoned in the Cosmo Girl's fashionable I-belong-only-to-me mindset, she found herself unspeakably lonely. After a series of empty non-relationships and several abortions, she at last found tentative interior peace in decades of celibacy. But she never married or had children and died in her sixties of breast cancer, which some medical research suggests may be linked to abortion and the Pill. Shortly before her death, in one of our many late-in-life phone conversations, C— recalled her Cosmo lifestyle years with sad regret. She lamented, "We had sex like barnyard animals."

For her part, Betty Friedan justifiably called *Cosmo* "quite obscene and quite horrible."[18] As the mother of the women's movement, Betty hoped to broaden and deepen women's lives. *Cosmopolitan's* shallow sex-revolution philosophy narrowed women's lives to what Betty called "an immature teenage-level sexual fantasy," promoting "the idea that woman is nothing but a sex object, that [she] is nothing without a man, and there is nothing in life but bed, bed, bed."[19]

I agreed with Betty. Although I was willing to use *Cosmo's* prestige to further my own ambitions and promote my magazine-writing career, from my vantage point, it seemed clear to me that sex outside of marriage was fraught with hazards for women. All contraceptives have rates of failure. If you happened to get pregnant by surprise (as I had with Dustin), the man who had sworn to love you 'til death do you part would very likely be there for you when you had the baby, as Walter was for me. A man who cared so little for you that he refused to make that promise would be far more likely to walk out the door. And then where would you be? A pregnant woman alone in the world with no way to get a job and no support system? Certainly not the sort of "freedom" I wanted to deal with! No thank you. Even as I manufactured copy to promote the supposedly care-free singles lifestyle, I disdained *Cosmo's* sex-revolution philosophy.

Yet one cultural social force I just knew in my heart to be unquestionably true and worth my steadfast support was the women's movement.

Why? Because I'd been fired for being pregnant. Just when a mother needed a paycheck most to support a new baby, it was legal and even considered "business as usual" for her employer to kick her out the door.

I'd taken being fired from the *Daily Breeze* in stride. But I knew I'd been subjected to a grave injustice. And so did Betty Friedan. What's more, Betty stood up in the public square and boldly promised that she and her new National Organization for Women (NOW) would get laws passed, so injustices like this would never happen to any woman again. By 1968, women made up 35 percent of the U.S. workforce, and every working woman I knew wanted to hear and support what Betty had to say. I was a loyal foot soldier in the women's movement's media army. Even as I rejected the sexual revolution lifestyle as a sham, I scrambled to climb aboard NOW's freedom train.

Chapter 4

The Deceiver Becomes the Deceived

We are governed, our minds are molded, our tastes formed, our ideas suggested, largely by men we have never heard of.

—Edward Bernays, *Propaganda*

In the mind unanchored to the One who is God, nothing amid the tempests of life is real. Reality can become just an "idea" you've made up in your head. With no measure of truth against which to test them, ideas can float free, take on a non-life of their own, and become very dangerous.

Unknown to me, a series of malevolent events led by "ideas" detached from reality had derailed the women's movement even before Walter, our baby, and I arrived in New York. If I'd known what had happened, I like to imagine I would have questioned the women's movement as my ticket to freedom more closely than I did. But that, too, at this late date is just an "idea." Instead, let us move on with what actually happened.

At *Cosmo*, in my arrogance, I thought I was capable of discernment. I was lying in print by making up anecdotes about "civilians," that much was true. But even so, I genuinely believed I could tell the difference between the truth that would set me free and the deceptions that would keep me in bondage. Other women, in their small-town narrow-mindedness, might not know the truth of things as they really are. But I did. Or so I thought. But in fact, I had already been taken in as much or more by the world's deceptions as anyone around me. Unfortunately, the free press is only as free as the minds of those journalists, editors, and writers who work in the field. I had already become that strange paradox of mankind that's especially commonplace among journalists: I had become both the deceiver and the deceived.

How did this paradox come about? Well, for one thing, I wasn't as smart and self-aware as I thought I was, or I wouldn't have been puking on the subway. But for another, there were many propaganda spinners in New York far more sophisticated than I. One of the subtlest of them all was Lawrence Lader, a Harvard grad, heir of old money, and close friend of Betty Friedan.

I never met Larry. Until my fifth decade of life, I hadn't even heard his name. Yet my willingness to be seduced by his secret schemes and cleverly crafted "special idea" would lead me to embrace, defend, and market a false path to freedom that was not just reprehensible but evil. What happened behind closed doors between Larry Lader and Betty Friedan would misguide my thinking in such a way that it would change my whole life and the lives of millions of other Americans. So even though it may appear at first glance that we are now leaving my story, in fact we are entering into it more deeply.

Larry and Betty: Birds of a Feather

Described by a physician who knew him well as "a cadaverous-appearing man with a rasping voice,"[1] Larry met Betty Friedan in 1942 through mutual friends from Vassar.[2] The two magazine writers, both atheists with old-left leanings, continued to see each other frequently during the 1950s in the New York Public Library's Frederick Lewis Allen writers' room.[3] An inner sanctum of literary camaraderie, the marble-and-wood-paneled Allen Room provided working space for eleven resident writers. The only requirement for receiving a coveted key to the tall dark-wood double doors was a contract from a book publisher. In this secluded literary hideaway, Betty wrote much of *The Feminine Mystique*, and Larry started his first book, a biography of Planned Parenthood founder Margaret Sanger. During three years of interviews, as Sanger poured out her most intimate thoughts to Lader, she would become in his words "the greatest influence" in his life.[4]

It was while working on Sanger's biography in the Allen Room that Lader first became obsessed with abortion as the royal road to sexual freedom. Lader scorned pregnancy as "the ultimate punishment of sex" and idolized abortion as the ultimate way for a man and woman to enjoy "the pleasure of sex for its own sake" without having children.[5] The idea of death before birth—for that is what abortion is—fascinated him.

Lader and Friedan shared many ideas in common. For example, both would one day sign the Humanist Manifesto II, an ideological statement written in 1973 for the American Humanist Association (AHA). The motto of the AHA is "Good Without a God." If I had read the Humanist Manifesto in my twenties, since I considered myself an "educated and sophisticated person," I probably would have signed it too. In many of its tenets, the manifesto differed little from our *Cosmo* philosophy. Both shared the same core belief: that human beings are entirely in charge of the universe, and each isolated individual, operating independently, must make up his or her own private rules. In many ways, humanism as it was laid out in the Humanist Manifesto II was just our *Cosmo* philosophy dressed up in a tweed jacket with a college diploma.

Much of the manifesto sounded quite noble. It urged the "recognition of the common humanity of all people" and stated, "We must learn to live openly together or we shall perish together." Yet it also alluded to traditional religions as "obstacles to human progress," stated that morals "derive their source from human experience" and "need no theological or ideological sanction," and called for the "rights" to abortion, birth control, euthanasia, and suicide.

Hidden within the Humanist Manifesto II also lay an unspoken assumption about an individual's *personhood*. The document reflected the fashionable belief that the human person is a non-worshipping being, abandoned in a vast universe to wander lost, lonely, and afraid with neither the ability nor the need to relate to an all-loving God. Explicitly denying man's deep longings for a relationship with the God Who is Love, the manifesto claimed that traditional religions "separate rather than unite peoples" and "cannot cope with existing world realities."

Denying the existence of "the prayer-hearing God, assumed to love and care for persons, to hear and understand their prayers and to be able to do something about them," the manifesto both Larry and Betty signed stated, "No deity will save us; we must save ourselves."[6]

Yet even though Betty signed the Manifesto, the memory of her Jewish roots would remain with her and call to her throughout her life. In her memoir, *Life So Far*, published when she was nearly eighty years old, she wrote that "there's something in Jewish theology about your duty to use your life to make life better for those who come after. I felt that mission strongly. It wasn't enough just to start a movement for women's rights. You had to make it happen."[7]

Lader, too, was Jewish. But in all the years one of his closest allies knew him, "he never discussed his Jewishness."[8] He was also a staunch believer in the eighteenth-century Malthusian notion that the world's growing population would soon lead to global famine. He had worked for a brief stint as executive director of the Hugh Moore Fund, which poured millions of dollars into the population-control movement during the 1960s.[9] Perhaps the second greatest influence in Lader's life, Hugh Moore was a multimillionare who had parlayed his idea of a disposable cup into the Dixie Cup Company, which he then sold. Moore believed the United States needed to fight the looming threat of communism in third-world nations by keeping the poor from having "too many" children. To mold public opinion and sway public policymakers to adopt his way of thinking, Moore wrote and self-published a fear-mongering little pamphlet entitled *The Population Bomb*. In his pamphlet, he declared, "Today the population bomb threatens to create an explosion as disruptive and dangerous as the explosion of the atom, and with as much influence on prospects for progress or disaster, war or peace."[10] Moore predicted a coming "population explosion" which, as Population Research Institute president Steven Mosher put it, "would be the mother of all calamities, leading to widespread famine and crushing tax rates, the spread of communism and the scourge of war, plus every other imaginable environmental and social ill in between."[11] In Moore's mind, too many babies (particularly among the poor) were the root cause of poverty, crime, and wars. If people weren't stopped from reproducing like rabbits, Moore insisted, the horrible consequence would be worldwide starvation. Lader agreed with him. "It is now recognized," Lader ominously warned in his biography of Moore, "that we must reduce birth rates or await the inevitable disaster. We are on the way to *breeding ourselves to death*" (italics his).[12]

Larry's surefire solution to this terrifying Malthusian idea of impending disaster was abortion, not just for the poor, but also for any woman who wanted to call herself free. Betty's special idea, you'll recall, was that creative work of her own would set a woman free. Larry's special idea was that unrestricted abortion would set a woman free. In this conviction, Lader had far more in common with *Cosmo*'s Helen Brown (hard work and sex without the kids will set you free) than he did with Betty.

Betty supported the legalization of abortion—for other women. Yet, personally, even when she was fired from her newspaper job for being pregnant, the possibility of aborting her own baby to save her job seemed never to have entered her heart.

"Ideologically, I was never for abortion," Betty wrote in the year 2000. "Motherhood is a value to me, and even today abortion is not.... I believed passionately in 1967, as I do today, that women should have the right of chosen motherhood. For me the matter of choice has never been primarily the choice of abortion, but that you can choose to be a mother. That is as important as any right written into the Constitution."[13]

Larry said he tried to persuade her otherwise, that women needed abortion to be free. Yet for many years, Betty remained unconvinced.

The Secret Plan Unveiled

We would never have known it was Lader who at last persuaded Betty to insert abortion into NOW's package of "women's rights" if it weren't for the written testimony of a third party who eye-witnessed events as they unfolded behind the scenes. This eyewitness was Bernard ("Bernie") Nathanson, M.D. As director of one of the world's largest abortion clinics, Nathanson worked with Lader in the late 1960s to found NARAL, the first national organization set up to repeal U.S. abortion laws.

In his book *Ideas Triumphant*, Lader observed: "When Arthur Schlesinger, Jr., concluded, 'Ideas are great educators,' he was paying little attention to those special ideas that sneak into history almost surreptitiously."[14] Lader knew how to sneak his special ideas into history, and he taught Nathanson his secrets.

In the early days of the abortion movement, Nathanson and Lader frequently took short trips together out of the city. On a typical outing on October 7, 1967, they took a drive down to Bucks County, Pennsylvania. The conversation turned, as usual, to abortion. "If we're going to move abortion out of the books and into the streets, we're going to have to recruit the feminists," Larry observed as they drove along. "Friedan has got to put her troops into this thing—while she still has control of them."[15]

Betty, who always insisted the women's movement had to speak for mainstream women who wanted children, was locked in a bitter power struggle for control of NOW. Her adversaries were several groups of militant radicals, whom Bernie characterized as "the Trotskyite left, the Lesbian libbers, and the more rabid pro-abortionists."[16]

Bernie initially objected to the idea of recruiting Friedan for their abortion cause. He regarded abortion as "a broad social issue that feminists shouldn't abrogate to themselves." At that time, most abortion advocates were white, upper-middle-class men, primarily doctors and lawyers. If a bunch of radical women appeared to take over the abortion movement, Bernie feared that moderate legislators and judges (again the vast majority of them men) would dismiss abortion reform without a fair hearing.[17]

"I was dead wrong, of course," Bernie later admitted. "Larry's marriage with the feminists was a brilliant tactic."[18]

On another memorable occasion, over a fish dinner and a bottle of cold white wine in a small harborside restaurant on Saint Croix in the Virgin Islands, where they'd rented a beach house getaway to work out NARAL strategies, Larry began to unveil the fabricated story he planned to use to market abortion to women, the media, and the American public.

"Historically, every revolution has to have its villain," Larry told Bernie. "It doesn't really matter whether it's a king, a dictator, or a tsar, but it has to be *someone*, a person, to rebel against."[19]

Larry's villain of choice—his "favorite whipping boy,"[20] in Nathanson's words—was the Catholic Church.

But Larry warned Bernie they shouldn't try to tar and feather *all* Catholics. "First of all, that's too large a group, and for us to vilify them all would diffuse our focus," he observed. "Secondly, we have to convince liberal Catholics to join us, a popular front as it were, and if we tar them all with the same brush, we'll just antagonize a few who might otherwise have joined us and be valuable showpieces for us. No, it's got to be the Catholic *hierarchy*. That's a small enough group to come down on, and anonymous enough so that no names ever have to be mentioned, but everybody will have a fairly good idea whom we are talking about."[21]

Locking his jet-fighter radar directly onto the Catholic hierarchy, Larry said, "That's the *real* enemy. The biggest single obstacle to peace and decency throughout all of history."[22]

During their road-trip conversations on their way home from Bucks County to Greenwich Village, Larry continued his diatribe, launching into what Bernie described as a "chilling indictment of the poisonous influence of Catholicism in secular affairs from its inception until the day before yesterday." Increasingly discomforted by Lader's violent anti-Catholic bigotry, Bernie offered a mild protest: "But, Larry," he objected, "the Catholic Church isn't *all* bad. Don't forget that among other things they did more or less keep the intellectual world together in the Dark Ages."[23]

Undeterred, Larry continued to portray the Church as Public Enemy Number One.

"Well, Larry, what do you think?" Bernie persisted. "Is the Catholic hierarchy identical with the anti-abortion forces? Aren't there *any* others opposed to abortion?"

At this point, Larry "set the intellectual tone for the next eight years with a single word."

"No."[24]

Larry habitually referred to the Catholic hierarchy as the *opposition*, and Bernie remembered, "That was how Trotsky and his followers habitually referred to the Stalinists."[25]

During another NARAL strategy meeting, Larry told Bernie, "We've got to keep the women out in front. You know what I mean . . . and some blacks. Black women especially. Why are they so damn slow to see the importance of this whole movement to themselves?"[26] (It apparently did not cross his mind that perhaps black women did not regard his crusade to eliminate their babies as their path to true freedom.)

All revolutions also need a clever propaganda slogan to use as a rallying cry, and Lader had a humdinger of a slogan in his pocket. The slogan was "No woman can call herself free who does not own and control her own body." On its face, the slogan is true. Who could deny it? But what does it mean? "Owning and controlling one's own body" is one of those empty phrases that could mean anything from dieting to lose weight to schussing gracefully down a mountain slope.

"That's the whole point of good propaganda," media critic Noam Chomsky points out. "You want to create a slogan that nobody's going to be against and everybody's going to be for. Nobody knows what it means because it doesn't mean anything. Its crucial value is that it diverts your attention from a question that *does* mean something: Do you support our policy? That's the one you're not allowed to talk about."[27]

Lader claimed Margaret Sanger invented the "control your own body" slogan. But if she did, she did not mean by it what Lader said it meant. Sanger so vehemently opposed abortion that, by Lader's own admission, his abortion advocacy caused a rift between them which remained unhealed at her death.[28] Sanger called abortion "barbaric." It wasn't until after Sanger died and abortionist Alan Guttmacher took the helm that Planned Parenthood (the organization Sanger founded) publicly began to advocate legalized abortion.[29] Dismissing Sanger as behind the times, Lader created his own lexicon in which a woman's freedom "to own and control her own body" meant her right to unrestricted abortion on demand.

A Masterpiece of Persuasion

To Lader's frustration, Friedan was almost as reluctant as black women were to accept his idea that women needed to abort their children to be free. To Larry's disappointment, the first edition of *The Feminine Mystique* mentioned neither contraceptives nor abortion. His cleverly crafted *Abortion* book, however, seems to have finally convinced Betty that America's abortion laws needed to be changed.

Published in 1966, the 212-page hardcover had on its cover a sinister red-and-black op-art design which appeared to conceal yet at the same time reveal two malevolent eyes. Under a pretense of love for women (particularly the poor), Lader wrote, "The complete legalization of abortion is the one just and inevitable answer to the quest for feminine freedom."[30] His book was tantalizingly subtitled: "*The first authoritative and documented report on the laws and practices governing abortion in the U.S. and around the world, and how—for the sake of women everywhere—they can and must be reformed.*"

In a back-jacket endorsement in praise of *Abortion*, Betty raved: "Lawrence Lader's book is the first daring revelation of the cruelty and damage inflicted on American women by our antiquated abortion laws. It is not only an authoritative study of the hypocrisy and absurdity of abortion practices; it is a courageous blueprint of what women must do to abolish the state's power to force them to bear a child against their will."

A masterpiece of persuasion, *Abortion* likened the abortion movement to the civil rights movement, suggesting that women's "bondage" to pregnancy was as unjust and evil as eighteenth-century slavery. This emotionally intense but logically false analogy appealed strongly to undiscerning readers during the 1960s civil rights era. Under the guise of objective journalism, in collusion with eminent New York pro-abortion attorneys Harriet Pilpel, Ephraim London, and Cyril Means Jr.,[31] Lader methodically laid out in his book a persuasive and powerful legal argument for abolishing all abortion laws.

In addition, he desacralized the baby in the womb by claiming that even the Catholic Church has always been confused about whether or not the "fetus" has a soul and, that therefore, the fetus probably doesn't have a soul, at the very least not until its mother feels the baby kick. Splitting spirit from matter and creating a verbal smokescreen to make the issue seem as complicated as possible,[32] Lader ignored or overlooked Christ's sanctification of the flesh. He also ignored or overlooked *The Didache* or *The Teaching of the Twelve Apostles*, written in the first century and often considered the Church's first catechism, which plainly and simply states: "Do not kill a fetus by abortion, or commit infanticide."[33]

To create the largest possible media splash for his book, Larry pulled out all the stops. In May 1966, the same month *Abortion* was released, he published an article containing excerpts of his book in *Reader's Digest* (the magazine which at that time I most admired and trusted). Independently wealthy, Larry also hired his own publicist to make sure key journalists heard about *Abortion*. One used copy of the book, which I obtained years later when it was out of print,

was personally autographed to nationally syndicated New York
City radio host Casper Citron, "with deep appreciation," penned
in Lader's slithering handwriting. The inside dust-jacket copy raved,
"Lawrence Lader has written an angry book, but a book completely
informed and documented, a book to change the attitudes and laws
of a nation."

Unfortunately, Lader's "completely informed" and "documented"
story was laced with poisonous half truth, limited truth, and truth out
of context. Much of the bogus abortion history in his angry book
was invented by Cyril Chestnut Means Jr., a New York Law School
professor who later became a NARAL attorney. Means arbitrarily
destroyed legal precedent, replacing it with a history of his own making. According to Villanova University law-history professor Joseph
Dellapenna, author of a meticulously researched, 1,283-page volume
titled *Dispelling the Myths of Abortion History*:

> Means propounded two hitherto unsuspected historical "facts": First,
> that abortion was not criminal in England or America before the nine-
> teenth century; and second, that abortion was criminalized during the
> nineteenth century solely to protect the life or health of mothers,
> and not to protect the lives or health of unborn children. Regardless
> of how many times these claims are repeated, however, they are not
> facts; they are myths.[34]

Because Dellapenna has so effectively laid out the intellectual case
against the distorted history upon which *Roe v. Wade* was based, he
has been publicly accused of being a Catholic, perhaps in the hope his
work will thereby be discredited. Dellapenna assures his readers, "I
am not a Catholic. I am and have been for most of my life, by choice,
a Unitarian. (Today, one might describe me as a lapsed Unitarian, for
I find even that church too restrictive.)"[35]

The Lader/Means/Nathanson pro-abortion campaign was a propagandistic tour de force. Means' highly imaginative history was a
convoluted blend of fact and fiction so intricately interlaced only an
extremely well-educated and diligent historian could pry the two
apart. After Lader published Means' fabricated history in his *Abortion* book, Means managed to get his misstatements of historic fact
published in a reputable scholarly journal, the *New York Law Forum*.

He then proceeded to present "his radical revision of the history of abortion—a history that had been unquestioned for centuries—to the Supreme Court in an *amicus* brief to *Roe v. Wade*."[36] Justice Harry Blackmun, in turn, relied "heavily and uncritically" on this history to write his abortion opinions (*Roe* and *Doe v. Bolton*).[37] Blackmun cited Larry's *Abortion* book no less than seven times and Means' history (but no other historian) another seven times.

By comparison, the petty lies we told at *Cosmo* were child's play.

To continue the ruse, many statistics in Lader's book—and later in NARAL's press releases—were completely made up. "Knowing that if a true poll were taken we would be soundly defeated, we simply fabricated the results of fictional polls," Nathanson revealed. "We announced to the media that we had taken polls and that 60 percent of Americans were in favor of permissive abortion. This is the tactic of the self-fulfilling lie. Few people care to be in the minority."[38]

The number of illegal abortions Lader alleged to be done annually in the United States was also fabricated. Although the actual figure was about one hundred thousand, Nathanson said, "The figure we gave to the media repeatedly [and the figure that appeared in Lader's book] was one million. Repeating the big lie often enough convinced the public."[39] As for the number of women dying each year from illegal abortions, the figure NARAL constantly fed to the media was ten thousand, when the real number was around two hundred to two hundred and fifty.[40] These fictitious figures, Nathanson reported, "took root in the consciousness of Americans" and convinced many "we needed to crack the abortion law."[41]

Part of the nature of propaganda is that it must be concealed and disguised. The difficulty of recognizing a propagandist at all is part of his success. With the publication of his *Abortion* book, Lader's fictional statistics hit the wire services and were spread as truth throughout the U.S. Newspapers from the *Oakland Tribune* in California to the *Cedar Rapids Gazette* in Iowa to the *Gazette-Mail* in Charleston, West Virginia, ran Lader's false statistics with no questions asked.

Soon Larry's statistics were just "in the air." You didn't even have to have read his book to hear and believe his numbers. I absorbed them as if by osmosis.

Propaganda is high-tech communication at its most dehumanizing: it steals away a person's freedom to make decisions based on

the truth without his even knowing it happened. By now, my conscience was so drowsy from the many lies I'd told, intellectual errors
could slither into my head and breed there entirely unnoticed. I made
a comfortable nest in my head for Lader's lies.

So did Betty Friedan.

After reading *Abortion*, Betty seems to have been sold at last on
Lader's "abortion will set you free" idea, impressed enough she even
considered putting a demand for the repeal of all abortion laws into
NOW's original 1966 Statement of Purpose.

Close friends wisely cautioned her not to. "You're doing something controversial enough," historian Carl Degler (who was later to
win the Pulitzer) told Betty. "Don't put abortion in there."[42]

So she didn't.

Yet just one year later—only six weeks after that Bucks County
road trip when Lader told Nathanson they needed to recruit her for
their cause—Betty created an uproar at the Second Annual NOW
Conference, when, in her characteristic domineering style, with a
voice like a foghorn, she demanded that NOW take a stand in favor
of contraception and for total repeal of all abortion laws.

What's more, Betty demanded that abortion, contraception, and
sex education be inserted into the women's movement not to further
her own agenda (or so it was said), but only to serve all women's best
interests. She did it to shield me from injustice and to set me free.

Chapter 5

A Fly on the Wall of the Chinese Room

Ours has become an incredibly violent time. Our people are involved in acts of violence both in our streets and in Southeast Asia. Meanwhile, all mankind exists under the dark shadow of the strategy of nuclear terror with its threat of sudden death for all of us.

Has life ever been held more cheaply? Has there ever been greater indifference to the taking of life? Are we really aware of just how hardened we have become?

I wonder if, in this atmosphere, we are capable of making a wise decision on this issue [of abortion] involving our very attitude toward human life. Perhaps we should wait for a more compassionate and less callous time.

—Senator Alan Cranston,
Rockefeller Commission Report on
Population Growth and the American Future, 1972

At *Cosmo*, the one assumption I never thought to question in my confusion was whether or not abortion and contraception were good for women. Among journalists working for any publication (especially among freelancers, but it also happens on-staff), a subtle kind of self-censorship tends to set in. If I heard anything negative about abortion or the Pill, I automatically shut it out of my mind, because I knew *Cosmo* would never publish it, even if I dared to write it. In Helen Gurley Brown territory, it was an automatic given that separating women from children (through abortion and contraception) was required for women to be free. How could a woman have sex "just like a man," work sixty-hour weeks "just like a man," and devote her life to the corporation "just like a man" if she kept taking time off to have babies? Plainly, she couldn't. That's why I believed the *Daily Breeze* fired me for being a mother, and why *Baby Talk* refused to hire me with a new baby at home.

But—and this was the fine print in the social contract—an allegedly smart woman *could* biologically neuter herself (temporarily or permanently) through the Pill, the IUD, abortion, sterilization, or hysterectomy. Then *voila!* Suddenly, she could behave like a man both in bed and at work. Many people "in the know," not just Helen Gurley Brown and Hugh Hefner but a bevy of other great thinkers of the hour, thought this population-wide neutering of women sounded like a splendid idea—good for men, good for business, good for America. Since our poor planet Earth was (erroneously) thought to be staggering under the weight of too many hungry people, making women's bodies more like men's was even thought to be good for the world.

Rhetorically framed as a "right" all "strong, independent women" desired and needed to be truly free, abortion became in my mind an intrinsic plank in the women's movement platform—as sacrosanct and necessary as, say, the right to apply for credit in my own name, the right to serve on a jury, or the right to receive equal pay for equal work.

Yet if I had known the full story about what happened one November night in the Chinese Room of Washington D.C.'s Mayflower Hotel, I would have had to scrutinize this idea more carefully.

What happened that November night will soon play a central role in my story. So come with me now as I become a fly on the wall and together we listen in on that meeting.

A Place Where Power Resides

Proclaimed by Harry Truman to be Washington, D.C.'s "second best address" (after the White House), the Mayflower Hotel when it opened in 1925 was said to have "more gold leaf than any other U.S. building except the Library of Congress." Calvin Coolidge held his Inaugural Ball here. FBI director J. Edgar Hoover ate lunch here every day for twenty years. It was also while staying in the Mayflower that President Franklin D. Roosevelt dictated his famous speech containing the prophetic line: "We have nothing to fear but fear itself."

It is November 18, 1967, and a small contingent of NOW members have gathered in the Mayflower for their second national conference. Although eighty-nine persons (excluding officers) formally registered for the conference, according to NOW president Betty Friedan, one hundred and five persons have arrived.[1] By midnight tonight, they will have voted on and adopted a "Bill of Rights" that will set the political agenda of NOW and the mainstream women's movement for decades to come. Held in several rooms, including the Mayflower's opulent Chinese Room with its spectacular carved ceiling and ornate, gold-leaf filigreed mirrors, the two-day conference is closed to the press. The only journalist here is a fly on the wall.

The women milling about the Mayflower Hotel this seasonably brisk Saturday morning include lawyers, business owners, labor-union organizers, suffragists, and student radicals. A handful of men are also here. Each attendee can see a tiny part of what NOW needs to accomplish to make America a better place for women. But only a few possess the broad worldview required to see the big picture and understand where the fault lines lie. Approximately one hundred passionate, strong-willed individuals have come together this day, with their own individual hopes, dreams, and fears—and that's the beauty of it, and the terror of it.

Two Power Houses

The two powerful women seated side by side at the head table as the meeting is called to order at 9:00 A.M. are both founding members of NOW, but they could not be more different.

Known for her flamboyant, combative style and domineering bursts of energy, Betty Friedan at age forty-six is a force to be reckoned with. "She walks like a tipsy penguin, carrying herself belly forward like a woman in the third month of her pregnancy," a writer once described her. "With her slim arms and legs, her pregnant posture, wearing her no-bra bra under clinging jerseys, she could be the fertility icon of a pagan tribe. It is, perhaps, a reflection of a mercurial personality that she never looks the same twice. At a lectern she is sometimes earth mother, sometimes bitch, sometimes child. People who admire her find her attractive. To her enemies she is all the witches from Macbeth."[2] In the words of Betty's comrade Larry Lader, "She sweeps through meetings ... and speeches with frantic bursts of energy as if each day might be her last. Everything is in motion, not just her words which come so fast she seems to ignore the necessity of breathing. Her hands gesticulate, wave, flail. Her eyes are deep, dark, charged, and violent as her language."[3]

In stark contrast, the tall, dignified, lavender-blue-eyed retired IRS attorney seated next to Betty has "a deep aversion to hostility and confrontation."[4] At seventy-two, Marguerite Rawalt is a veteran Washington insider—a personal friend of Eleanor Roosevelt and one of the few independent activists President John F. Kennedy appointed in 1961 to his new Commission on the Status of Women. A connector, Marguerite corresponds with professional and business women all over the country. One of her longtime friends is eighty-two-year-old, Washington, D.C., resident Alice Paul, the main leader and strategist of the women's suffrage campaign which resulted in the 1920 passage of the U.S. Constitutional amendment that gave women the right to vote.* By comparison, Betty is a newcomer to the women's rights movement, a media celebrity who only recently entered the inner sanctums of Washington power through the door of a best-selling popular book.

As you'd expect, these two women have come to the table from radically different backgrounds. Betty grew up, according to Lader, as "a fumbling, precocious Jewish girl in Peoria, Illinois, a lonely outcast from the dates and sororities essential to Midwest conformity."[5] Marguerite crossed the plains in a covered wagon as a child, lived among Indian tribes, and never forgot the lessons she learned as a Texas farm girl from her dependable dad.[6] She works as easily with men as with

---

*Alice Paul, a Quaker, had led her peacefully protesting Silent Sentinels to picket the White House to gain women the right to vote. Having previously been jailed along with others, she knew being arrested would bring her cause the media attention it deserved. A firebrand, she deliberately walked the picket line, knowing she would be arrested and face a harsh jail term. She was jailed, went on a hunger strike, and was force fed—all to win women the right to vote. Paul strongly opposed linking the Equal Rights Amendment to abortion. She said, "Abortion is the ultimate exploitation of women." Other suffragists who opposed abortion included Susan B. Anthony, Dr. Elizabeth Blackwell, and Elizabeth Cady Stanton. "Without known exception," observes Feminists for Life president Serrin Foster in *The Feminist Case against Abortion*, "the early feminists condemned abortion in the strongest terms." See http://www.feministsforlife .org/herstory/ and http://feministsforlife.org/-taf/2001/summer/Summer01.pdf.

women.[7] And when she went duck hunting two years ago at age seventy with her brother Louis, she shot six ducks, bringing down two ducks with one shot.[8]

As for their private lives, Betty's marriage to Carl Friedan (who runs his own advertising firm) has been "volcanic almost from the start, a succession of brawls that often [reach] physical violence."[9] Betty has been known to "black out during fights with Carl and wake up with a bruised face and a black eye." But she's no shrinking violet. One dark night, she cut a gash in Carl's head by hitting him with a curtain rod.[10] Another time "Carl showed up for an important job interview with a scratched face. The woman who set up the appointment with him told him that he looked as if he had been mauled by a tiger."[11] Predictably, this violent marriage, during which both Betty and Carl are alleged to have had extramarital affairs, will soon end in divorce.

Marguerite, on the other hand, was married for twenty-six years to mild-mannered Harry Secord, a retired Air Force major and the love of her life. Although Marguerite had no children, she still struggled valiantly to balance her brilliant career with her marriage. "When she had to choose, she put Harry above everything else—without regret," her biographer wrote. "She needed Harry to temper the force of her own drive. When he wasn't there, she pushed too hard, tried to do more than was possible for one person to do."[12] Now a widow, Marguerite referred to Harry after his death in a poignant letter to a friend as her dear comrade, friend, partner, and pal.[13]

Regarding God, Friedan turned away from Judaism while she was still in high school and will one day sign the atheistic Humanist Manifesto II, which denies the existence of a prayer-hearing God. Marguerite is a Presbyterian, whose deep faith guides her behavior and how she sees the world. In 1961, in a Christmas letter to her family, she wrote: "In today's world with the Communist shadow, it is more important than ever to remember that Christ was born and that we are Christians. It is the only thing we can cling to as we contemplate nuclear possibilities."[14]

So how did these two disparate souls wind up sitting side by side on November 18, 1967, jointly presiding over such a historic meeting? In this case, their differences have brought them together. Betty couldn't run an orderly meeting if her celebrity depended on it. Marguerite is "an expert on parliamentary procedure."[15]

Before the meeting begins, one NOW board member, Mary Eastwood, overhears Betty say to Marguerite, "So tell me about Robert's
Rule's of Order" (referring to the recognized guide to running meetings smoothly, orderly, and fairly).[16]

Having attended a board meeting the previous evening in Friedan's
hotel room where an angry dispute erupted over the Equal Rights
Amendment, and perhaps hoping to avoid a similar cat fight, Marguerite volunteers to sit beside Betty to act as her parliamentarian—
on the condition that she (Marguerite) will still be permitted to participate in the discussions.[17]

A "Bill of Rights" for You *or* Me (but Not Both of Us)

The Saturday morning session of the NOW convention goes
smoothly. Everyone in the room agrees American women should
be allowed equal rights under the law (including equal pay for equal
work) and should stop doing the "menial housework" of politics
(such as stamp licking and coffee pouring) until they share in political
decision making. As a fly on the wall, I don't much like the enthu-
siastic vote in favor of a national network of child-care centers for
working mothers. I'd rather find some way to earn a living at home,
so I can bring up my children and not farm them out to strangers.
That's just one reason why the goal of earning a living at freelance
writing appeals so much to Walter and me. Be that as it may, the vote
in the Chinese Room is unanimous in favor of government-funded
child-care centers.

The afternoon meeting, which opens at 2:00 P.M. after a darling
lunch, is a less friendly affair. Hostile debate breaks out over support-
ing an Equal Rights Amendment to the U.S. Constitution. Pauli
Murray, age fifty-seven, a strong-minded civil rights and labor activ-
ist, who has known Eleanor Roosevelt since the 1930s and will one
day leave academia to become an Episcopal priest, opposes the ERA.
The first black American to graduate from Yale Law School, Pauli
was on the original steering committee that laid the groundwork
for NOW. Predating Rosa Parks' historic protest in Montgomery,
Alabama, by fifteen years, Pauli was arrested in 1940 for violating
Virginia segregation laws after she and a friend sat in a whites-only
section of a bus. At the Founder's Dinner at NOW's 1971 national

conference, Pauli will also be given public credit for writing much of NOW's stirring, five-page "Statement of Purpose," which had the ring of the Declaration of Independence and which declared that "human rights for all are indivisible." She deeply opposes the idea of splitting women's rights off from others' rights and firmly believes the vitality of the Fifth and Fourteenth Amendments are sufficient to cover all human rights. Whenever human rights are divided, hate and violence erupt, as one person's rights are pitted against another's.

Sharp-eyed and keenly alert, Pauli senses a dark spirit at work in the Chinese Room. Friedan, in her usual combative style, listens politely to those who speak in favor of the ERA and rudely "calls time" on those who oppose it. Pauli angrily stalks out of the meeting and immediately fires off a telegram to withdraw her name from nomination to NOW's national board. In a seven-page, single-spaced letter sent the following Tuesday to give reasons for her decision, Pauli will observe this conference was "not broadly representative of women in the same sense" the 1966 NOW conference had been.[18] She saw no Catholic sisters, no women of ethnic minorities (other than about five black women), no women who represented the poor. Although she didn't mention it, she also saw few if any young mothers like me. Friedan had already raised her children; many others there, including Pauli and Marguerite, had no children at all. Eye-witnessing what clearly appeared to be a "commando attack" at the meeting, Pauli will later say she observed "an organized force at work which had no intention of permitting calm and reasoned discussion." Although singling out Marguerite Rawalt as "imminently fair throughout the proceedings," Pauli will state the way Betty conducted the meeting filled her with "revulsion."[19]

But that's far from the end of the story.

The Mere Fifty-Seven

Friedan has saved the vote over the abortion resolution for last. Without warning, she suddenly shocks many delegates, including Marguerite Rawalt, by belligerently pressing for full repeal of all abortion laws. Abortion is not an issue to which Marguerite has devoted much time. On the one hand, she believes abortion should probably be decriminalized. Yet, on the other hand, she has "serious reservations" about NOW endorsing abortion as a woman's legal right. She's more politically experienced than Betty, and she believes NOW "should define their territory precisely and postpone controversial issues. They had their hands full with job discrimination, low wages, poor representation on the bench, on juries, and in Congress."[20]

The abortion plank sparks bitter, strident controversy.

Soon the meeting spirals once again out of control. Of the one hundred or so members in attendance, students and radicals have shown up in unexpected numbers to cast their votes for abortion. Using Lader's slogan about "a woman's right to control her own body,"[21] they repeatedly stand up and shout, "We've got to have an abortion plank!"[22] In a microcosm of the abortion controversy that still rages in our nation today, here are just a few of the points we hear amid the hysteria:

"[Abortion] is the constitutional right of each woman," one speaker says. "This is part of the sexual revolution."

"This resolution would be a step to overcome the plight of the poor," says another.

Pro-abortion sociologist Alice Rossi declares, "If no harm will come of it, people should be free to do as they choose. If they want pre-marital relations, then let them."

"NOW should not support pre-marital relations," constitutional lawyer Phineas Indritz retorts.

"The Catholic members of NOW will quit," warns Elizabeth "Betty" Farians, a Catholic. She adds, however, that some "avant-garde theologians" are already debating the question of abortion.

Another declares, "I am against murder."

"This stand on abortion is not especially controversial," one speaker intones. "People are very interested in the question of abortion."

"There are other organizations devoted to this question," argues another. "Why does NOW have to be? Show me another organization, and I'll back out of this one."

Many press for delays until the abortion question can be more carefully studied. Another sampling of comments:

"... I recommend we bring this question up next year."

"We must be cautious," urges another. "We don't want to be considered a NUT group."

"To influence the legislature we must be a strong, large, powerful organization. This organization will never be large and powerful—but we can be controversial. Our ideas will be heard. NOW will be in the forefront. We have to take a stand *now*."

"... Psychiatrists rarely tell the real reason abortions have such an emotional effect on women," sociologist Rossi opines. "It could be because it is unlawful and they feel guilty, but instead they say it is sado-masochistic: a woman wants an abortion so she can feel guilty about the sexual act. This is silly."

"To be against abortion is the clergy's idea—not God's decision," says yet another. "There have been so many reforms in the Catholic Church. These reforms have not been made by God but by men...."

"All things concerned are decided by the individual," declares another. "This is the age of the individual, not the age of tutelage by dogma."[23]

On and on the battle rages.

Marguerite Rawalt is furious. She deeply opposes the "radical and irresponsible" turn the Mayflower Hotel meeting is taking and fears abortion will upstage the genuine legal battles for equality women are fighting. What's going on? Why was she not told ahead of time that abortion would be on the table? Things are happening too fast. Who's calling the shots?[24]

Finally someone moves that a "new statement" be written on abortion. The motion is seconded. The vote goes 42–32 *against* writing a new statement (the motion is *defeated*). The meeting is adjourned. Yet two women leave the room and go out to rewrite the abortion statement, anyway.

What was that all about?

I haven't a clue. Very strange.

When the meeting reconvenes in the Chinese Room at 8:30 P.M., the resolution to support repeal of all abortion laws is withdrawn. The newly written substitute resolution reads: "NOW endorses the basic policy of women to control their own reproduction. We therefore encourage sex education, distribution of contraceptives, and the reappraisal of existing abortion laws." And the war continues.

Alice Rossi reads the substitute resolution and says, "We offer an alternative. We withdraw the first resolution and offer [this] instead."

The first person to speak in the discussion from the floor is Ti-Grace Atkinson, twenty-nine, a tall, blond, divorced Columbia

University philosophy major, whose language is peppered "with the Marxist jargon of the student peace movement."[25] Within a year, Ti-Grace will split off from NOW and become active in the more radical left-wing Women's Liberation movement, popularly known as "Women's Lib." She will state in a speech given on March 4, 1970, at the University of Rhode Island "that all institutions and practices that are founded on inequitable principles . . . must be destroyed. *Some of these institutions are marriage, motherhood, sex, love, prostitution, religion*" (italics added). Further, in a speech she will make at Catholic University of America on March 10, 1971, she will refer to the Catholic Church as "the greatest organized crime ring the world's ever seen."[26]

But tonight in the Chinese Room, her rhetoric is less heated. "This substitute is a questioning," she says, "not a stand, not a principle."

Among other points we hear in the debate:

"Rights and equality come with responsibility. If women want rights in other areas, they must be responsible for their own reproduction," says another member.

"The revised statement is good," says a third. "It can benefit the progressive state of New York and also the others."

"The words of the resolution should be changed," a male Constitutional lawyer pipes up. "Instead of *reappraisal*, use the word *challenge*."

"People are worried about the press image. We must go onward."

"We should not compromise," Friedan declares. "We must pioneer."

"All laws penalizing abortion should be repealed," the male attorney asserts.

"NOW should endorse the principle that [a] woman [should] control her reproductive processes and that it should be a matter between her physician and herself."

"We either take a stand on abortion or not. Why do we need a conscience all of a sudden?"

On and on the bitter controversy rages, until one NOW officer later recalled she felt emotionally "drained."[27]

In the end, the vote is 57–14 in favor of the first resolution, calling for the repeal of all abortion laws.[28]

Yet once again, puzzling questions arise in my mind. The 57–14 vote represents the views of only seventy-one people. Friedan reported one hundred and five people attended the conference. *What happened to the other thirty-four votes?* Did those people abstain? Did they get tired of the fight and go home? The minutes of the meeting don't say. A total of ninety-seven votes were recorded for and against the ERA resolution, so perhaps only ninety-seven voting members were present. And yet only seventy-one votes were recorded either for or against the resolution to repeal all abortion laws. *Where are the other votes?* A great mystery remains.

The intensely emotional meeting finally ends around 11:00 P.M.

When the dust settles at last and her side has won, Friedan feels "gooseflesh." She believes the Mere Fifty-Seven who voted "yes" for legalized abortion tonight have "the authority to speak for women" over all generations, both for the suffragists who had gone before and for generations of women to come.[29]

One of Marguerite's dear friends, attorney Elizabeth ("Betty") Boyer from Cleveland, leaves the conference "in despair over the abortion vote."[30] She came to D.C. with such high hopes. Boyer has a "strong sense of right and wrong,"[31] and she and others who attended the meeting suspect it was intentionally "stacked with students and radicals" to ram through the abortion vote.[32] She knows the women she recruited to join NOW in Ohio will be as appalled at the abortion plank as she is. In Boyer's words, a new life is a "sacred trust."[33] Boyer will return to Ohio to "face complaints and outrage over the abortion plank."[34] She will later resign from NOW's board of directors after what she describes as "a shouting match" and go on to give Ohio women the organization she promised by founding the Women's Equality Action League (WEAL). Proving that advocating legal abortion was not a necessary precondition for winning women's rights, WEAL would fight successfully to abolish "Help wanted (male)" and "Help wanted (female)" classified ads in newspapers and to end sex discrimination in colleges and universities. WEAL would also be instrumental in the passage of the Equal Credit Opportunity Act of 1974, a law allowing a married woman to apply for credit under her own name.[35]

In her disgust over what happened in the Mayflower Hotel, Boyer was hardly alone. Television broadcaster Paige Palmer, NOW's

director of women's activities, wrote a scathing letter to Betty Friedan in which she stated she had looked forward to the conference and
set aside other plans to attend, but she departed "wishing I had never
heard of N.O.W." Sharply criticizing Betty's overbearing behavior
during the abortion debate, Palmer noted, "For an intelligent woman
to show such disrespect for parliamentary law was most disappoint-
ing. A presiding officer never shows her feelings whether she is for or
against a speaker from the floor. I feel that because of the president's
facial expressions, she was able to persuade the group to vote according to her desires." Observing that "there was a group who came
only to see to it that the abortion question was discussed and passed,"
Palmer added: "This is known as 'railroading.'" Further, Palmer
pointed out that Dr. Shepherd Aaronson, the only M.D. present who
could speak intelligently from a medical standpoint on the abortion
issue, was "shut up in no uncertain terms," while women who knew
nothing about abortion were allowed to voice their opinions freely.[36]
Before the dust completely settled, one-third of the women who
attended the Mayflower Hotel convention resigned from NOW.

Betty felt "utter confidence" that human history was made at that
meeting in the Chinese R ⌐ ⌐ [37] And indeed it was.

For on that tragic night, in ⌐he paltriness of an earthly moment,
the women's movement was sharply scissored into two irreconcilable
factions: women for legal abortion on demand, and women who
opposed it.

In the hours before midnight on November 18, 1967, NOW
simultaneously became both the national organization *for* women and
the national organization *against* motherhood, a living contradiction.

Yet the following Monday morning, NOW held a nine o'clock
news conference in the Mayflower Hotel and handed out a press release
in which all the uproar in the Saturday night meeting was glossed over.

Controlling the Press

Never shy when standing in the media spotlight, Betty Friedan proclaimed on Monday morning via a press release to reporters (and
through them to the American public) that through its new Bill of
Rights, NOW was speaking for "the New Woman power block

[*sic*]," a massive force which she claimed included "28 million American working women, the millions of women emerging from our colleges each year who are intent on full participation in the mainstream of our society, and mothers who are emerging from their homes to go back to school or work."[38]

In reality, of course, regarding abortion and contraception, Betty was speaking only for herself and fifty-seven other individuals in the Chinese Room. Self-appointed and unelected, she had rammed through the vote for abortion in a totally undemocratic process. Yet she claimed to have her finger on the pulse of America. Such is the *hubris* of the "intelligent few" who craft and use propaganda for their own glory.

On Tuesday, Marguerite Rawalt's worst fears were realized: the *Washington Post* headlined the abortion vote. In an interview, Ti-Grace Atkinson declared that "the abortion stand seeks to free women really from their own notions of themselves as 'slaves' to their reproductive processes." Further, the *Post* reported: "NOW supports the furthering of the sexual revolution of our century by pressing for widespread sex education and provision of birth control information and contraceptives, and by urging that all laws penalizing abortion be repealed."[39]

Thus, at the very moment the Mere Fifty-Seven received Lader's abortion plank into their political platform, the women's movement and the sexual revolution became united as one in the eyes of the media and the world. The unholy marriage was consummated.

When news of NOW's abortion vote reached Larry Lader's ears, of course, he was elated. "Once the National Organization for Women and Women's Liberation groups joined the abortion movement," he jubilantly rejoiced, "we were ready to shake the country."[40]

In 1968, emboldened by NOW's surprising demands, many organizations which had previously endorsed only abortion law *reform* (allowing abortion only in "extreme" cases of rape or incest, for example) now came out for full *repeal* of all existing abortion laws. These organizations included Planned Parenthood World Federation, the American Civil Liberties Union (ACLU), and the governing council of the American Public Health Association. Meanwhile, Lader continued to shape public opinion through his freelance magazine articles. Two of his stories to appear in 1968 were "The Mother

Who Chose Abortion" (*Redbook*, February) and "The New Abortion Laws: A Discussion of the Ethical and Medical Considerations That Underlie Them" (*Parents Magazine*, April).

Also in 1968—that historic year of "America's Suicide Attempt"— Lader and his accomplices began to hatch a plan to "bring together every abortion group in the country—religious, political, feminist, medical" for a three-day conference with the "ultimate purpose" being "to swing moderate reformers to complete repeal."[41]

The next year, at a conference held February 14–16 in Chicago's posh Drake Hotel, NARAL was born.[42]

The sexual revolution's abortion train was chugging full steam down the tracks. It was time to bring public opinion more firmly aboard.

The Women's Strike for Equality

Edward Bernays, author of *Propaganda*, advised those "invisible governors" and "intelligent few" who aim to shape the minds and hearts of the masses to "create events" to grab media attention.

NOW's first major manufactured event was designed to produce the greatest national media splash: it was called the Women's Strike for Equality. The march was held on August 26, 1970, the fiftieth anniversary of women's winning the constitutional right to vote. It took place just a week or so before Walter, Dustin, and I arrived in New York. In the largest women's rights protest ever held in the United States at the time, Betty (who, because of her "explosive personality and habit of irritating her associates," had not been reelected NOW president and "wanted an inspiring project to crown her career")[43] proudly led a police-estimated crowd of more than twenty thousand women along with some sympathetic men marching curb to curb down New York's Fifth Avenue. The women carried signs and banners displaying slogans like "Don't Cook Dinner—Starve a Rat Tonight!" and "Don't Iron While the Strike Is Hot". With thousands more marching in other cities, including Boston, Chicago, San Francisco, and Washington, D.C., the strike captured huge media attention and established the women's movement for the first time as a powerful political force in the public eye. Years later in his book *Ideas Triumphant: Strategies for Social Change and Progress*, Lader would boast, "The women's march was an impressive example of how ideas could be turned into reality."[44]

Cosmopolitan's Helen Gurley Brown was there to march for women's "freedom" right along with Betty and the others.

Immediately following the march at a rally in Bryant Park behind the New York Public Library, Betty gave an impassioned speech to a cheering crowd in which she laid out NOW's political platform, calling for, among other things, passage of the ERA, "a system of twenty-four-hour day care centers for the children of working mothers, equal education and employment opportunities"[45]—and, of course, free abortion on request. NOW's powerful endorsement clothed abortion in a respectable garment small-town America had never seen it wearing before. NOW also urged women across the nation to boycott products whose advertising was degrading to the image of women and, in an ironic twist, named *Cosmopolitan* as one of the worst offenders.

Helen Gurley Brown didn't flinch. She perceptively suggested to a *New York Times* reporter that her sex-revolution magazine *was* part of the women's movement.[46]

And, indeed, thanks to Betty, it now was. Intellectually brilliant as she was, the mother of the women's movement simply did not have the eyes to see what she had done. By inserting demands for abortion, contraception, and sex education into NOW's "Bill of Rights," she had inadvertently bound the women's movement and the sexual revolution so tightly together in many people's eyes that the two movements would forever after be seen as one and the same. With no small pride, Betty later recalled it was only "when women took up the issue of abortion that it became a really big issue."[47]

And once again she was right.

NOW's abortion plank gave the U.S. government, universities, and all of corporate America (including the major media monopolies) a convenient, expedient way to escape from having to provide day care, parental leave, and other benefits for mothers and families. Corporations could now freely choose to hire women from two mutually exclusive pools of applicants: there were sexually "free" *women* (the *Cosmo* type, unencumbered by children), and then there were *mothers*. *Women*, if they took the Pill and played their cards right, could

earn M.B.A.s and Ph.D.s and be groomed for the corner office with
their eyes focused on breaking through the glass ceiling. A *mother*
unwilling or unable to give an employer 24/7 dedication could leave
college without a degree (*her* choice), drop out of the workforce to
raise children (also *her* choice), or be relegated to the mommy track
(no comparable daddy track existed).

The cultural dynamic shifted so dramatically that in the 1980s Betty
discovered to her alarm that, in her own words, "in cities like Boston, New York, Los Angeles and San Francisco, where feminist consciousness was supposedly at the cutting edge, women of childbearing
years were dividing into bitter antagonistic camps as they were forced
into no-win, either-or choices, motherhood vs. career."[48] Betty had
an "uneasy sense" something had gone terribly wrong with the wom-
en's movement, so much so that she wrote another book, *The Second
Stage*, in which she called for the women's movement to set aside
its divisive anger, stop overemphasizing abortion rights, and reaffirm
the importance of the family. While promoting the book, she told a
reporter that saying you're for abortion is "like being for mastectomy.
We are for the choice to have children, for affirming the generative
roots of women in families."[49] Noting that women were now suffering from a "new problem that had no name," Friedan declared, "The
women's movement . . . has come to a dead end. . . . Our failure was
our blind spot about the family."[50]

But by then the sexual libertines had seized control of NOW,
and Betty had lost her media-ordained authority. The dirty deed was
done, and there was no turning back. With NOW's pro-abortion
vote in the Chinese Room on November 18, 1967, Lader had
secretly orchestrated one of the greatest backstage propaganda tri-
umphs in American history. Working mothers and single women of
childbearing age had been betrayed. And history was on the march.

Meanwhile, dutiful little *Cosmo* writer that I was, I followed the
branch of the women's movement that garnered the most favorable
publicity.

Chapter 6

Good-bye to Glamour

Glamour is a youth's form of blindness. . . . Like the rainbow, it is a once uplifting vision that moves away the closer you come to it.

—Playwright Arthur Miller, *Timebends: A Life*

After two years in the Big Apple, Walter and I skedaddled from New York, the city of our dreams. There were deeper reasons why we left, and I'll get to those soon.

But, on the most superficial level (where most of my major decisions at that time were made), it was the pink-feather gown that did it.

The prelude to the pink-feather gown business was this: One day at *Cosmo*, in the lobby, I happened to meet two tall, slender women who had just stepped off the elevator. Asking me for directions to the ladies' room, they explained they were models who'd just arrived for a photography shoot. I was amazed: They looked so ordinary. It was women like *these*—just ordinary women—whose photographs I had so greatly admired in the glossy magazines on the racks at the Rexall Drug in New Hampton? It seemed to me most men wouldn't turn their heads to look at them twice. And yet somehow in their ordinariness they were more real, truer to themselves, than the pictures in the magazines.

The two models disappeared into the ladies' room with their makeup bags in hand. When they emerged half an hour later, transfigured by the magic of Revlon and L'Oreal, they were both knockouts. Now everyone—man or woman—would look at them twice!

I didn't think to myself, *Wow, they used to be plain Janes, and now thanks to all that lipstick, eye shadow, mascara, and blush, they're gorgeous. Isn't that marvelous?*

Instead, I thought, *How beautiful each appeared when she was uniquely herself. How sad to have to put on a mask to hide one's true self in order to earn a living and win the praise of the world.* The glamour I had so foolishly hungered for as a small-town Iowa girl turned out to be not just a sham but a betrayal of the truth of women's lives.

But there was more.

The Cover That Wasn't

My favorite *Cosmo* cover of all time featured an elegant blonde model adorned in a splendid pink-feather gown. Breathtakingly delicate, the gown was the sort of dress Cinderella might have worn to the ball. Or so I imagined. I could just picture the sophisticated blonde cover girl (or perhaps even myself) dancing at the Prince's Ball in that stunningly gorgeous gown.

Then I learned the truth. There was no pink-feather gown. The pink feathers were fluffed up and arranged around the model's shoulders only long enough for photographer Francesco Scavullo[1] to get just the right photogenic effect he needed to achieve the perfect cover shot. There was no gown. From the waist on down, the model wore blue jeans and sneakers.

This discovery, added to my encounter with the two models in the lobby, permanently freed me from my passion for glamour. It became clear to me all glamour was just a man-made illusion, a façade—sheer make-believe manufactured entirely for profit. A little glamour may be fun. But if it's taken too seriously, it can distract women from the deeper truths of their lives. Along with the fantasy feather gown, the life I once imagined I would lead if only I could work for a glamour magazine like *Cosmopolitan* popped like a bubble and vanished in a puff of pink smoke.

This was the shallower reason I found it easy to leave *Cosmo*'s editorial office and launch out as a self-employed freelance writer.

On a deeper level, I'd found working eight-plus hours a day in an office to fulfill other people's dreams to be intensely disagreeable. *Cosmo* was Helen Gurley Brown's dream, not mine. I wanted to be free to walk outside on a sunny day whenever I pleased, to think my own thoughts (not Helen's), to use my time for what I most valued and not be enslaved to gathering pleasures and profits for somebody else. My time was my life. Although I didn't articulate it then, I think I realized on the deepest level of my being that all time is God's time and, therefore, all time is sacred. I certainly didn't want to be chained all day to a desk in an office, writing *Cosmo* claptrap.

So that's why, when we lost our cushy free-rent deal in Riverdale (Walter wasn't willing to be as much of a servant as Andrea wanted him to be), I was ready, even eager, to leave the unhallowed halls of *Cosmo* and move cross-country with Walter and the baby back to Los Angeles.

Why L.A. again?

Because the apartments we could afford on my measly $105-a-week salary in New York were horrifying places to raise a child. One eighteenth-floor apartment for rent in the Bronx had a guardrail-encircled outdoor patio little bigger than a large desk. Dustin was just starting to walk and climb. Walter and I peered over the metal patio rail down to the ground far below and ... well, that ended our apartment hunting in New York. We knew we could find a lovely, safe, *ground-floor* apartment in southern California for a fraction of the exorbitant rent the landlord was asking for the Bronx Death Trap.

We once again packed all our belongings in the Bug and headed back to LaLa Land, where the livin' was easy and the sunshine was free.

Three for the Road

As we drove merrily back across the Great Plains, singing "On the Road Again" at the top of our lungs along the way, Walter and I took stock of what we had accomplished in New York City. Our two years there had been satisfyingly productive. Walter had finished his first novel, *The Sand Castle*, a coming-of-age story about a seventeen-year-old boy who builds a giant sand castle on the beach. The story was good. The first agent who saw the manuscript offered to represent it, and the first editor who read the manuscript bought it. Dial Press was preparing to publish *The Sand Castle* hardcover in 1973. Busily at work on his second novel, Walter figured he could write as easily in California as in New York for a fraction of the expense.

Meanwhile, I had landed my first full-length article assignment
from *Cosmo*. I'd also gotten to know Peter Workman, an offbeat
entrepreneur with a quirky grin, who was just starting what would
one day be the phenomenally successful Workman Publishing Company. Peter was looking for a writer to pull together what he originally called "The Third-World Baby Name Book." Most baby-name
books at the time contained only names like Susan, Fred, and Sam—
names everyone had heard. Peter wanted this book to include unusual names from Africa, Latin America, and Asia. This project, while
not yet a firm deal, offered yet another possible source of income.

It can be hard for young college grads in today's world to imagine
how easy it was to get jobs in those days. The economy was flourish-
ing, and boomers, particularly college grads, had our choice of positions. It was no wonder we all felt so free. The day I graduated from
J-school on full scholarship (no student loans to repay), I received a
surprise $1,000 from my scholarship just to go job hunting when, in
fact, I already had a job at a magazine put out by the Missouri State
Teachers Association. An accountant friend of mine had eleven job
offers to choose from the day she graduated from college.

So it was no problem to find work once we arrived in L.A. When
you were young and cute (that is, sexy and unpregnant), you essentially just had to show up at an office and smile. As long as no one
knew I was a mother, I got and quit jobs as readily as I changed
my hairstyle.

Walter and I had taken an apartment just off the 405 in the San
Fernando Valley. We moved so often we had no furniture, not even
a bed. So we were sleeping on the floor. I had just quit a perfectly
fine editorial position with a house organ (a company magazine) for
the petroleum industry, because it didn't quite suit my tastes. Cheerfully unemployed, I was scouting around for another position.

One morning at nine o'clock, the telephone rang in the next
room. Still "in bed," I got up off the bedroom floor to go answer
it. The voice on the other end of the line was Peter Workman. I'd
submitted a proposal for the baby-name book. He liked it and was
ready to offer an advance against royalties of $3,500. Unbelievable!
Of course, I said yes on the spot.

I returned to the bedroom, where Walter was still sound asleep on
the floor.

Leaning down, I gave him a tender little wake-up kiss, and grinned, "Guess what?"

My first book contract! Eventually, the book would grow to include names from all over the world and would be called *The New Age Baby Name Book*.[2]

It was a red-letter day, a turning point in our lives. Now at last Walter and I could stay home together with baby Dustin and still earn a living. It was the opportunity we'd been waiting for. What joy!

We soon moved again, this time to a cozy two-bedroom stucco house in Pomona, with a sprawling oak tree shading the backyard and with plenty of space where Dustin could play. Walter (who never thought small) built tiny Dustin a sandbox twelve feet square.

To our surprise, I got pregnant again. In this modern age of Perfect Planned Parenthood, you might think I was a reproductive neanderthal to get "accidentally" pregnant not just once, but *twice*. In fact, however, the Pill was (and is) only about 99 percent effective at best, and according to the U.S. Centers for Disease Control, in typical use, the Pill is only 92 percent effective. In plain English, this means if one hundred women take the Pill for a year, in "typical use," eight will get pregnant. And that's just for one year. What happens in years three, four, and five? After three years, will twenty-four women in a hundred have gotten pregnant? Who figures out these statistics? Do different couples have different odds? What if a woman makes love almost daily? Is she more likely to get pregnant on the Pill than a woman who has sex once a week? Who crunches these numbers that slither into people's heads and nest there, thereby changing their family dynamics?

Had I been in genuine pursuit of the truth, I could have asked all these questions and more. After all, I'm a reporter. Asking tough questions is supposed to be part of my job. But I skipped over such questions. Just as I was skating over the surface of life, not taking anything else too seriously, I wasn't taking my sexuality or my body's ability to bear life seriously, either. The love between Walter and me wasn't supposed to be so concrete and real—so completely *embodied*—that our sexual communion could actually result in the real presence of a third person. Sex was just supposed to be fun. Unfortunately, by irresponsibly writing sex-revolution propaganda for *Cosmo*, I not only misled myself. I also helped to mislead millions of others.

When Walter and I found out we were expecting a second child, we both thought I must have forgotten to take the Pill—and perhaps I did.

Or perhaps not. Perhaps it was perfectly planned, after all.

Chapter 7

Philosophy of a Little Gray Man

The trouble with life isn't that there is no answer, it's that there are so many answers.

—Anthropologist Ruth Benedict,
An Anthropologist at Work

It was in Pomona, in my quest for truth, freedom, and meaning, that I first began to struggle with two great questions of life: Who am I? And what am I doing here? My reasoning powers were weak. Cut off from tradition and uneducated in history, I was like a ragpicker in a cultural junkyard, picking through popular ideas, discarding some, tucking others into my scruffy rucksack, trying to find a few that might work. Needless to say, this is not the best way to acquire a quality education. As a result of my ragpicker method of inquiry, my mind was polluted with intellectual error.

I can't say my intellectual pollution began in college, but it certainly escalated there. In my junior year at the University of Missouri, I'd taken a class called "Introduction to Philosophy," taught by a thin, gray-faced, bespectacled little man in his sixties who seemed chronically depressed and lectured for fifty minutes three times a week from a stack of dog-eared note cards that appeared to be as old as he was. He mumbled into his dark sweater the entire period, seldom looking up at anyone in the class. I took careful notes and got an "A."

But years afterward I could remember only one thing the little gray man taught me. He said that some people thought God was like a Master Watchmaker, who had wound up the universe like a clock and then walked away. He seemed to like this idea a lot. A sardonic

81

little smile would play at the corner of his old lips when he talked about it. At age twenty-one, I found this idea immensely impressive. I imagined this was the way to think "philosophically" about God.

Although I didn't know it at the time, my sad, gray-faced professor was teaching a Christian heresy called *Deism*, which gained prominence during the seventeenth and eighteenth centuries, and was particularly popular among Enlightenment intellectuals raised as Christians who believed in one God, but found fault with organized religion. This idea of a Watchmaker God strongly appealed to me, since it dovetailed perfectly with my childhood fantasy that God was far away up there in a place called "heaven" while I was down here in this world struggling to get by on my own.

Like nature, of course, the mind and heart abhor a vacuum. Not knowing the Father, the Son, and the Holy Spirit, and therefore unable to worship Him as only He deserves, I began to redesign the empty altar inside myself, setting it up to worship another god. Some people set up the interior altars of their hearts to worship idols such as sex, money, power, or perhaps some charismatic leader (Hitler and James Jones come to mind). I chose myself and my ambitions as my gods. I chose to set up my interior altar as a place where I could go anytime I pleased to worship me and my career.

My Self, My God

Like all worship, self-worship benefits from having a catechism. I found this catechism in a book I read in Pomona, which left a deep impression upon me and profoundly influenced my thinking for the next several decades. The book was Abraham Maslow's *Farther Reaches of Human Nature*. A self-proclaimed atheist who'd been born Jewish, Maslow created a humanistic psychology that appealed not only to me but also to millions of others, including Betty Friedan. Of the many influences on *The Feminine Mystique*, Maslow's self-as-god theories were among the most influential, providing what one biographer called the book's "intellectual underpinnings."[1]

Today, *The Farther Reaches of Human Nature* appears to me to be an empty attempt to create a Christian-sounding religion without Christ at its center. That is to say, Maslow's humanistic theories contained strong elements of Christianity—but placed hope and trust in man's achievements (not in Christ) at the center of one's faith. In Maslow's worldview, the glorified human "self"—not God—was in charge of the universe. Dr. Paul Vitz, professor emeritus of psychology at New York University, has dubbed the religious-sounding psychology Maslow and others developed in the 1960s and 1970s "the cult of self-worship" or "selfism."[2]

Maslow's selfism was understandably popular among people like me who considered ourselves to be broad minded, enlightened seekers. As long as I put Christ at the perimeter of my faith and not at the center, God couldn't ask too much of me, certainly not anything I didn't already want to do. Nor could He condemn anything I'd already done. I could call myself a *good person*—even a *Christian*, if such a word amused me. Yet I could still continue comfortably along my way, not rocking the boat in any meaningful way and doing business as usual.

Maslow's selfism also dovetailed perfectly with my search for who I was meant to be and my belief in the Watchmaker God. Being a Christian in name only, I picked up Maslow's theories in the junkyard of contemporary thought and tucked them into my rucksack.

As role models for anyone wanting to follow his new religion, Maslow selected and studied a group of allegedly "psychologically superior" people, whom he called "self-actualizers." He claimed these "superior people" he'd identified knew how to make choices in life that could be used "as possibly the ultimate values for the whole [human] species."[3] Christ had no place in Maslow's theories. Nor did the saints. His self-actualizers were to be the role models for all of mankind.

Self-actualizing people, as Maslow described them, had many admirable traits I longed to possess and express. They were sensitive to beauty, detached from petty socializing, had a good-natured (rather than cruel) sense of humor, and were kind, caring, and dedicated to a "higher" cause or mission outside themselves. Self-actualizers were also frequently capable of having a "peak experience" (which Maslow described as "a moment so wonderful it made you weep or get cold shivers of ecstasy"[4]). Maslow placed the peak experience (not worship of God) at the heart of organized religion.[5] At the same time, in a peculiar twist, he warned against the self-absorbed search for peak experiences for their own sake as not only selfish, but potentially evil.[6]

Maslow, who had studied the monkeys with University of Wisconsin primatologist Harry Harlow, based his bright and beautiful-sounding psychology on a false anthropological view of man as a self-creating, non-worshipping being who could be supernaturally good with no help from the Father, the Son, and the Holy Spirit. Assuming the human person to be not a being made in the image of God but "a choosing, deciding, seeking *animal*" (italics added),[7] Maslow's theories had the forms of religion without the power of religion. He spoke of religious-sounding "peak experiences," "religious values," and "love knowledge."[8] But his theories had no ability to reach the truly transcendent or to transfigure me or anyone else in any way that would draw us closer to God.

When Friedan adopted Maslow as her psychological guru and made his theories the underpinnings of *The Feminine Mystique*, she inadvertently invented a feminism that talked the talk of human freedom but walked the walk of the monkeys in the jungle. She created a feminism based upon a false humanism that did not elevate a woman but degraded her to the level of an animal, a feminism founded upon a psychological theory with no God and without authentic love, a brand of feminism that talked about love in the family but did not exclude bashing her husband over the head with a curtain rod or scratching his face so deeply he looked like he'd been mauled by a tiger.

Although he paid lip service to love, Maslow defined "self-actualizing" largely in terms of worldly success. Self-actualizers were people who longed to write the great American novel, become President of the United States, or be Secretary-General of the United Nations.[9] Maslow did not encourage his disciples to follow the humble "little way" of Saint Thérèse of Lisieux. Being "the very best you are capable of becoming," in Maslow's view, seemed largely to mean becoming rich, famous, and successful in the eyes of the world. Maslow reduced the Christian sages and saints, "the most beautiful men and women in our world,"[10] to humans who were merely "good choosers."[11]

You can see why this egocentric, therapeutic pseudo-religion appealed so highly to Betty and also to me. I wanted to be rich, famous, and successful in life. Maslow seemed to know how to do it. These "superior people" of his were highly creative, which made his theories doubly appealing. Creativity was one talent I definitely believed I needed to set me free to use my own time for those pursuits I most valued.

The Longing to Be Fearless

Maslow wasn't the only intellectual who influenced me in Pomona in my search for freedom. A second book also profoundly affected me— *The Female Eunuch* by Australian feminist Germaine Greer. Although much of the book bored me, I skipped those parts. The chapter that most spoke to my heart was titled simply "Security." Later in the chapter, in one part I didn't agree with, Greer urged women to have sex outside of marriage (which is probably why Helen Gurley Brown chose to excerpt this particular chapter in *Cosmo*). But the part of the "Security" chapter I liked best had to do with being set free from slavery to money and the corporate office.

"There is no such thing as security," Greer wrote.

> There never has been. And yet we speak of security as something which people are entitled to.... Although security is not in the nature of things, we invent strategies for outwitting fortune, and call them after their guiding deity insurance, assurance, social security.... We know that money cannot repay a lost leg or a lifetime of headaches or scarred beauty, but we arrange it just the same....
>
> Probably the only place where a man can feel really secure is in a maximum security prison, except for the imminent threat of release.... Security is when everything is settled, when nothing can happen to you; security is the denial of life....
>
> The search for security is undertaken by the weakest part of the personality, by fear, inadequacy, fatigue and anxiety.[12]

It seemed to me Greer was onto something here. In her views, *fearlessness* was the path to freedom, and I agreed with her.

Slowly, imperceptibly, something in me had changed. I now saw not simply the women's movement *per se*, but an intrepid determination to earn a living by freelancing (the fulfillment of "the dream" Walter and I shared) as my ticket to freedom. Freelancing was the way I was going to be able to combine work and family—to have a big-time career and still be home 24/7 with Walter and the children— without sacrificing either to the gods of commerce. I was blind to how much I'd already sold out. The lies I told in print in order to get paid seemed small and petty compared to the great benefits I believed

I could reap. *Cosmo*'s checks, when they came in the mail, seemed to me like a lifeline. I should have known you're never going to win when you start dancing with the devil.

Unfortunately, Walter, the Episcopalian, seemed equally confused.

So on we trudged, pilgrims traveling side by side on the same road, with no reliable moral compass to guide us.

Not Poor, Just Broke

Walter had been teaching math in a private girls' school in Pomona, but the school suddenly closed its doors, and he was out of a job. Meanwhile, the OPEC oil crisis struck, the economy took a nose-dive, and jobs were far less plentiful than they'd previously been. To supplement our roller-coaster freelance income, Walter had taken a little job in a shoe store, but it didn't pay much. It was frustrating for him, after all the excitement of selling his first novel, to be back spending his days selling shoes. Still, he had high hopes for *The Sand Castle*, yet to be published. So he just kept on moving, working non-stop on his new novel whenever he got the chance.

Meanwhile, I had finished *The New Age Baby Name Book*, and we were waiting for the last installment of my advance to arrive. We waited . . . and waited . . . and waited. Peter Workman had just editorially acquired a book entitled *Your Check Is in the Mail*, and he kept promising me the check would arrive any day. Robert Benchley put it well: "The freelance writer is a man [or woman] who is paid per piece or per word or perhaps."

Finally, Pacific Gas & Electric would wait no longer and turned off our electricity.

Walter, who'd grown up like Abraham Lincoln reading at night by a coal-oil lantern, had lived without electricity until he was fifteen. Spoiled and coddled as a child, I was much more upset with the lights-off situation than he was. Here I was pregnant, with a three-year-old, and with no lights or working refrigerator. I don't remember whether the stove was gas or electric. I only recall thinking that when Germaine Greer wrote that it was a trap to worry about security, I doubted that she meant for us to sink quite this low.

The baby name book had taken me only about three months to write and would over the next thirty years earn a total of nearly

$300,000 in royalties. So at the moment we had our electricity disconnected, although we didn't know it at the time, I had just finished a book that would eventually pay off quite well.

One of Walter's favorite lines was: "We're not poor, we're just broke."

What was the difference?

"Poor is a state of mind," he'd firmly declare. "Broke is a temporary condition."

Many days and months I felt poor, but all that time we were really just broke.

Eventually, the check from Workman arrived, and we got our electricity turned back on. But what Walter seemed to consider just part of the adventure was for me an unforgettable financial trauma. I wasn't nearly as ready as he was to make sacrifices for our writing careers. Ever the poet, Walter saw himself as Thoreau at Walden Pond, cutting his life down to the bare necessities to get to the Truth of Things as They Really Are.

I was more inclined to agree with Samuel Johnson: "No man but a blockhead ever wrote except for money." I was an angst-filled wreck. I felt totally trapped. I was five months pregnant, so no one would hire me, and we had no money to pay the hospital when it was time for me to give birth. The Workman check, when it at last arrived to my great sigh of relief, was just enough to catch up on our bills.

To top it all off, our landlord was having the inside of our house painted, and I was stuck alone at home all day with a loquacious housepainter, a chubby old fellow in a paint-spattered white cap who wouldn't shut up and kept trying to engage me in conversation. When I finally began to talk with him and I revealed we had no idea how we were going to pay the hospital for me to have the baby, he jovially launched into a horror story about his sister-in-law who was once in the same predicament. She eventually had to go to a slum hospital where they took what he called "welfare cases," and she experienced some sort of hideous disaster (I forget the details). Detached from God, I was ready to listen to any blowhard who came my way. Images of being a "welfare case" in some filthy Third World–like hospital, giving birth on a dirty cot without anesthesia, flooded my mind, and I panicked.

Young women often feel most vulnerable when they're with child. Taught that I was supposed to be a strong, independent woman, the thing I feared most was vulnerability. I longed to be fearless. Yet at the same time I felt more helpless and vulnerable than I'd ever felt in my life.

Couldn't we ask my good parents for financial help? No, because they had also fallen on hard times. The shoe store in Iowa had burned to the ground, and Dad and Mom had moved with my two younger brothers to California, where they, too, were struggling to start their lives over.

I don't think Walter ever fully understood how terrified I felt during that second pregnancy. An inveterate problem solver brimming with hope, he had a plan to deal with the hospital situation. A credit card had recently arrived in the mail, but we weren't using it because our income was so dicey. If all else failed, he'd decided we could put the hospital bill on that credit card. A few weeks before I gave birth, Workman also offered me a contract for a new book (*The American Biking Atlas and Touring Guide*) with a $10,000 advance. So, as usual, someone was watching over me, but I didn't know who. So I was filled with alarm—over nothing.

To make a long story short, we used the credit card to pay the hospital, and I gave birth to a perfectly beautiful baby girl. When the nurse in the delivery room handed her to me, a sweet bundle in a blanket, she had already fallen peacefully asleep. We named her Erin Kimberly.

Walter and I had decided if we were to make a success of our writing careers, we needed to be on the East Coast. We'd been hasty and reckless to leave New York City so soon, because we were now too far away from the hub of the publishing world to keep in regular personal contact with publishers and editors.

So six weeks after baby Erin was born, after the first installment of the advance for the *Biking Atlas* arrived, we packed up the Bug once again. We hopped on the I-10, caught the I-15 north to Barstow, picked up the I-40, and headed east. This time we hoped to find a farm in Connecticut, some place where the kids could play outside and run free and we could plant a vegetable garden.

Chapter 8

Harry's Dilemma

. . . ours is a tragic century where men are faced with tremendous decisions that shake the souls of the strongest.

—Catherine Doherty,
Poustinia: Encountering God in Silence, Solitude and Prayer

We arrived in Connecticut in autumn, just as the leaves were changing. New England was everything we had hoped for and more: picture-postcard villages, antique shops, apple-cider mills, farm stands, charming back roads meandering through gently rolling hills, splashed with scarlet, persimmon, and amber fall foliage.

Taking a small, two-story house in Storrs, close to the University of Connecticut, we soon settled into a comfortable routine. After breakfast, cups of steaming hot coffee, and plenty of good conversation, we retired to our respective upstairs studies to work. Dustin played with his Matchbox cars and other toys at our feet. Erin, the easiest baby imaginable (she seldom cried), slept and cooed most of the day. Writing while raising children at home together was a merry difficulty we were more than happy to embrace. I was deeply touched one day when Walter showed me the dedication he'd written for *The Sand Castle*: "For Sue, friend and fellow cohort, who also just happens to be my wife."

Dustin Remembers God

There was a very steep staircase in our house that ran up between the living room and the kitchen. One day, three-year-old Dustin was sitting perched on the bottom stair. Suddenly, he looked up at me with his big, innocent brown eyes framed in golden curls and said: "When I was with God ..."

Then he fell silent.

I was amazed. "What?" I asked in wonder. "What did you say?"

Then, afraid I was so overly eager I might close him down, I prompted more gently, "Tell me, Honey, ... what it was like when you were with God?"

A puzzled look came over our little boy's sweet face, and he said no more.

In amazement I called out to Walter: "Dustin just said ... *when I was with God!*"

"Can you tell me more, Dusty?"

But the three-year-old just sat quietly and looked up at me in wide-eyed innocence, as if Mom had gone a bit loopy.

It was as if a flash of light had briefly lit up Dustin's mind and then vanished, or as if a door had opened just a crack and then softly closed.

The Church inspired by the Holy Spirit, of course, teaches we have no preexistence in heaven. But our little boy spoke so matter-of-factly he didn't seem to be making up a story. Could he have briefly recalled some moment when he was "with God" before he could talk or even perhaps when he was in the womb?

To this day, whatever Dustin meant remains a mystery.

Some may say I was making far too much of a child's babblings. Perhaps so. But I was unconsciously struggling to understand my relation to God and to neighbor, and I was grasping at straws in the dark.

I was hardly alone. Amid the general collapse of all traditional values taking place around us, many were losing their moorings.

Women struggling to find a firm footing in the slippery sands of the cultural chaos of the '70s frequently declared: "The personal is political!"

But the political is also personal.

So let us shift our focus now for a few minutes and flash back to look at yet another political struggle which happened largely behind the scenes but which will soon move to the front and center of my personal story.

A Good Solid Republican

To the ordinary American, the National Organization for Women's newfound claim that sex without the kids will set you free was a completely foreign concept. The Bolsheviks had legalized abortion on demand in Russia in 1920. But nothing of that sort had ever happened in the United States.

Perhaps no one in 1971 was more perplexed by women's cries for abortion on demand than Richard Nixon's latest appointee to the U.S. Supreme Court. In his early sixties, salt-and-pepper haired and married with three grown daughters, Harry Blackmun was a churchgoing Methodist, steady and reliable. He had grown up in a working-class neighborhood in Saint Paul, Minnesota, the son of a father who struggled to make ends meet by wholesaling fruits and vegetables, a business that eventually failed. Harry wrote in his diary, "Never can I remember a time when Dad was ever a step ahead of the world; he was always worrying and stewing about when he should get the instant batch of bills paid off."[1]

Talented as an orator, Harry won a scholarship to Harvard at age sixteen, but separating from home for him had been tough. The night before he left for his sophomore year at Harvard, both he and his mother Theo wept. In his diary, he wrote that "parting with the best home folks available and with one's greatest pals in the world, was one darn hard job."[2]

Harry worked his way through college and, even years later as a Supreme Court Justice, typically took a full briefcase of work home after putting in a twelve-hour day. When his daughters were small, he would cuddle them in the rocking chair and sing what one of his daughters called "deeply comforting songs" like "Tooraloora-loora." He was a loyal Harvard man, but his favorite piece of music was the Yale "Whiffenpoof Song": "We're poor little lambs who have lost our way."[3] He was certainly not the sort of man to advocate "sex-without-the-kids" as the ultimate path to anyone's freedom.

So how did Republican Harry Blackmun (by all accounts a loving son, devoted husband, and good dad) wind up writing the Supreme Court opinions that legalized abortion throughout the nation, thereby fulfilling Larry Lader's wildest dream?

To put it mildly, it wasn't easy for Harry. The assignment to write the opinions for *Roe v. Wade* and its companion case *Doe v. Bolton* had fallen on Harry by surprise. Chief Justice Warren Burger assigned him the task of writing the opinions even though Harry's craftsmanship lacked finesse and he was "by far the slowest writer on the Court."[4] What's more, Burger believed the Justices' votes on the abortion cases in the closed-door conference after oral arguments had been too close to call and the Court's final decision would "stand or fall on the writing" of Blackmun's opinions.[5] Further, Harry thought the oral arguments in *Roe* had been weak. To write an opinion that would sway his colleagues, he believed he needed a lot more facts, information, and insights than attorneys on either side of the case had provided.

Harry Seeks Guidance

To sort out the abortion mess, the first person Harry turned to for help was his old friend Tom Keys, head of the Mayo Clinic Medical Library in Rochester, Minnesota. Blackmun had spent nine of the best years of his life working at Mayo as a "doctor's attorney." Tom immediately rallied his library staff and began sending Harry articles on the Hippocratic oath and abortion history.

Harry also sought advice from the women in his family.

One evening, shortly after he'd been assigned to write the abortion opinions, Harry was having dinner at home with his wife Dottie and their three daughters.

"What are your views on abortion?" Harry asked the four women seated around the family dinner table.

His daughter Susan, the youngest, recalled:

> Mom's answer was slightly to the right of center. She promoted choice but with some restrictions. Sally's reply was carefully thought out and middle of the road, the route she has taken all her life.... Nancy, a Radcliffe and Harvard graduate, sounded off with an intellectually leftish opinion. I had not yet emerged from my hippie phase and spouted out a far-to-the-left, shake-the-old-man-up response.
>
> Dad put down his fork mid-bite and pushed back his chair. "I think I'll go lie down," he said. "I'm getting a headache."[6]

Although Harry claimed to be unsure of his wife's position on abortion, Dottie told one of his law clerks (a young male attorney who favored laissez-faire abortion) that she was doing everything she could to further the cause. "You and I are working on the same thing," she told the law clerk. "Me at home and you at work."[7]

To write his opinions, Harry retired to the Justices' second-floor library, where he spent most of his waking hours in silent solitude, laboriously working at a long mahogany desk. Months passed. As the winter snows melted into spring and D.C.'s cherry blossoms burst into bloom, Harry remained squirreled away in the library.

When at last in mid-May Harry showed a draft of his *Roe* opinion for the first time to one of his politically leftist law clerks, the clerk claimed to be "astonished" the draft was so crudely written and poorly organized.[8] When he circulated the draft on May 18, 1972, to the other justices, Harry's more liberal colleagues on the bench—Justices William Douglas, William Brennan, and Thurgood Marshall—were disappointed, whereas conservative Justice Byron White strongly dissented.[9]

Why were Douglas and Marshall so disappointed? Catholic feminist Mary Meehan suggests one possible reason. Meehan reports, "Justices Douglas and Marshall had been lacking in sexual restraint—to put it mildly—well before the '60s, and the problems of both were aggravated at times by heavy drinking. Perhaps they realized that legal abortion could be extremely helpful to *men*—enabling them to escape paternity suits, years of child support, social embarrassment, and the wrath of betrayed wives. But none of this, of course, would be mentioned in the Court's opinions." Meehan reports that in 1961 Justice Douglas had also written to *Population Bomb* pamphleteer Hugh Moore, saying, "I have seen some of the literature ... all of which I thought was excellent."[10]

In any case, when Harry failed to produce a competent pro-abortion draft of his opinions, he got flak from his colleagues.

Having vowed to do his best "to arrive at something which would command a court,"[11] Harry withdrew the draft, asking that all copies be returned to him. He planned to do more work on his opinions over the summer.

In late July 1972, Harry flew to Rochester to immerse himself in research at the Mayo Clinic medical library. Meanwhile, his politically liberal, $15,000-a-year[12] law clerk George Frampton Jr., age twenty-eight, volunteered to stay in Washington until early August to help research and draft the opinions. The two talked by phone almost daily.[13]

An Unexpected Guide Appears

An early draft Harry wrote on the history of abortion in his small, cramped longhand reveals he was still struggling.[14] Writing is difficult, and Harry wasn't much of a writer. On the subject of abortion, Harry was finding it hard to think clearly.

Young George, on the other hand, was an excellent writer. He'd graduated from Harvard Law School in 1969 (where he was managing editor of the *Harvard Law Review*), and he had at his fingertips an extraordinarily handy resource—a highly persuasive book entitled *Abortion: The first authoritative and documented report on the laws and practices governing abortion in the U.S. and around the world, and how—for the sake of women everywhere—they can and must be reformed.*[15] Yes, indeed. It was Larry Lader's masterpiece of propaganda, the same book that had so greatly impressed Betty Friedan.

Lader's masterpiece of propaganda supplied much of the historic background Blackmun's opinion had previously lacked. But more important, Lader's book provided a coherent form or template that tied together the many disconnected fragments of thought that had previously kept Blackmun's abortion opinions from working. In all-new sections on the history of abortion written by George and dated August 10, 1972, Lader's book suddenly appears in the footnotes for the first time.[16]

In a lengthy five-page, single-spaced letter, typed on legal-size paper, which he sent to Harry along with the draft, George made an unusual suggestion. He suggested that Harry consider circulating this new draft before it was cite-checked by a clerk. Cite-checking is detailed fact-checking to ensure that a judicial decision is sound. Why would a junior law clerk suggest circulating a draft that hadn't been cite-checked?

George was eager for Harry to circulate his draft before oral arguments were reheard in October—for three reasons: He wrote that circulating the revised draft before oral argument would "nail down [Blackmun's] keeping the assignment," "should influence questions and thinking at oral argument," and "might well influence voting." Though George stated he would not recommend delayed cite-checking "as standard operating procedure," he thought that in this particular case the benefits strongly outweighed the disadvantages.[17]

We don't know when or even if the history section in Blackmun's abortion opinions was ever cite-checked. But we do know that if it happened, the fact-checking was faulty. For when Blackmun accepted Larry Lader, a mere magazine writer, as a reliable authority on history, philosophy, and theology, he became as a blind man following a blind guide. Despite his best efforts, Harry failed to see he had embraced a well-crafted verbal mirage, mistaking it for the truth.

Let us be very clear about what happened here. The picture that emerges from Blackmun's papers, available for public inspection at the U.S. Library of Congress, is that of a justice who, in the words of Pulitzer Prize–winning, pro-abortion historian David J. Garrow, "ceded far too much of his judicial authority to his clerks." It is plain from an inspection of Blackmun's papers that his clerks made "historically significant and perhaps decisive contributions to *Roe* and *Doe*"—a degree of involvement Garrow calls "indefensible."[18]

Lader set himself up as an authority on centuries of abortion legal history and also on two millennia of Catholic teachings about abortion—and Blackmun and his clerk fell for the ruse. In the final version of the *Roe v. Wade* decision, Lader's masterpiece of propaganda is cited at least seven times, and Cyril Chestnut Means' scholarly papers are cited another seven times.

Cyril Means, you'll recall from Chapter 4, was the NARAL attorney who falsified abortion legal history, fabricating his own version almost entirely out of whole cloth.

Lader, of course, was just a clever wordsmith—certainly no expert on history.

And yet as the late Notre Dame theologian Father James Burtchaell observed, it is "clear in the record that Justice Blackmun was indebted for the innards of his argument to two of the major strategists of the abortion movement"—Means and Lader.[19]

Why would anyone on a judicial body as intellectually respected and erudite as the U.S. Supreme Court give a man who was little more than a popular magazine writer such high credibility as a historian?

On the one hand, perhaps no one will ever completely know.

On the other hand, Ellul in his *Propaganda* book suggests the well-educated intellectual may be more vulnerable to propaganda than the common man is. "Naturally, the educated man does not *believe* in propaganda; he shrugs and is convinced that propaganda has no effect on him," Ellul explains. "This is, in fact, one of his great weaknesses, and propagandists are well aware that in order to reach someone, one must first convince him that propaganda is ineffectual and not very clever. Because he is convinced of his own superiority, the intellectual is much more vulnerable than anybody else to this maneuver."[20]

Ellul observed that intellectuals who consider themselves to be well-informed may, in fact, be "the most vulnerable of all to modern propaganda, for three reasons: (1) they absorb the largest amount of secondhand, unverifiable information; (2) they feel a compelling need to have an opinion on every important question of our time, and thus easily succumb to opinions offered to them by propaganda on all such indigestible pieces of information; (3) they consider themselves capable of 'judging for themselves.'"[21]

Do Ellul's insights explain what happened to Harry and George as they laboriously wrote and rewrote *Roe v. Wade* and *Doe v. Bolton* until they finally succumbed to a propagandist's falsified version of history to get the job done?

Maybe. Maybe not.

In any case, Harry was deceived by Lader's propaganda, six other black-robed men on the bench went along with the ruse, and the tragic result was the U.S. Supreme Court's most controversial decision since the *Dred Scott v. Sandford* decision denied personhood to black Americans in 1857.

The Scholars Don't Buy It

"The immediate academic response to *Roe v. Wade*," observed *New York Times* pro-abortion reporter Linda Greenhouse, "ranged from tepid to withering." The first critiques came from the left.

In a scathing *Yale Law Journal* article titled "The Wages of Crying Wolf: A Comment on *Roe v. Wade*," liberal law professor John Hart Ely (an abortion supporter) declared, "*Roe* lacks even colorable support in the constitutional text, history, or any other appropriate source of constitutional doctrine." The opinion "is bad," Ely added, "... because it is *not* constitutional law and gives almost no sense of an obligation to try to be."[22]

Ely's critique was soon joined by other influential voices. "One of the most curious things about *Roe*," Harvard law professor Laurence Tribe observed in *Harvard Law Review*, "is that, behind its own verbal smokescreen, the substantive judgment on which it rests is nowhere to be found."[23]

In their essay "*Roe v. Wade*: No Justification in History, Law, or Logic," Americans United for Life Legal Defense Fund attorneys Dennis J. Horan and Thomas J. Balch state: "Virtually every aspect of the historical, sociological, medical, and legal arguments Justice Harry Blackmun used to support the *Roe* holdings has been subjected to intense scholarly criticism."[24]

Ironically, a year after *Roe* was released, Harry still wasn't completely comfortable with the Court's decision. Speaking in February 1974 to *The Washington Post*, Harry prophetically stated the *Roe v. Wade* ruling will be regarded "as one of the worst mistakes in the court's history, or one of its great decisions, a turning point."[25]

Chapter 9

Just Broke—Again

Freedom is essential to self-respect ... but not all choice enhances freedom.

—Barry Schwartz, *The Paradox of Choice*

Unfortunately, even the most avid news consumer picks up only flotsam and jetsam of everything that's happening in the world. Although, of course, I heard plenty about *Roe v. Wade*, the legal scholars' adverse reactions to the Supreme Court's decision raised not even a blip on little *Cosmo* writer Sue's radar. I wasn't trying to keep up with the latest abortion news. I was busy trying to earn a living, so Walter and I could stay home together and raise our two children.

Although our life in Connecticut was largely idyllic, our only bugbear was, once again, too little money. I had failed to ask for a large enough advance for the biking atlas, and the freelance income I received from *Cosmo* was too unreliable to count on. After I finished writing an article, it could take months for *Cosmo*'s editors to read it, approve it, and put through payment, plus another long month for the check to arrive.

Meanwhile, our high hopes for *The Sand Castle* evaporated. For some inexplicable reason that forever baffled us, the novel that had been picked up by the first agent who saw it and sold to the first editor who read it was released by Dial Books for Young Readers with absolutely no publicity on December 26, 1973—one day after Christmas.

Despite this less-than-stellar beginning, *The Sand Castle* went on to garner good reviews, including a coveted starred review in *Kirkus*. The only other book in that issue of the magazine to earn the Kirkus

Star (one of the most prestigious designations in the book industry) was *The Honorary Consul* by Graham Greene.

The Honorary Consul became a twentieth-century American best seller.

The Sand Castle sold fewer than one thousand copies.

Considering our little family's dire financial situation, Walter was briefly devastated. But this was the man who'd fearlessly enrolled in college with only twenty bucks in his pocket. He wasn't even close to giving up our dream.

The Temps

Our finances were in such desperate straits that we realized we both needed to get jobs again until our writing began to pay off. At least we now had three books in print, so we figured *something* should eventually come together to allow us to continue on our path.

After a difficult search to find a decent sitter, we finally located a warm-hearted mother of two who ran a day care center out of her home. One paycheck wasn't enough for us to make ends meet, but with two we figured we could squeak by. We both signed up with Manpower, a temporary employment agency.

When you work temp jobs, all sorts of interesting experiences come your way, but Walter's experiences were inevitably more interesting than mine.

I got an insurance-company job as a file clerk. After months of struggling with the uncertainties of putting words on a page, I found the certainty of alphabetically filing little white index cards all day (B *always* comes after A) to be somewhat therapeutic. I worked alongside another temp, an ex-convict just released from prison. A short, muscular, dark-eyed young man not much older than I, he intimated he'd been imprisoned for robbery and seemed earnestly determined to make a fresh start in his life.

Meanwhile, Walter went to work in a bill-collection agency. He sat in a room with a group of collectors who spent all day on their phones, nastily harassing poor debt-ridden souls about their past-due accounts. One collector gleefully gloated to everyone in the room that he'd just repossessed the car of an immigrant who could barely speak English when the man was only one month past due on his payments. Considering the sorry state of our own finances, it was a horrible place to work.

One day Walter got fed up. The manager, a loud, brash man, was standing in the middle of the roomful of bill collectors, having a hissy fit over something. Walter had just finished emptying out a large cardboard box, and he was carrying the box across the room to deposit it in the trash, when the manager started raging.

Strolling past the red-faced manager, Walter calmly and gently placed the empty box over the poor man's head and just kept on walking.

Shocked into silence, the angry man stood there stock-still in the middle of the office with a cardboard box over his head.

Walter wasn't fired on the spot. He couldn't be, because strictly speaking he was employed by Manpower, not by the bill-collection agency. But that job assignment quickly ended, and the temp agency moved him on to a new position in an insurance-company typing pool filled with a bunch of blue-haired ladies.

Older women generally adored Walter, and he fit in there just fine—except, of course, when he came back from lunch and regularly lit up a big, black, stinky cigar, which he smoked in its entirety, contentedly blowing smoke rings until it was time for him to get back to work. (In those days, the joy of smoking in the office was still legal, but not always greatly appreciated by others.)

A Medical Misunderstanding

Since we certainly couldn't afford another baby right now, we decided there was only one sensible thing to do: I had to go on the Pill again.

In those days, almost all ob-gyns were men. So I made an appointment with a man I had never met to get a prescription for the birth-control Pill.

The day of my appointment, in the doctor's private little office, I confided that I'd been on the Pill in the past, but I hated it because it always made me so depressed. I was hoping perhaps he could pre-scribe something else that wouldn't give me the blues.

The doctor looked at me knowingly over his reading glasses. Then he condescendingly replied, "Could it be things in your life aren't going so well right now?"

How can you answer a question like that? There are *always* things in life that aren't going so well. I wanted to scream: "No, you don't understand, Mr. Amateur Psychoanalyst. I am relatively happy by nature. But when I go on the Pill, I *always* get miserably depressed."

Instead, seeing no way to break through his medical armor of superiority, I simply snatched up the prescription and left.

Unfortunately, our unpleasant exchange was so brief that the doctor failed to inform me I needed to take the Pill for an entire month before it would be effective, and (because I'd been on the Pill before and therefore imagined I knew how to use it) I failed to read the instructions.

Guess what?

Within a month, I was pregnant.

Walter had been concerned about the second pregnancy. But this time he was really upset. How in the world were we going to afford another baby? He saw his already fragile writing career going up in smoke before his very eyes.

I was contrite. I should have read the damned directions.

What were we going to do?

Well, of course, due to *Roe v. Wade*, we now had a choice. I could either have this third baby, or get an abortion.

The one choice I did not have available to me in 1974 was the ability to remain gainfully employed while I was pregnant. Four years later, Congress would finally pass the Pregnancy Discrimination Act, an amendment to Title VII of the Civil Rights Act of 1964. This law, had it been in effect in 1974, would allegedly have prevented me from getting fired for being with child. I say "allegedly" because in reality pregnancy discrimination did not disappear in 1978. The war against pregnant mothers simply went underground, hidden under a propagandistic verbal smokescreen that presented contraception and abortion as a woman's "choice," an empty and meaningless liberty that would not allow a woman's body to be left in her natural state but would only allow her to be doctored up with chemicals so she would be more like a man.

What about adoption? After giving birth to two beautiful babies, I knew I just couldn't do it. Giving a baby up for adoption would have been unthinkable. Abortion, which after all was my right as a liberated woman, seemed to me to be an easy escape hatch out of an impossible situation.

Of course, we weren't really poor. We were just temporarily broke. But as *Dune* author Frank Herbert put it: "Fear is the mind-killer. Fear is the little-death that brings total obliteration."[1] Scared and confused, I found it hard to think clearly.

A Rational Option

Walter, who no longer attended the Episcopal Church (perhaps my indifference had rubbed off on him), found a passage in the Old Testament (Ex 21:22), which he interpreted to mean that if two men are fighting and one hits a pregnant woman and she miscarries her child, he just has to pay a fine. If he kills the woman, however, it's "an eye for an eye, a tooth for a tooth." His own interpretation of this passage assured him that from a Christian perspective abortion is not really that serious.

In his personal misinterpretation of one Old Testament biblical passage taken out of context, Walter was hardly alone. A remarkable number of believers, Protestants, Jews, and Catholics alike were searching for ways to support abortion—and they found them. Those churches and religious organizations who published official statements in support of abortion either shortly before or after *Roe* included the American Baptist churches, American Friends Service Committee, American Jewish Congress, American Lutheran Church, B'nai B'rith Women, Central Conference of American Rabbis, Disciples of Christ, Church of the Brethren, Episcopal Church and the Women of the Episcopal Church, Lutheran Church in America, National Council of Jewish Women, National Federation of Temple Sisterhoods, Presbyterian Church in the United States, Reformed Church in America, Reorganized Church of Jesus Christ of Latter-Day Saints, Union of American Hebrew Congregations, Unitarian Universalist Association and Women's Federation, United Church of Christ, United Methodist Church (Blackmun's church), United Presbyterian Church (USA), United Synagogues of America, Women's League for Conservative Judaism, and Young Women's Christian Association.[2]

In his scheme to abolish all abortion laws, Lader had scornfully calculated that "a few" liberal Catholics would join his abortion cause, thereby becoming "valuable showpieces" for him. How right he was. Among these valuable showpieces were members of Catholics for a Free Choice, who received funding from many private abortion-supporting foundations.* The high percentage of Catholics who chose to dissent from Church teachings about love for others, when it came to abortion, must have exceeded Lader's wildest dreams.

As a lukewarm Protestant, of course, I was indifferent to all this. Mine was a watered-down Christianity. I believed in God—that is, I believed in the existence of God—but I did not believe God to be with us. Neither Walter nor I thought to say, "We'll get through this somehow. God will provide." What's more, in my mind, abortion was an integral part of the women's movement, a right as fundamental as equal pay for equal work.

As Walter and I struggled with our anxiety over this latest pregnancy, it occurred to me I wouldn't even consider having an abortion if it weren't for *Roe v. Wade*. Looking up some sleazy criminal abortionist in a back alley would be too hideous a prospect for words. I wouldn't know how to do it, even if I wanted to (which I certainly didn't).

But now that I could have an abortion done in a bright, clean hospital in Hartford—in the very hospital where I had already given birth, no less—abortion seemed like the most reasonable option.

Of course, there was nothing reasonable about the decision I was making. I was in a panic. I knew if I was to have an abortion, I'd have to get it done quickly before that "little blob of tissue" grew so big I'd start to feel him kick. I didn't think of myself as *killing a child*. I thought of myself as *solving a problem*. If I took time off from work to have another baby, I didn't know how we'd ever be able to make ends meet. As strange as it may sound to those who see reality with

---

*In an eye-opening report, *Catholics for a Free Choice Exposed* (published by Human Life International in 2001), Brian Clowes tracked down Catholics for a Free Choice funding and found millions of dollars had been donated by abortion-supporting foundations, including: $5,095,800 from the David & Lucile Packard Foundation, $1,066,700 from the Sunnen Foundation, $6,380,760 from the Ford Foundation, and many others, including much smaller grants from *Ms. Magazine* and the Playboy Foundation. Although Clowes' book is now out of print, at this writing it was still available, used, on Amazon.

more clarity, abortion seemed to me at the time to be the *responsible* thing to do. I told myself I was responsible for the two children we already had. We were struggling to feed and clothe two. If we had a third, all three would suffer. On and on the rationalizations went.

***

The abortion-intake nurse at Hartford Hospital is a heavy-set black woman in her forties with genuine warmth. She regards us with compassionate concern. Here we are, a young married couple clearly in love. Are we *sure* we want an abortion? She doesn't try to talk us out of it, not directly. But she gently asks many probing questions to try to get us to *think* about this step more seriously than we seem to be taking it.

We parry her kindly questions at every turn. Yes, we're sure. Yes, we've talked this over together. No, we don't want to think about it any longer. Yes, we want an abortion soon, as quickly as possible.

Finally, seeing how headstrong and determined we are on the matter, she sighs and gives us some consent forms to sign. "When can you come back?" she asks. We make an appointment for the following Wednesday—at noon.

I don't recall having a pre-op exam, but I probably did. A lot of what happened I've blocked out of my mind. Now, forty years later, much of it is just a blur.

What I do remember is this: We were both on our lunch hours from our temp jobs at the insurance companies. Walter went with me. He was welcomed with joy into the delivery room when I gave birth in this hospital. This time he was told he must wait for me in the lobby.

I'm ushered into a small room furnished with several brown couches, where I'm told to wait until I'm called in for the abortion. A pretty young woman is also here. She has just had her third abortion. The doctor comes in to see how she's doing. I don't recall why, but somehow I conclude she's a prostitute. He jokes around with her and seems quite pleased with the way the surgery went.

Later I will find it hard to understand why he was so flirtatious with the prostitute and so terribly ugly to me.

I'm wheeled into the surgical room on a gurney, draped in a white sheet. The black nurse who scheduled the abortion stands near my head and holds my right hand. The doctor refuses to wait long enough for the anesthesia to go into effect before he begins. I'd been led to believe an abortion was easy. The pain is excruciating, almost as piercing as giving birth.

The doctor is bitter and angry. He does not want to be doing this. Suddenly he snorts, "I usually deliver them *alive.*"

I freeze. I catch my breath and stop breathing. My eyes stare straight ahead without blinking.

"Sue!" the black nurse cries. "Sue! Sue!"

For a moment, she thinks I have died, and in a way I have. It's not only a tiny little life who dies on this gurney. Part of my heart dies along with him.

The pain ends as quickly as it began. Soon it's over. I'm wheeled out and sent back to the room with the brown couches to rest for a few minutes. Then I'm told it's okay to leave.

Walter meets me in the lobby.

"How was it?" he asks.

"Fine," I say.

We walk silently side by side along the sidewalks of Hartford back to our respective offices. I feel relieved and empty at the same time. Emotionally numb.

When I arrive back in the office, no one seems to notice or care I'm a few minutes late.

I have just snuffed out a tiny life over my lunch hour. I have betrayed the bond of love that holds the universe together. And no one I work with seems any the wiser.

Chapter 10

Two Roads Diverge

Even in falling away from God, the world remains nestled in the supernatural.

—Hans Urs von Balthasar, *The Christian and Anxiety*

After my abortion, I don't quite know how to say this, but somehow the story inside me changed. From that bleak hour on, I would never again be the naïve little girl from Iowa. I had done the unspeakable, and I had done it rashly and boldly, almost without a moment's hesitation or doubt.

At a pivotal moment in our lives, when we most needed to embrace the freedom born only of hope and trust in God, Walter and I had succumbed to mind-shrinking fear. Blind to truth, we had sought a false freedom—a transitory freedom from duty rather than the eternal freedom to love. As a result, we made a contemptible choice that resulted in the catastrophe of death.

I usually deliver them alive.

Amid the business of struggling to earn a living, the aftermath of the abortion went underground. That is to say, we distracted ourselves from our fears with the busyness of business. Although Walter was my soul mate and we frequently talked about everything else under the sun, the abortion was one off-limits subject we almost never discussed. Even when my unaddressed grief surfaced in odd ways, I said nothing.

My parents had three children—my two younger brothers and I—so there were five in our family. After the abortion, as I set the dinner table, I would sometimes find myself unconsciously counting out five dinner plates and setting them on the table.

106

Five, I'd puzzle. *Why five? We need only four. Ah, of course.* Realizing what I had done would send a sudden electric jolt through my body. Then without a word, I would silently remove the plate I had set out for the child who was no more.

A relentless, low-level angst tormented me. Back on the Pill, depression became my constant companion. Refusing to face up to and grapple with my own faults, I blamed my heightened emotionality only on our money problems.

Still Broke ...

After the abortion, of course, our financial situation did not immediately improve. On the contrary, it continued to deteriorate. Our car broke down so we could no longer drive it, and Hartford was twenty-five miles away.

Stripped of transportation, I stayed home with the kids. Meanwhile, Walter persevered with his typical fortitude. One memorable day, the skies opened up and unleashed torrents of rain. The storm was what Missourians call a real gullywhumper. Walter had holes in the soles of both his shoes. Undeterred, he cut thick pieces of cardboard from a heavy cardboard box and placed them in the bottoms of his shoes in an attempt to keep his socks and feet dry. Then he hitch-hiked to Hartford in the downpour. All this just so he could work for a few bucks an hour to support our family.

Eventually, we got the Bug repaired, and I also went back to work.

Then, quite suddenly, God provided for our little family in a new and surprising way. The U.S. economy plunged deeper into recession, and Walter and I were both laid off by Manpower on exactly the same day. It happened on Christmas Eve.

The blow hit us hard. We were shocked and dismayed. *Whatever were we going to do?*

Still, it was Christmas Eve—no time to worry. We had work to do. The neighborhood kids had been filling Dustin's and Erin's sweet little heads with stories about Santa rewarding good girls and boys with toys and leaving naughty children with nothing under the tree. Broke and unemployed as we were, the last thing we wanted was for our Christmas tree to be barren.

Fortunately, we'd just received our last Manpower checks and we'd also been collecting Green Stamps for years. So before heading home from Hartford on Christmas Eve, we stopped at the Green Stamp store and loaded up on toys to place under the tree. We also stopped at Barker's (a Target-like discount department store), where to our delight all toys had just been marked down to half price.

Consequently, when Erin and Dustin awoke on Christmas morning, they marveled at the delightful treasures jolly Saint Nick had brought.

A Gift in Disguise

Getting laid off turned out to be a fortuitous blessing in disguise, a turning point in our lives. We had both worked long enough for Manpower that we were eligible to collect unemployment checks for six months—long enough to give us time to jump-start our writing careers. With *The American Biking Atlas and Touring Guide* at last in Barnes & Noble, I became an overnight authority on bicycling. It was admittedly a small victory. But when you're trying to earn a living at freelance writing, you take victories wherever you can. As OPEC put on the squeeze and Americans lined up for hours to fill up their gas tanks, bicycling suddenly became hot and trendy. A *Saturday Review* editor phoned me one day out of the blue to commission an article on the joys of bike touring. *Connecticut* magazine, *Colorado* magazine, and the travel section of *Newsday* on Long Island all bought bicycling articles from me. Even *Cosmopolitan* commissioned a story titled "Biking in the City." (Walter said it was the best article I had written for *Cosmo*—probably because it was one of the few that was completely true.)

In June 1975, in the same issue my biking story appeared, *Cosmo* also ran teasers for July's upcoming sex-revolution-propaganda pieces. One teaser for an article titled "The Sexually Aggressive Woman" asked the reader: "Are you far enough along the liberation road to take charge of lovemaking? Is he far enough along to lie back and enjoy your sensual declaration of independence?" The teaser for another article ("The Naked Truth about the Morning After") read: "The two of you almost danced [sic] all night, came home glowing with wine and passion, discovered each other in bed. *But*—in the A.M.'s early light, when reality shines bright, how do you keep romance going with the comparative stranger ... or do you *want* to?"

In the same issue, the magazine soft sold the dubious "joys" of divorce with an article titled "Self-Renewal: Divorce's Surprising Dividend," promising the gullible reader that if she were just "strong enough," a divorce crisis could open her up "to new stirrings of personal growth." In a clever turn of phrase only a skilled propagandist could craft, *Cosmo* promised to "present guide lines on how to switch from being half a couple to a self-sufficient majority of one." How many women that month bought and acted upon this false call to freedom? How many divorces did I help facilitate? Only God knows.

Certainly, Helen Gurley Brown didn't listen to the nonsense we were peddling at *Cosmo* any more than I did. She was married and by all accounts faithful to the same man for fifty years (she called David her "pussycat"). Nevertheless, the profit-driven sexual revolution demanded that a woman be single to be "sexy" and "free," and *Cosmo* provided the persuasive rhetoric required to sell women on this empty dream and to help grease the wheels of commerce.

Meanwhile, back in Connecticut, once editors saw and liked my work, they began calling me with assignments. Before long, Walter and I were able to earn a living by writing full-time. An article titled "Bike Tours in Fall Foliage Country" led to my becoming a regular contributor to *Connecticut* magazine and to many family adventures. Each month, the four of us would pile into our new yellow-and-black Datsun and travel throughout the state, seeking out "the very best" doughnuts, breads, candy shops, toy stores, Christmas barns, and hand-churned ice creams we could find.

I also began writing about bargains and other hidden treasures for *Yankee Magazine's Travel Guide to New England*. To write a story on children's zoos, we took our miniature Doctor Doolittles on an outing to Willington Wild Animal Farm, situated deep in the woods at the bottom of a steep hill in the northeastern corner of the state. Dustin, eight, was delighted to discover that the peacock with its iridescent blue chest and sleek green back walked "like a tightrope walker—with one foot in front of the other" and that the woolly monkey looked like he had "an army hat on." Three-year-old Erin shrieked with joy as the grivet monkey swung on his rope and chattered at her, while Dustin watched the blue-eyed spider monkey swinging effortlessly through his cage and sighed, "I'd just love to have a prehensile tail."

It was a good time in our lives. We took many happy day trips together through the Connecticut countryside and got paid for it all.

Meanwhile, Walter finished and sold his second novel, a thriller about a Nobel-Prize-winning physicist who goes mad and hijacks an airplane with a nuclear bomb aboard. Entitled *The Accident*, the book garnered good reviews, and the publisher expressed high hopes it would be picked up for a movie. (Instead, the potential movie deal fell through and the publisher went broke, but that's another story.)

The New Age Baby Name Book also began to pay off, and we filled our apartment with furniture, even purchasing an antique upright grand piano for a mere $50 from a couple who had inherited the piano and just wanted to get it out of their living room.

Suffice it to say, being laid off on Christmas Eve turned out to be a gift in disguise. Working at home, we were able to order our days in ways that allowed us to earn a living and also raise our children together. Writing for a living was not the meaning of our existence. But it freed up our time so we could pursue the meaning of our existence. If only we had been more diligent about our pursuit of that meaning ...

But I'm getting ahead of myself.

Two Roads Diverged

Although writing success did not please or fulfill me as much as I had imagined it would, bringing up children was sheer delight. Little moments still stand out: making divinity, finger painting, baking homemade bread on a rainy day, putting up a tire swing, planting a vegetable garden, playing softball in the backyard. The sweet little child kisses that leave your cheek wet and your heart filled with joy. Our children were not a *block* to the adventure; they helped give *meaning* to the adventure.

I have a peculiar memory—strange that it should have stuck with me all these years. And yet it was one of those little moments of truth you never forget.

I was rinsing out a dirty diaper in the toilet, of all things, when my thumb slipped into the poop. As I cleaned myself off, it occurred to me how far I now was from leading the sophisticated lifestyle we preached at *Cosmo*. *Helen Gurley Brown would be appalled if she knew one of her writers was living like this*, I thought to myself. *She would shudder with horror at the thought of living like this herself.*

Then I smiled quietly and happily added: *Poor Helen has no idea what she's missing.*

In fact, of course, the millionaire I called "poor Helen" thought she knew exactly what she was missing, and she wanted no part of it. Driven by desires for money and success, she called *Sex and the Single Girl* "my first baby."[1] One story she told about herself revealed how determined she was not to sacrifice her own needs for the greater needs of others, especially some pip-squeak of a kid.

On a transatlantic flight from Paris to New York City, Helen was seated in business class with two *Cosmo* editors when a baby across the aisle started to cry. Awakened from what she called "a serious sleep," Helen wrote:

> I went to the mother, reasonably, graciously, said I knew what a challenge it must be to care for a baby in flight (I hadn't a clue), but I hoped she'd do her best to quiet the child ... , that I had a long day ahead when we got to New York. Mommy, while not totally hostile, was totally disinterested, said not a cooing word to her baby who finally did quiet down; I went back to sleep. At the second wake-up ... baby now has his second wind, yelling up a storm ... I grittily stayed in my seat. How often can you remonstrate with a mommy who hasn't got the word *soothe* in her vocabulary and is also apparently deaf, but I am pissed. Other passengers don't seem to mind baby or be particularly sympathetic with me.... Glowers at mother get me nowhere, naturally, but the baby finally stops crying again.... I will myself to sleep again.... At the third wake-up—yowl, yowl!—I blast out of my seat, fly over to mother and baby, scream at baby, "Shut up"!

The two *Cosmo* editors with her try to pretend they don't know her.

"I guess it was quite a sight ... grown woman screaming at tiny infant," Helen admitted. "When I told [my husband] David this story his first words were, "Oh, my God, what if she was a *Cosmo* reader!"[2]

Years after I heard this story, I found myself wondering: Was Helen's bizarre behavior, her angry eruption over a little baby crying in business class, born of her own unacknowledged post-abortion wounds? Helen admitted late in her life that during her early days in Los Angeles in the advertising business, when she was earning money to support herself, her mother, and her wheelchair-bound sister, she'd been a kept woman. She didn't go to college and, in fact, had to drop out of secretarial school for lack of funds. How many abortions did she feel compelled to have to keep her various jobs before she met and married David, who urged her to write *Sex and the Single Girl*? Helen has justifiably been called one of the architects of the culture of death.[3] Her ideas and the propaganda she invented to spread those ideas were certainly deadly. And yet on a personal level, was she just a talented, small-town girl from Green Forest, Arkansas, who'd managed to make it big in the world by having one or more abortions along the way?

I was relieved to be living far from the day-to-day dreariness-mixed-with-angst I had encountered while working on staff at *Cosmo*. With God's grace, I was beginning to learn that a life spent chasing transitory pleasures will never satisfy the human heart. It was at home that I first began to taste the true freedom born only of lasting love, the type of freedom Friedan and the Mere Fifty-Seven seemed to have overlooked that fateful night in the Mayflower Hotel.

Although the NOW-led women's movement made much of who does the dishes and who mows the lawn, Walter and I refused to waste our time fussing over day-to-day sex-role duties. There was more than enough drudge work to go around, and we split it up along the lines of who could do what most efficiently. Since Walter knew how to repair a car, fix a flat tire, and mow the lawn, those were some of his jobs. Since I loved baking, I did most of the cooking. Oddly enough, Walter ironed better than I did. The dishes got done when the dishes got done. We settled into a comfortable routine that left us both plenty of time to retreat to our studies and write. We didn't ask ourselves who was doing the most work or who was getting the short shrift. We made no attempt to divvy up the work so we would be "equal." We both just dived in and worked as hard as we could. Our marriage wasn't a 50-50 deal. We both gave 100 percent and tried to do whatever we could to set one another free. Together, we made a great team.

An Idol in Person

Of course, sometimes I had to leave Walter and the children and venture forth alone into the world. To promote my books and articles, I had to appear on television, go on radio talk shows, and ride in limousines. Don't get me wrong. I'm not complaining. I'm just saying schlepping the book wasn't the glamorous thrill this small-town girl from Iowa once imagined it would be.

A sense of absurdity and emptiness pervaded many tasks I was assigned to do. Without Christ at the center of my heart, I was wandering lost in a wasteland, where nothing outside my love for Walter, Dustin, and Erin seemed to have any significance.

I especially loathed appearing on television.

If I'd cared about what I'd written, I suppose being on TV might have been worth the effort. As it was, I was just going through the motions because some publicist asked me to do it. Unlike Helen Gurley Brown, I was never on Johnny Carson's *Tonight Show*. But I was on *Geraldo*, *QVC*, *Oprah*, the *Today Show* with Matt Lauer, and others. (More about *Oprah* later.)

I was once on live TV in Hartford with a famous multimillionaire film star. A comedian, director, producer, and one of the all-time greatest headliners in Las Vegas history, he had been a childhood hero of mine, so I was fascinated to meet him in real life. He carried around with him a huge briefcase filled with videotapes of every television show on which he'd ever appeared. I found the way he cherished those tapes strange and somehow grotesque. It was as if he were carrying himself around in a suitcase so he could remember who he was.

Backstage (the Hartford studio had no green room in those days), this famous Hollywood clown spent all his time entertaining the stagehands and revving himself up for that magic moment when the camera would be aimed only at him, and he would once again come to life.

I felt sorry for this little man with the big name as he strutted his stuff, feeding hungrily off the adoration he saw in others' eyes. For all his funniness, he seemed to me very sad.

Of course, I was just skimming over the surface of this man's life. Everyone and everything contains a deeper, interior reality invisible to the eye. I wasn't who I appeared to be. So why judge *him* by his appearance? But I habitually judged my neighbor harshly in those days in an attempt to ignore my own flaws.

In any case, the real-life backstage encounter with one of my childhood idols hammered yet another nail into the coffin of my dying love affair with celebrity. Behind the mask, what I once thought would be fun didn't seem to me to be fun at all.

An Empty Atonement

Once I made an empty attempt to imbue one of my TV appearances with some deeper meaning. For nine years, I wrote a monthly "Bargains" column for *Connecticut* magazine, in which I sought out factory outlets and other secret hideaways all over the state where readers could buy everything from designer dresses to billiard tables for a fraction of the regular price. Because I was The Bargains Lady (one of my many dubious achievements), a Hartford television channel asked me to do a spot on their *PM Magazine* show about where to find the best discount lighting fixtures in town. The producer paid me forty bucks for a tedious day's work that made me feel as if I were a barker in a used-car commercial. That old feeling which had started when I was on staff at *Cosmo* swept over me again, and I felt that day I had betrayed everything a real journalist should be.

Even then, I must have unconsciously realized my lack of journalistic ethics was linked in some unseen way to my abortion.

In a futile attempt to atone for both, I used the forty dollars I received as blood money.

I'd seen an advertisement for a pro-life center in a local hometown shopper. So I decided to spend the ill-begotten forty bucks on a new crib and mattress to give to some unknown woman more courageous than I was, some struggling mother who, despite her poverty, had chosen to keep her baby and to reach out humbly to others for help.

In my mind, I had to give away a *new* crib. That was important. I thought: *It can't be a bed that has ever been used before.*

As I buy a wooden crib, the thought occurs to me: *At least some poor young mother—someone for whom there is "no room at the inn" in our society—will have a brand-new crib for her brand-new and perfect little baby. Perhaps late some night, as she watches her baby lying there, sweetly sleeping, she will find comfort and take courage in realizing that someone she never met cared enough to give her this crib, and she will know she is not alone.*

The pro-life center is on the second floor. To reach it, I have to maneuver the crib and mattress up a narrow stairway. I'm short and weigh 112 pounds. The crib and mattress are heavy and awkward for me to carry. It's quite a struggle. When I arrive at the top of the landing, the center is closed. The door is locked. No one is there.

I am suddenly torn with indecision. *What shall I do now? Let's see: the hours are posted. Oh, sh—! No one will be here until tomorrow. Should I come back then when the office is open? If I do, what will I say? I could say, "Well, you see, I paid this doctor to kill my own baby. He wasn't happy about it, but he did it, anyway. So now I've brought you this crib, so some other innocent little baby will have a place to lay his sweet head. To tell you the truth, I don't even know if it's a crib. Maybe it's a coffin." No, I certainly can't say that. Should I drag the bed back down the stairs and take it home with me? No, I can't bear to do that, either.*

Finally, I just leave the crib and mattress propped up against the wall in the hallway and flee.

Later, I tell Walter what I did. No drawn-out, dramatic detail. Just the quick, basic facts: I took the forty dollars I got from *PM Magazine*, bought a crib with the money, and gave it to a pro-life center.

"I wish you had told me," he replies. "I would have liked to have gone with you."

A New Feminism Rises

As Walter and I struggled, each alone, to come to terms with the aftermath of the abortion, the pro-life women's movement was slowly building behind the scenes. Even before *Roe*, in April 1972, the seed for Feminists for Life was planted when two NOW members, Pat Goltz and Catherine Callaghan, met at a judo class at Ohio State University. A year later, on April 9, 1973, the two founded Feminists for Life in Columbus, Ohio. According to pro-life feminist Cindy Osborne, "Pat and Catherine were deeply disturbed because the women's movement was caving in to the demands of the patriarchy by allowing itself to be used by rich industrialists, the population control movement, and the playboy movement. They believed feminist organizations were failing to provide viable alternatives to abortion for individual women and abandoning them to abortionists and abortion referral services who would exploit their misery. Because the single-minded focus of the movement was on abortion, they were not developing workable solutions to the problems of poor and minority women."[4] Teaming up to fight for life in their NOW chapter in Columbus, Pat and Catherine soon learned their pro-life views were anathema. After Pat courageously criticized NOW for promoting abortion as a solution for everything from sexism to poverty, her local chapter "disciplined" her by formally kicking her out.[5] So much for freedom of speech.

Although the news that a new pro-life women's movement was sweeping like a tsunami across the land went largely unreported or, if reported, downplayed, the trend did not pass unnoticed by abortion-industry supporters, who found this grassroots uprising greatly disturbing. At a Planned Parenthood of America, Inc., event held September 14, 1979, at Rockefeller University to honor the late Margaret Sanger, author Michael Harrington (a Catholic-turned-atheist) drew a gasp from the well-heeled crowd of more than four hundred (including some Hollywood elites) when he stated that his travels around the United States had convinced him the right-to-life movement was "one of the few genuine social movements of the 1970s."[6]

Referring to the pro-life movement's unequivocal success "in capturing an ideal and mobilizing people in support of it," Harrington called the new pro-life feminism "the anti–women's movement women's movement."

"If the tone of the evening was any indication," the *New York Times* reported, pro-abortion factions "are worried that their own movement lacks that kind of vitality."[7]

The *Times* reporter was more correct than perhaps even she knew. When the Mere Fifty-Seven in the Chinese Room created a women's movement that overfocused on sexual, economic, and political power as the paths to freedom, they overlooked the essential element women require to be fully free: the power of love. As the decade rolled by, a growing army of Americans, who had the eyes to see what NOW's sex-revolution agenda was doing to women and children, mounted impassioned protests. Year by year, on January 22, at the annual March for Life in Washington, D.C., the numbers of

protesters against *Roe v. Wade* (the Supreme Court's legal enshrine-
ment of the unholy marriage between the women's movement and
the sexual revolution) continued to grow. As *New York Times* op-
ed columnist Gail Collins observed, "By the end of the 1970s, the
National Right to Life Committee claimed more than eleven million
members."[8] Meanwhile, in 1979, according to a history of the wom-
en's movement put out by the Feminist Majority Foundation, NOW
boasted only one hundred thousand members.[9]

NARAL'S Co-Founder Sees the Truth

Meanwhile, in one of those strange twists of history only God can
arrange, the pro-abortion movement lost one of its most zealous supporters. In the late 1970s, NARAL cofounder Dr. Bernie Nathanson
saw a living fetus on an ultrasound monitor.

This led him to quit the abortion business.

After founding NARAL with Lader and being personally responsible for more than seventy thousand abortions, he became a fervent,
indefatigable advocate for life. That's when he told the truth about
the propaganda he and Lader had so carefully crafted to sell abortion
to women, politicians, the American public, and ultimately to the
U.S. Supreme Court.

Two decades later, in 1996, Bernie would carry his search for the
truth even farther, and he would convert from Judaism to Catholicism. Telling his story in *The Hand of God: A Journey from Death
to Life by the Abortion Doctor Who Changed His Mind*, Bernie wrote:
"Although my fears are great, I know something now that I did not
know ... I am no longer alone. It has been my fate to wander the
globe in search of the One without Whom I am doomed, but now I
seize the hem of His robe in desperation, in terror, in celestial access
to the purest need I have ever known."[10]

He fell asleep in the Lord on February 21, 2011.

Even Bernie in the end knew that the grassroots pro-life movement, which had escaped being hijacked by Lader, represented the
most authentic liberation for women and children. Pro-life feminism represents the true legacy of the suffragists. But the NOW-
and-NARAL-dominated branch of the women's movement, with

its propaganda mills churning, continues to pretend to speak publicly for all women everywhere, even for poor, voiceless women in other countries.

What's worse, I bought, and most of my media colleagues to this day continue to buy, into the deception.

As a *Cosmo* writer, I was so deeply deceived and blind to the truth that I even refused to see the evidence of my own tragic personal experience with abortion, when it was right before my eyes. I was a prime example of cognitive dissonance in action. As I silently grieved the loss of my third child, I continued to beat the politically correct propaganda drums, loudly crying out that abortion was every expectant mother's right. Internally torn with stress and anxiety, I continued to claim that NOW and NARAL were a woman's true friends, and they were leading me and all my other "liberated" sisters down the road to freedom.

Chapter 11

The New Woman Asks New Questions

Today I see feminism as the Great Experiment That Failed, and women in my generation, its perpetrators, are the casualties. Many of us, myself included, are saddled with raising children alone. The resulting poverty makes us experts at cornmeal recipes and ways to find free recreation on weekends. At the same time, single men from our generation amass fortunes in CDs and real-estate ventures so they can breeze off on ski weekends.

—Kay Ebeling,
"The Failure of Feminism," *Newsweek*, November 18, 1990

Being married to a writer can be a challenge. Mario Puzo once recalled that when he was writing *The Godfather*, his wife claimed she'd never seen him writing; all she'd ever seen him do was lie back on the sofa and stare at the ceiling. He said, "I don't know what it is. You sort of go into a trance." Writers walk about the house, stare out the window, wander through the garden, and say *nothing* to anyone. Yet their minds are filled with fiends and angels, curses and prayers, demonic shrieks and love songs. The professor who taught me magazine writing at the University of Missouri said that when his wife left him forever, as she stormed out the door, she snapped, "You'd rather sleep with your typewriter than with me." Although he swore it wasn't true, this taught him a writer should only marry another writer.

Walter and I were ideal for each other in that we could be deeply intimate with each other, but we also knew when not to intrude. We'd be immersed in a conversation about God, quantum physics, or the distance to the farthest star one minute and the next minute be sitting side by side lost in silent contemplation. Sometimes when

Walter and I were both writing, we'd take a coffee break and sit together, just the two of us, alone in a room, saying nothing. Realizing we hadn't spoken for twenty minutes or more, one of us would suddenly laugh and say, "We've got to stop meeting like this." Then we'd arise and go back to work.

When we were working, our daily routine varied little. After bundling the kids off to school and pouring second cups of coffee, we'd retreat to our separate studies at about 9:00 A.M. We'd break for coffee around 10:30 and pause again for lunch. Our workday ended around 3:30 when the kids came home from school. Often I had just taken a batch of chocolate-chip cookies or a loaf of homemade bread from the oven when Dustin and Erin arrived. Then the four of us would gather comfortably around our kitchen table and chat about what had happened that day. It was sheer bliss.

On those rare weekdays when we weren't writing, Walter and I couldn't get enough of each other's company. Sometimes our breakfast conversations would become so absorbing we'd continue talking until noon. Walter was a fathomless depth. The more I knew of him, the more I wanted to know. He was my best friend, lover, comrade, pal, travel buddy, and writing partner. We were way beyond good for each other.

Victims of Deception

Sadly, not every career woman was as happy as I was. In February of '85, I published an article in *Connecticut* magazine entitled "Ah, Romance ... Where Has It Gone?" It was a sentimental but nonetheless true piece about the loss of romantic love across our land. As women increasingly focused on their careers at the expense of love as the way to "actualize" themselves, balancing love and work had become the new juggling act. A day contains only 1,440 minutes. Will we devote this minute right now to caring for others—or to earning money? Although it can be done, it's hard to do both at once. Work schedules cut into time for love until some couples had no time for each other at all. For many women and men, the unholy marriage between the women's movement and the sexual revolution had spawned loneliness and discontent. The "Ah, Romance ..."

story struck a chord with many readers. Soon a *New Woman* magazine editor contacted me and began giving me assignments to write articles on love, intimacy, and troubled relationships.

In 1963, Betty Friedan had written about the idyllic relationships with men the self-actualized New Woman would enjoy. Yet by the 1980s, if there was one word to describe how real New Women felt about the sexualized women's movement, that word was *ambivalent*. It was one thing to insist upon equal pay for equal work (an eminently reasonable request), quite another to insist that now, thanks to the Pill and abortion, women were sexually, biologically, and emotionally no different from men and should act accordingly.

A single young woman, if she was to be regarded as strong, intelligent, and independent, was now expected to hop into bed with a man at least by the third date, to have multiple sex partners without remorse, and to reject saving sex for marriage as unliberated and old-hat. All the sexual rules had been broken, or so women were told. But the new unspoken sexual rules were even more domineering. For all the public talk about the New Woman having "control of her own body," she was allowed to say *yes* to sex, but she wasn't allowed to say *no*. In January 1985, I published *Cosmo*'s first article on the horror of date rape, that most unreported of all crimes.

It turned out, of course, that women *weren't* just like men (*hello?*), and women who struggled to follow the tyrannical new sexual rules in the name of what passed for freedom frequently felt angry, insecure, and angst-ridden.

Of course, women were hardly alone in their dissatisfactions. Men who had their adolescent fantasies of sex without responsibility fulfilled often found themselves unspeakably lonely. It turned out that empty sex without authentic love brought no one peace but often only bred an insatiable craving for more. Porn addictions erupted not just among men on the societal fringes, but among millions of ordinary guys.

As a new generation of difficulties arose, thoughtful women began asking new questions. *Where did it all go so wrong?* In a 1988 essay in *The New York Times Magazine* titled "When Feminism Failed," Los Angeles *Herald-Examiner* editor Mary Anne Dolan observed, "What was missing in the 'new' women I saw at *The Herald* and elsewhere was the joyful 'I am.' What remained was the fearful 'I want.'" Bemoaning the rampant "devotion to success" she witnessed among women "at the expense of personal well-being," she added, "The question, to me, is not whether women can be as ruthless as men; we all know the answer to that. But is it so unreasonable to expect, as we did during the height of the women's movement, that women can be humanizers? ... We ought to ask again: what do we want?"[1]

Meanwhile, relationships between women and men were in tatters. In *Newsweek*, Kay Ebeling observed that from her perspective, "The main message of feminism was: woman, you don't need a man; remember ... the phrase: 'A woman without a man is like a fish without a bicycle'? That joke circulated through 'consciousness raising' groups across the country in the '70s. It was a philosophy that made divorce and cohabitation casual and routine. Feminism made women disposable."[2]

In fact, of course, it wasn't feminism *per se*, but *the secret marriage of the women's movement with the sexual revolution* that persuaded many misguided women to allow themselves to be sexually used and then disposed of (along with their babies).

By the early 1980s, victims of the sexual revolution began to appear everywhere. Previously crisp, black-and-white guidelines about how men and women should treat one another seemed to have faded into dim, wavy lines of gray. Single women who wanted to marry couldn't find suitable mates. Married women were getting divorced. Many career women who'd waited until their midthirties to have children discovered they'd waited too long and now either had to accept lifelong childlessness or go through the torments of in-vitro fertilization and other tortuous medical procedures just to get pregnant. As Ruth Institute founder Jennifer Roback Morse put it, sex without babies had been fun; babies without sex turned out to be not so much fun. Men, stripped of the maturity that comes with responsible fatherhood, were becoming self-absorbed Peter Pans who couldn't grow up.

Walter and I, of course, had already caved in to the mainstream women's movement's abortion rhetoric, and our hidden choice silently continued to haunt us. But now the sexual revolution had also spawned a divorce revolution. Divorce spread invisibly like a virus from one family to the next, and no one was immune.

New Friends and Musical Beds

Walter and I met Roy and Melanie* one chilly spring afternoon under a high blue New England sky at a Little League practice field.

An avid Boston Red Sox fan, Walter had signed up to coach Dustin's Little League team that spring, and I volunteered to help. Roy was a graduate student at the University of Connecticut, and his wife Melanie was a stay-at-home mom. Their son Shawn was Dustin's age, and their daughter Polly was eight, the same age as Erin. Our two families immediately hit it off, and we began to see each other socially.

A tall, boisterous academic with a bushy red beard and a lumber-jack physique, Roy habitually dominated conversations by talking loudly over the top of everyone. Short and thin, with light-brown hair, Melanie had a quick smile and loved to laugh.

Although we tried not to let it show, both Walter and I preferred Melanie's friendly company over Roy's belligerence. When she came to us one day in tears and told us Roy was having an affair and he'd asked for a divorce, our sympathies naturally poured out to her.

Soon Melanie and I were like sisters. She phoned me at 1:00 A.M. when she couldn't sleep, stored her furniture in our garage, and gave me a play-by-play description of the bitter court battles with her ex. When she mustered the courage to start dating again, I babysat with Polly.

Brown-eyed with long dark hair, Polly tried to put on a brave face. But she was no longer the happy little girl she'd been when we met her. One evening when her mother was on a date and she was staying overnight at our place, she teared up as I tucked her in. "I just wish I could sometimes sleep in my own bed," she moaned softly.

Roy's self-centered game of musical beds had led to musical beds for his children.

I gave Polly a tender little hug, but I had no way to relieve her grief. It was heart-wrenching to witness what the marital breakup was doing to her.

The situation went from bad to worse, and one day Roy kid-napped Shawn and Polly and hustled them off to Pennsylvania.

* Not their real names.

Melanie was hardly the carefree divorcee depicted on the pages of *Cosmo*. Left to her loneliness, she was unspeakably sad. When she had no family with whom to share the holidays, Walter and I invited her to spend Thanksgiving and Christmas with us.

Moving Out and Moving In

Finally, Melanie got up the energy to move out of her old house into a new apartment. We helped her move.

The next day, she phoned and asked Walter to come over to her place to set up her stereo. She seemed so defenseless. Of course he agreed to help.

That was the day she tried to kiss him.

Sometimes love calls you to open up to others. Sometimes love calls you to draw a clear boundary line over which others can't cross. Walter did not kiss her back. On the contrary, he was so disgusted by her seductive behavior he immediately came home and told me every grisly detail.

I felt betrayed and annoyed. But I wasn't angry, because I had no reason to be. After all, no harm was done. Love had won, and deception had lost.

Rather than apologize, Melanie phoned me one day as if nothing had happened and began whining as usual about her nonexistent love life.

Maybe she was just testing the waters to see how much or how little I knew.

Suddenly, with no apparent regrets, she boldly blurted out, "I like Walter."

"So do I," I firmly replied.

Well, of course, that ended our poisonous friendship. We still occasionally spoke, but our old intimacy was gone. Later I published an article in *Woman* magazine, in which I posed the question "When is a friend not a friend?" I chose to use as my lead anecdote the true-life story about Melanie's betrayal (changing her name, of course). The piece was titled "Eight 'Friends' You Can Do Without."

Our experience with Melanie taught me a valuable lesson: the single, childless "autonomous self" the sexualized women's movement worshipped was—in her "freedom" from others—a lonely and frightened self, a false self cut off from God and man. Our true selves emerge only when we're part of an ever-deepening web of love. Personally witnessing Melanie's tragic divorce also enabled me to see how one broken marriage can spread like a virus through a community, threatening to infect and destroy other relationships it touches.

One day, as Erin and I cuddled together on the living-room sofa of our Connecticut country home, Erin suddenly declared, "*We're* not getting divorced, are we."

She said it not as a question, but firmly and confidently, as if she were stating an indisputable fact.

"No, Honey," I agreed, giving our nine-year-old a reassuring squeeze. "*We* certainly are *not* getting divorced."

Erin's innocent claim of ownership over "our" marriage opened my eyes. She made me see the marital union belongs to more people than the woman and man who tie the knot. Marriage belongs to the entire interconnected community and most especially to the children. Although I still supported the women's movement's pleas for equality at work and in education, I rejected the movement's radical claim that marriage was a trap from which I needed to escape if I wanted to be self-fulfilled and free.

Much later, however, I began to wonder: What if our marriage had been on the rocks when Melanie and Roy came our way? What would have happened then?

Love in a Time of Trial

Life is seldom easy, and Walter was suffering a prolonged and particularly difficult period in his writing career. Perhaps the writer who most deeply influenced Walter's novels was William Faulkner. The influence came not so much from the stories and novels Faulkner wrote, good as those were, but from something he said. On December 10, 1950, in Stockholm, Faulkner gave his Nobel Prize acceptance speech in which he observed:

> Our tragedy today is a general and universal physical fear so long sustained by now that we can even bear it. There are no longer problems of the spirit. There is only the question: When will I be blown up? Because of this, the young man or woman writing today has forgotten

the problems of the human heart in conflict with itself which alone
can make good writing because only that is worth writing about,
worth the agony and the sweat.

He must learn them again. He must teach himself that the basest of
all things is to be afraid; and, teaching himself that, forget it forever,
leaving no room in his workshop for anything but the old verities and
truths of the heart, the old universal truths lacking which any story
is ephemeral and doomed—love and honor and pity and pride and
compassion and sacrifice. Until he does so, he labors under a curse.
He writes not of love but of lust, of defeats in which nobody loses
anything of value, of victories without hope and, worst of all, without
pity or compassion. His griefs grieve on no universal bones, leaving no
scars. He writes not of the heart but of the glands.[3]

Faulkner closed his speech with, "The poet's voice need not merely
be the record of man, it can be one of the props, the pillars to help
him endure and prevail."[4]

Walter took these words to heart. Writing in a post-World-War
world under the shadow of the bomb, Walter tried to tell stories that
would lift the heart and help mankind not just endure, but prevail.

Tragically, during the heydays of the sexual revolution (and I
would say the trend continues today), commercial publishers were
far more eager to invest their money in stories written for the glands.
Lust sells. Stories about love, honor, pride, compassion, and sacrifice
are less predictably profitable.

Walter had finished a new novel, "The Rubaiyat of Ernie Barnes,"
the tale of a young Harvard man whose heart was in conflict with
itself. Ernie's violent intellectual and spiritual journey leads him from
the hallowed halls of Harvard deep into the coal mines of West
Virginia and, ultimately, into a hellish confrontation with his own
demons and fears. The 417-page typewritten manuscript took three
years to complete. To write the story, Walter drew upon the darkest
moments from his childhood, traumas so deeply hidden he refused to
talk about them even to me.

Before we were married, Walter made a statement I'll never forget.
He said, "I'd rather hurt all my life than never feel anything at all."

This intimate revelation, which greatly puzzled me at the time,
now seemed to be coming to pass. Walter's writing path was one of
sweat, toil, and anguish.

One way to be taken seriously as a literary artist in the 1970s was to include early on in one's book (at least by chapter two) the requisite reference to the "irrational superstition" of all religion or to poke fun in some way at the Catholic Church. A disparaging comment or two about Christianity or God gave you credibility as an artist among those handing out the checks. If one could create a scene dwelling in detail on the insensitivity or stupidity of a character who happened to be a priest, so much the better. I'm not saying Walter's refusal to play this game was the sole reason his novels kept getting rejected. But it certainly didn't help.

One day a high-wattage Manhattan literary agent rejected the manuscript of "The Rubaiyat" not because the story wasn't good but simply on the cavalier ground he "didn't like first-person novels."

When he opened the agent's letter with eager hope only to find yet another crass rejection slip, Walter in fury and frustration picked up his thirty-five-pound manual typewriter and threw the machine through a wall. The heavy, old Smith-Corona crashed through an ersatz maple-wood panel in our bedroom, shattering it into splinters.

The wall wasn't ours to smash. The house was a rental.

Walter had taken a risk. He had gone deep into those silent, hidden places of his heart where the demons lie and God speaks the truth. He had tried to bring out of those places gifts of love, beauty, and light. He had poured out his heart's blood in black words upon a white page. And this agent viewed it all with a jaded eye and scornfully turned away simply because he disliked first-person stories?

I was playing games with my life, but to Walter nothing about life was a game. The artist, to be true to his form, must always take the risk of being ignored, laughed at, or misunderstood. Walter wasn't quite ready yet to take that risk. Things mattered too much to him. He was struggling too hard to support a family to suffer fools lightly. On that fateful day the typewriter hit the wall, he took "The Rubaiyat of Ernie Barnes" and stored it away in a cardboard box, where it lay untouched, gathering dust, for the next two decades.

Chastened and chagrined after his temper cooled, Walter spent the next several days searching every lumberyard and hardware store in the area until he at last found a matching maple panel to replace the one he'd destroyed. The panel was in a discontinued color, and when he finally found it, it cost him only $6, a genuine bargain. Then he dutifully went to work and carefully repaired the wall. (By the way, the typewriter survived unscathed. Those old Smith-Coronas sure were made to last.)

Life is not easy, and no marriage is perfect. My Walter was plainly a passionate man. What if he had been tempted that day in Melanie's apartment just to chuck all the difficulties of his current life the way he'd chucked his typewriter? What if he had decided, as Roy had, that the only way he could "fulfill himself" was by starting anew?

What if he had said yes to her kiss?

At the moment, it could have seemed an action of small note, so easy, so simple, a choice made in the blink of an eye . . .

What violently shattering consequences would have followed such a kiss of betrayal? Would we have become just another broken family, shipwrecked on the shoals of the sexualized women's movement I was so ardently promoting on the pages of *Cosmo*? The sexual revolution, through media megaphones like *Cosmo*, said other women's husbands were fair game. Melanie was doing nothing more—nor less—than what Helen Gurley Brown (and I by collusion) preached in the name of setting women free. But what about me? How free would I have been had her seduction succeeded? Cast alone into the world with two children to support, would I once again have become an unwitting victim of my own propaganda? Our whole family was spared this tragic outcome not because of my virtues (for I had none), but because my dear Walter believed in the truth and beauty of lasting love and had the integrity to defend it in one of life's small, fleeting moments.

Lest anyone dismiss me as a sentimental romantic who's giving Walter far more credit than he deserves, let me quote Christian psychiatrist M. Scott Peck, author of *The Road Less Traveled*, who observed in his book on human evil:

> He who behaves nobly in easy times—a fair-weather friend, so to speak—may not be so noble when the chips are down. Stress is the test for goodness. The truly good are they who in time of stress do not desert their integrity, their maturity, their sensitivity. Nobility might be defined as the capacity not to regress in response to degradation, not to become blunted in the face of pain, to tolerate the agonizing and remain intact. As I have said elsewhere, "one measure—and

perhaps the best measure—of a person's greatness is the capacity for suffering."[5]

When the mainstream women's movement leaders miscast all men as the enemies of women's freedom, they had apparently never met a man like my pal Walter. Ibsen's much-ballyhooed line, "He is strongest who is most alone," denies the unseen power of love. Divided, Walter and I would have fallen even more frequently than we did. Together, we stood stronger than either of us could ever have done on our own.

Chapter 12

From *Cosmo* to Cosmos (and Back Again)

We are not sent into this world to walk in solitude. We are born to love, as we are born to breathe and eat and drink.

> —Kenneth Boulding, Cofounder of General Systems Theory,
> William Penn Lecture 1942

Near the beginning of our life journey together, Walter and I had set out to find a little bit of heaven on earth. In Roxbury, I thought we'd almost found it. We moved to Roxbury in 1985 for the local high school, which after much careful research we'd concluded was one of the best in the state. A charming colonial village situated in the northwest corner of Connecticut's gently rolling Litchfield Hills, Roxbury (incorporated in 1796) had only 1,468 residents, among them actor Dustin Hoffman and playwright Arthur Miller. Roxbury was comprised of a library, a general store, a gas pump, a post office, and a one-teller bank. It felt to us as if a magical spell of protection had been cast over the charming little town. We called it "The Shire."

In Roxbury's tightly knit little community, the American spirit of independence was still vibrant. Roxbury residents were both fiercely independent *and* interconnected. On election day, if you hadn't made it to the town hall by 4:00 P.M. to cast your vote, you would get a phone call from a clerk. If you still hadn't made it by 6:00 P.M. (*mea culpa*), you would get another call. I didn't personally check the figure, but I was once told our percentage of voter participation was something like 97 percent.

When the Iroquois Natural Gas Company decided in the mid-1980s to install a pipeline from western Canada to Long Island and tried to bring it through Roxbury, all hell broke loose. The united little community rose up in arms, and Iroquois plainly had a tough fight on its hands. The night an Iroquois spokesman came to speak at a meeting in our tiny wooden town hall, he was met with roaring protests from irate local citizens. Arthur Miller stood up in the meeting and announced in a stentorian tone, "This is our field, and we're not going to let you boys plow in it." Iroquois was reportedly unprepared for the intellectual rigor of Roxbury. (The gas company dropped the Roxbury plan and put the pipeline through New York State instead.)

The year we moved to Roxbury was, not coincidentally, also the year we went back to church. We had never, to my recollection, taken Dustin and Erin to church, and I was aware I'd neglected my duty as a mother. Organized in 1740 and believed to be the oldest Anglican parish in Litchfield County, the whitewood Christ Church with its red double-door was near the town green, within walking distance of the late-nineteenth-century farmhouse we'd rented.

The Reverend Bruce Shipman, balding with a ruddy complexion, welcomed us warmly. Oxford-educated with degrees in theology and philosophy, Father Bruce generously offered to give the four of us lessons together. Attendance had dropped, the church was just hanging on, and he was plainly eager to have more young families with children in the parish.

One day in class Walter said he'd always thought of his body as "a suit of clothes" he would one day discard. To our surprise, Father Bruce firmly declared this notion of the body as disposable to be a heresy, because Christ sanctifies our flesh and will raise our bodies up on the last day. As I would later learn, any "spirituality" that opposes matter to spirit is ultimately contrary to the Gospel: non-Christian.

Although Walter and I had been baptized, neither of us could produce our baptismal certificates. So Father Bruce insisted upon baptizing us again "just to be sure."

The Sunday we entered the church, Guyana-born Bishop Clarence Coleridge (the first black to become an Episcopal bishop in Connecticut) came to oversee the service and confer confirmation.

Alongside others, the four of us knelt together before the altar.

When Bishop Coleridge came to us, his eyes widened quizzically above his mustache. "Is this a whole family?" he asked.

Father Bruce nodded.

The bishop anointed our foreheads with holy oil and claimed us as Christ's own forever. Then he gave our family a special blessing.

New Beginnings

After we returned to church, everything in our lives seemed fresh and new. Never had we been so happy. One morning as Walter and I sat together at the kitchen table, sipping cups of hot coffee, my husband of twenty years looked deeply into my eyes and said, "I'm falling in love with you all over again." And I realized I was falling in love all over again with him too.

On snowy winter evenings, the four of us would gather around our living-room fireplace to roast marshmallows and tell stories. These intimate evenings led us to conclude we each had our limitations: Dustin couldn't tell a short story, Erin couldn't make a little sandwich, I couldn't pop a little popcorn, and Walter couldn't build a small fire.

One spring morning when we got up and looked out our north kitchen window, we saw a white deer nibbling at the greenery in our backyard on the edge of the forest.

On cool summer evenings, as Walter and I sat peacefully side by side on the back porch in the moonlight under a black canopy sparkling with stars, the frogs in our small garden pond merrily serenaded us. The frogs—one was blue—had a strange habit of floating on top of the water and allowing Erin to pet them. Our lives seemed imbued with wonder, beauty, and magic.

Something new was also happening to our writing. Walter began creating screenplays, and I was working on a parenting book with University of Connecticut psychobiologist Evelyn B. Thoman. To explain to you what happened next—an insight I gained which helped lead me to a profound change of direction on my spiritual journey—we need to talk briefly about physics.

This isn't quite as strange as it may at first sound. We all resemble those wooden Russian nesting or *matryoshka* dolls, with a story inside a story inside a story. The story I'm about to tell you next is one of those bigger stories within which my smaller story was embedded.

A Journalist and a Scientist Meet

I'd met Evelyn several years before we moved to Roxbury when we had rented a house from her just off campus near the University of Connecticut. A vibrant woman in her sixties who'd gotten her Ph.D. after raising six children, Evelyn invited me to act as her collaborator on a book titled *Born Dancing*. The book was about the wordless dance of unity that goes on between a mother and her baby. Although I didn't know it when I agreed to write the book with her, Evelyn was about to open my eyes to a new interconnected worldview that would begin to turn my whole way of thinking inside out and upside down.

Evelyn taught me that we are swimming—or perhaps drowning—in a sea of ideas that are so much a part of our lives we don't even see them. The "idea" of the universe as a Great Machine, for example, was a seventeenth-century idea I'd unwittingly inherited from René Descartes and Isaac Newton. Descartes envisioned the universe as a Great Machine. Newton provided the mathematics and laws of physics that made Descartes' Great Machine run.

It was this "idea" of the universe and everything in it as a Great Machine from which my misguided notion of the Watchmaker God had sprung. If the universe is like a machine, who manufactured it? Because I thought of myself as a Christian, my answer was that God made the Great Machine, and then He walked away into some magical place called "heaven," leaving me way down here by myself to muddle through on my own. I thought this was originally *my* idea, and it had only been reinforced by my university philosophy professor. But I was wrong. The Cartesian-Newtonian worldview and the analogous notion of the Watchmaker God were actually part of the sea of ideas I was born into.

I was longing for a unity or wholeness of being, a wholeness of *personhood*, much like the fullness of personhood Betty Friedan said the women's movement was all about. Evelyn offered me a glimpse into a new scientific worldview that almost seemed to provide it. She explained to me that the "new physics"—which began in the early 1900s with the discoveries of Albert Einstein, Max Planck, and Niels Bohr—had now revealed the idea of the universe as Great Machine *to be fundamentally flawed.*[1]

Of course I'm no physicist. So I was in no position then, nor am I in any position now, to critique what Evelyn told me. But as I sat at her kitchen table in Storrs, she explained to me that physicists can now take two paired electrons (one spinning right, the other spinning left) and separate them so far from one another it's impossible for them to "communicate" in any way. Yet at the instant—the very *instant*—physicists reverse one electron's spin, its partner will reverse its spin, as if the two were inextricably connected by some invisible cosmic force.

This introduction to the subatomic world made my head spin and left me deeply perplexed. *How could it happen? How could these two particles be so interconnected that one instantaneously appears to "know" what the other is up to?*

It defied common sense. Yet Evelyn insisted there was no question that it happens. In the invisible dimension of the very small—on the level of the unimaginably tiny particles out of which all the big things are made—*everyone and everything* appear to be inseparably interconnected.

As physicist and astronomer Sir James Jeans famously observed, "The universe begins to look more like a great thought than like a great machine."[2]

Or as another physicist put it, we are all involved "in a continual cosmic dance."[3]

When Evelyn told me this, something inside me began to change, and I slowly began asking new questions. As a journalist, it's my job to sniff out the latest news. Yet if the new physicists were right, my Cartesian-Newtonian worldview (the lens through which I tended to see all reality) was not just yesterday's news; *it was nearly a hundred years out of date!*

Further, Evelyn told me that because physics tends to orient all the sciences, her research field was also changing. A parallel to the new physics was general systems theory, one small branch of which involves the study of what are called microrhythms.

Split-Second Rhythms of Communication

The book I wrote in Roxbury with Evelyn, *Born Dancing*, was about the unseen microrhythmic communicative "dance" that goes on between a mother and her baby.

A pioneer in the study of microrhythms, a man named William S. Condon found in his experiments at Boston University in the 1960s that babies as young as one or two days old just naturally move their bodies synchronously in rhythm with human speech. Though the process is so subtle it can be measured only in microseconds and observed on slow-motion films, when a mother talks, her baby's body dances—not *in response* to her words, as if she were causing him to dance, but *in unison* with her words, almost as if the baby already knew what Mom was about to say before she said it.

According to Evelyn, the baby was not *reacting* to or *responding* to the mother. Rather, the baby was a *unity of one with* the mother. On a microscopic level, the rhythms of communication between a mother and her baby are so exquisitely entrained that the baby will shift position even when the sound of her voice changes at a rate of a *few hundredths* of a second. According to Evelyn, this happens because mother and baby are interacting with each other as a *system*, and not as a mechanistic cause-effect chain.

Equally mind-boggling, tiny babies seem able to tell real language from nonsense. When eight- and nine-day-old babies listened to tapes of disconnected vowel sounds, they stopped dancing, as if to say, "Why are you talking gibberish?"

What's more, mothers and babies aren't the only persons who do this. The same unseen phenomenon happens between a father and his baby, a teacher and an attentive student, or a woman and her husband at the dinner table.

Systems are all around us. But I learned you can't point to a system the way you can point to an oak tree. Evelyn taught me a system isn't a *thing* but a dynamic *process* by which many separate pieces work together as an orderly, organized whole that is greater than the sum of its parts. For example, the human body-mind-and-soul are one system, and it's this unified system working together (not just one broken-off, individualistic part of it) that controls the operation of "you."

What's more, I learned we're all part of many social systems (a social system merely being two or more persons interacting together as a whole over time). In *Born Dancing*, I wrote: "If you're happily married, you and your mate are one harmonious system. If you're divorced, you've felt how wrenching and difficult dissolving a complex social system can be." A strong social system, where everyone's rhythms are meshing smoothly together, is joyous. Just being part of it feels good. A disjoint system, in which one or more people feel separated, isolated, and lonely, isn't any fun. When you're rhythmically "out of step" with someone, when one or both persons' rhythms have become jerky or jangled, you're more likely to become irritated with each other and argue. It's no accident that good negotiators frequently share a friendly meal together before getting down to business. Being in sync promotes harmony. Stressed-out people in a disjoint system (or what Evelyn called an "asynchronous dance") push each other's buttons and get on each other's nerves.

Paul Byers, a Columbia University researcher on the rhythms of communications, found that in a harmonious system, when two or more people are moving in rhythm together (while rowing, marching, or singing, for example), their breathing will sometimes synchronize. Further, when a therapist and patient are communicating "in sync," their hearts have been observed to beat in unison.

One night, while we cuddled in bed, I rested my head on Walter's chest. As I reclined there, listening to his heartbeat, I felt in the dark for my left wrist and took my own pulse. Sure enough, our two hearts were beating as one.

Personhood and the Women's Movement

Systemic thinking opened my eyes to a new reality. Seeing myself as being deeply interconnected—even on microscopic level—with others around me gave me a very different understanding of my *personhood* than I'd previously had when I thought I was in fierce competition with other people to win fame, praise, and applause. In a mysterious, new way, I no longer saw myself as an isolated "I" alone in the universe. I no longer felt as disconnected from God and neighbor as I had before.

I loved the 1960s' women's movement as it was originally conceived, because it offered hope for correcting those *erroneous patterns of thinking* that had led to economic, educational, and social injustices and that had long bound women in chains.

But it now occurred to me that the 1960s' women's movement, at least as its political agenda had unfolded in 1967 in the Mayflower Hotel, did not correct these erroneous patterns of thought.

On the contrary, NOW's 1967 political platform seemed to me to have been rooted in a fundamentally flawed way of thinking: an overly mechanistic worldview that denies our profound interconnectedness, promotes competition for power, and falsely isolates a woman from God, from a true relationship of love with a man, and even from the dance of life in her own body. The political agenda of the women's movement pushed through by the Mere Fifty-Seven (and, unfortunately, still with us in the "official" women's movement today) was rooted in an overly narrow way of thinking about reality, one that denies the unseen *relational* and systemic dimension of women's lives.

In retrospect, now that I know how abortion and the Pill got inserted in NOW's political platform, I find myself asking even more questions: If Betty Friedan and the Mere Fifty-Seven in the Chinese Room had understood the interrelationship of everyone and everything the way the new systemic thinkers do, *if they had known about the invisible cosmic dance,* would they have been so determined to ram through the abortion vote to stop the dance by splitting mother and baby, who are a *unity of one* in the great dance of life?

Pauli Murray, the Civil Rights attorney who later became an Episcopal priest, was right on target when she left the Chinese Room that Saturday night and, as a matter of truth and justice, withdrew her name from nomination to NOW's national board, declaring as she resigned that human rights are "indivisible." She was more correct than perhaps even she knew. Human beings in love are, indeed, at one—systemically *indivisible*—even on a microscopic, physical level.

When feminists conducted consciousness-raising sessions in the 1970s to raise women's awareness of political and economic injustice, they had no clue how high women's consciousnesses would really need to be raised for us to be made truly free from the sea of ideas in which we all swim or drown.

So those were the two Big Events that happened to me in Roxbury: entering the Episcopal Church and writing a book that led me to see how deeply interconnected we all are in our unseen dance of relationships with others, especially with those we love.

A Verbal Duel

The much smaller event that happened in Roxbury, occurring in the shadow of the two Big Events, was that I quit writing for *Cosmo*. I'd like to say I quit writing sex-revolution propaganda for some noble reason, but I really did it because Helen wasn't paying me what I felt I was worth. I had conducted a writer's workshop in Norwalk on the Connecticut shore. After my presentation, many people came up to ask questions. One of them, a curly-haired woman from Westport, proudly told me she had just gotten her first assignment from *Cosmopolitan*, but she was confused about how to proceed. I asked her a series of questions to try to pinpoint her problem. Finally, in the course of our rather lengthy discussion, I asked how many words she'd been assigned to write.

"Twenty thousand," she said.

"Twenty thousand words?" I repeated in astonishment. "That can't be right. That's the length of a novelette. What are they paying you?"

"$5,000."

Now, I was even more astonished. This woman was such a newbie she didn't even know how long a feature-length article was, and she was being paid *$5,000*? For her *first* piece? I'd written for years for *Cosmo*, and I was getting only $2,750. Ouch!

After I helped sort out the Westport woman's confusion (she'd been assigned two thousand words, not twenty thousand), I was in a quandary. It appeared I was being severely underpaid. Here I was struggling to earn enough money to support a family, and these people who pretended to be my friends had apparently been shortchanging me for years. Weren't women who called ourselves feminists supposed to help each other, not stab each other in the back?

(Of course, you may well ask, what did I expect? When I'd worked as assistant to *Cosmo*'s articles editor, I'd seen that some writers were paid much more than others. Why did I think *Cosmo* would pay me more if they could get away with paying me less? To such a reasonable question, I can only reply that when I started dancing with the devil, I somehow believed I was the "special one" who wouldn't get her toes smushed.)

I had only recently submitted another article to *Cosmo*. Helen had already accepted the story. But, typically, I still hadn't been paid. To correct what I now perceived to be not just a creative slap in the face but a terrible social injustice, I complained to my agent Julian Bach, who suggested I write a letter to Helen explaining the problem. (To tell the truth, I don't think he wanted to get involved.)

Helen responded (through Julian) that I was *not* being underpaid. I was getting the "standard rate."

I countered with a "don't-try-to-fool-me-I-know-better" response.

As we exchanged moves and countermoves, it seemed to me this was becoming increasingly like a fencing match.

Finally, Helen stabbed at me with what may well have been her *coup de grace*: Ramming her sword through my little Cosmo Girl heart, she declared, "We pay Sue less, because she's a *boring* writer."

It was a deadly and bloody stab at my ego, and I began to stagger and fall, but Walter came to my rescue. "She's just bluffing," he declared, propping me up. "This is her Battle of Bulge. If you win this one, you'll win it all."

He sat down at his trusty old Smith-Corona and composed a letter in which he laid out a powerful case to "prove" Helen did not really believe I was a boring writer. Among other facts, he pointed out she had used something like twenty-seven of my articles as cover blurbs to entice readers to buy the magazine off the newsstands.

After Walter's bold counterattack, Helen seemed to back off.

A long silence ensued.

Finally, too impatient to wait longer, I composed and mailed another epistle, stating in essence: "Fine. Take all the time you please. Forget I asked for more money. Just give me back my manuscript."

This, too, was a bluff. From my vantage point, Helen's life seemed to be centered around the power of money. If there was one thing she'd be unable to tolerate, I figured it was this: *being unable to buy something she wanted.* The article we were dueling over, I must admit, wasn't one of my finer achievements. Even from a *Cosmo* standpoint, it wasn't top-notch. But by now I figured Helen wanted that article, and she wanted it bad.

At last, Helen agreed to pay me what I asked. Walter had apparently read her correctly: calling me a "boring writer" was, indeed, her last move.

The negotiation, of course, marked the end of my misery-filled relationship with *Cosmo*. After it was over, I felt a new lightness of being, as if I'd shed a heavy weight off my soul. The next month I landed my first assignment from *Reader's Digest*. The topic was "How to Build Better Friendships."

Unfortunately, my Battle-of-the-Bulge triumph was an ambiguous victory. I had won, but I had also lost. The negotiation had dragged on for months, and—you guessed it—once again we were broke.

Walter's New Plan

"The profession of book writing," Steinbeck remarked, "makes horse racing seem like a solid, stable business." During our extended negotiation with *Cosmo*, our income dipped so low we were serving the kids what we festively called our "vegetable dinners" (no meat—too expensive), and we got so behind on our bills our electricity was once again disconnected. With our money situation again urgent, Walter took a minimum-wage temp job in a Nestle factory that made Yoplait yogurt. He came home every night with his shirt, pants, and shoes reeking of chemicals. His supervisor (in charge of quality control, no less) was hooked on drugs, which she smoked or otherwise imbibed on her lunch hour—not a pretty picture.

Amid these exotic new miseries, Walter concluded he could set us free only by becoming, of all things—a Hollywood screenwriter.

Hey, don't laugh. Even Faulkner did a stint in Hollywood. It was worth a shot.

Walter's first screenplay, "The Quiz Show Girl," captured the interest (if not the checkbooks) of several producers. A quick trip to Los Angeles, which he'd made on a shoestring when we still had cash on hand, had netted him a Hollywood agent and a coveted pass into the private offices of Universal Studios. There he met an up-and-coming young story editor who loved "The Quiz Show Girl" and enthusiastically urged him to move West. After Walter returned to Roxbury from L.A., his new attitude was "Hollywood or bust." In his ever-hopeful heart, Hollywood offered a reasonable escape hatch out of an impossible, debt-filled situation.

I didn't want to move again. I loved Roxbury. But what better alternative plan could I offer? Roxbury wasn't exactly booming with employment opportunities. Worse, as inveterate freelance writers without steady-job resumes, we were becoming increasingly unemployable with each passing year.

To finance the trip, we sold all our furniture, every stick of it, even the chairs. We filled a small U-Haul trailer with our books, typewriters, contracts, and manuscripts and readied ourselves for yet another cross-country trek.

We planned to take nine days to drive cross-country, and we'd take the southern route (along U.S. 40), because we didn't want to risk trying to pull a trailer through the Rocky Mountains with our little Ford Escort. The distance from Roxbury to L.A. along our chosen route was about 3,200 miles. So we figured, if we left on September 1 and kept steadily moving, we could easily make it across the country in nine days. What's more, we *had* to make it in nine days—for two reasons.

First, before we could enroll Erin and Dustin in the top-notch magnet high school we'd located for them, they had to take a test to get in. They were both bright, so we thought they'd pass with flying colors. But they needed to take the test before school started the second week of September. We also had to locate and rent a house in Cerritos, where the school, Whitney High, was located. So to get settled once we arrived in L.A., we had a lot on our plates that we had to accomplish quickly.

Second, I had to hop on a plane ten days from now and fly back to Chicago to be on the *Oprah Show*. Oprah's producers were wrapping their September 11 show around an article I'd written for *Cosmo* entitled "Don't Be Afraid to Marry Down" (the woman attorney marries the bus driver, for example, or the female gynecologist marries the garbage collector). I had no legitimate claim to authority on this subject. The article wasn't even my idea. *Cosmo* had merely assigned it to me, and all the anecdotes were made up. But as the article's author, I was to appear as an alleged "expert" on the matter.

So we had to be in L.A. by September 9, so I could catch my plane at LAX on September 10 and fly to Chicago to be on the show. There was no time to lose.

As the four of us piled into our Ford Escort with our dog Baffles, Walter happily turned the ignition key. Quoting the silver-haired Colonel played by George Peppard on the television series *The A Team*, he quipped: "I love it when a plan comes together." Then he hit the accelerator, and off we sped toward the Western sky.

Chapter 13

Hollywood, Here We Come

*If my books had been any worse, I should not have been invited to Holly-
wood, and if they had been any better, I should not have come.*

—Raymond Chandler, Letter to Charles W. Morton,
editor of the *Atlantic Monthly*, December 12, 1945

We loved to sing as we were traveling. One of our favorite road
songs was "Charlie on the MTA." Another was the Willie Nelson
ditty, "On the Road Again"—

> On the road again
> Just can't wait to get on the road again
> The life I love is making music with my friends
> And I can't wait to get on the road again.
> On the road again
> Goin' places that I've never been
> Seein' things that I may never see again
> And I can't wait to get on the road again ...

Yet despite our initial enthusiasm and high spirits, getting to Los
Angeles by September 9 didn't turn out to be as easy as we thought
it would be. Our silver Escort had no air conditioning, and for much
of the trip the weather was swelteringly hot. By the time we reached
Oklahoma City, it was ninety-one degrees outside and unbearably
humid. Having just come from Connecticut, where one Fourth of
July was so cool we lit a fire in the fireplace, we all found Oklahoma's
heat and humidity insufferable.

The sun beat mercilessly down on us as we drove along. We had all the windows rolled down. Blistering hot wind was whipping through the car. Our mutt Baffles (who resembled a lop-eared German Shepherd) was in the way back, slobbering up a storm. Dog spit was flying everywhere through the air like an extremely unrefreshing sprinkler system.

Erin and Dustin, in the backseat, got the worst of it. Here's how Dustin later described the scene: "You'd turn around and you'd be hit in the face with that long, wet tongue. It was really weird and horrible. The back of the car was like a glazed doughnut. How can a dog slobber this much? They say a dog's mouth is cleaner than a human mouth? It sure didn't feel that way. If it's so clean, have a bite of *that*! I can't describe how bad it was. Think of the worst you can imagine—it was ten times worse. Dog slime, crusty slime all over the windows. The windows were almost white with slobber."

That pretty much sums it up.

About now, some kind-hearted animal lover may be thinking, "Oh, that poor dog." Not to worry. We gave Baffles plenty of water to drink. This was not dog abuse. She was just miserably hot, as were we all.

We experienced a little relief from the heat as we drove through the Texas panhandle. Then we hit the wide, flat, hot, empty deserts of New Mexico.

After we crossed into Arizona, things really began to go downhill or, rather, too steeply uphill. It was about ten miles east of Ash Fork, near milepost 155½, that the signs began to appear: "Trucks—vehicles pulling trailers check brakes and equipment—use lower gear" and "6% grade next 6 miles." Our poor little Ford Escort was not engineered for this challenge. As the car pulled the U-Haul trailer up the grade, an ominous red warning light flashed on the dashboard. The car engine was overheating. Walter, who was driving, pulled off to the side of the road to let the engine cool. Then he turned on the motor and started up the grade again—and again. Each time we pulled back onto the steaming pavement, the engine quickly overheated. Hot, hot, hot. Baffles continued to shower us with her saliva, although by now we hardly noticed. Would we be able to make it up the grade? It was our eighth day on the road. We had only about four hundred miles left to get to L.A. Had we come this far and endured so much only to be stopped short?

Finally, by driving about fifteen miles per hour, we slowly made it up the grade and over to the other side. By the time we made it, we were exhausted from the heat and tension. I'm not sure where we stopped to sleep that night. I think it was in Kingman.

The next morning—the ninth day—as we got up early and drove west, the sun was still beating down upon us, and even though the 6-percent grade was behind us, the car engine was still straining to pull the heavy load.

After being on the road only about an hour, we reached Needles in the Mojave Desert. The temperature was already approaching a hundred degrees. Fearing that if we kept pushing on, we could wind up stranded in the middle of nowhere in the scorching heat, we regrouped and sketched out a new plan. We decided we'd stop in Needles, take a motel room, and spend the day swimming in the pool and napping. Then we'd get back in the car in the cool of the evening and continue on to L.A. If we drove at night, we figured the car would be less likely to overheat, and with God's grace, we could still make it to L.A. by the end of the day.

To execute this new plan, we stopped at a Motel 6 in Needles. It was hardly the Beverly Hilton, but the motel pool that day offered the most refreshing swim I've ever enjoyed. Back in our room, we pulled the heavy drapes closed and stretched out. You could still hear the huge semitrucks roaring past outside. But lying on a soft double bed in the cool, darkened, air-conditioned room in the heat of the afternoon was pure bliss.

As soon as the orange sun began to sink like a flaming fire in the west, we got on the road again. It was still devilishly hot crossing the Mojave Desert. Dirt and sand filled the air, and you could feel the grit between your fingers and on your face.

At one point, shortly after it had become my turn to drive, I lost it. I went a little crazy. Ripping along U.S. 40 at eighty miles per hour, I yelled, "I've had enough of this! I'm sick of this! I'm getting us to L.A. as fast as I can."

The car was fishtailing all over the road, and Walter shouted at me to stop driving so fast—I was going to have a wreck and kill us all.

Finally, I regained control of myself, slowed down, and carefully eased off the highway.

Walter took the wheel and drove the rest of the way to L.A., piloting us safely into harbor. At about 11:30 that night, we reached

Bellflower, a town just northwest of Cerritos. We took the first motel room we could find. It was sleazy, but we didn't care.

It was the end of the ninth day. We had arrived on time after all.

It goes without saying, of course, that Helen Gurley Brown would have scorned the way I was living. She would never have lived this way herself. But that was her life; this was mine. She had chosen one road. I had chosen another, and for this I was grateful. Horrendous as our latest road trip had been, at least we had done it together. Despite all our difficulties, the feeling remained that somehow we were on the path to true freedom.

Although I was no longer tying myself up into knots struggling to write sex-revolution propaganda for Helen, *Cosmo* still had several of my unpublished articles in their backlog. So my byline would continue to appear in the magazine, off and on, for the next several years. For all practical purposes, however, I believed (erroneously, as it would turn out) that *Cosmo* and I had gone our separate ways.

I had just one small task connected with the magazine left to complete, a publicity gig that would not only help me earn a living without *Cosmo*'s checks but would also greatly promote my writing career. I had to go on the *Oprah Show*.

Chapter 14

Seventeen Minutes of Fame

I think everybody should get rich and famous and do everything they ever dreamed of so they can see that it's not the answer.

—Actor Jim Carrey,
Reader's Digest, March 2006

The next day, compliments of *The Oprah Show*, I flew first class back to Chicago. I traversed the distance it took us six sweltering-hot days to drive in the Escort in about three-and-a-half hours. The luxurious first-class seats were wide and comfortable. The flight attendants were friendly and attentive. The champagne was free.

Talk shows, sometimes called "tabloid talk shows" or "trash TV," were the way daytime television was staying relevant during the 1980s. At their best, these shows provided a national arena for airing controversial social and political issues. At their worst, they were the gladiator pits of America, where audiences booed and cheered as the gory spectacle of human brutality, betrayal, and suffering was unmasked and displayed before their curious eyes. On some shows, angry confrontations and fist fights regularly broke out between guests. When the national chairman of the Congress of Racial Equality and racist skinheads appeared on the same show, host Geraldo Rivera got his nose broken during an on-camera brawl.[1]

In this nitty-gritty entertainment medium, Oprah was queen. Millions of viewers tuned in every weekday to watch ordinary people confess their dirtiest secrets to the world, often for the first time they'd told anyone. Those at work during the day would tape the show so they could view it on their VCRs at night when they got

146

home. The *Oprah* world was big, big business, the peak of glamour, fame, money, and power. Oprah was arguably the most liberated woman on the planet—and I was about to become part of it all.

A uniformed limo driver meets me at Chicago's O'Hare International Airport. He holds up a sign with my name on it, so I spot him easily as I glide down the escalator toward the baggage claim. He whisks my luggage off the carousel and escorts me to a shiny black stretch limo, where he gallantly opens the door and ushers me into a seat with so much leg room it would accommodate Boston Celtics legend Larry Bird.

The limo driver smoothly covers the seventeen miles from the airport to Chicago's Magnificent Mile. As we slow to a crawl to make our way through the city's heavily trafficked streets, harried pedestrians strain their eyes, trying to peer through the limo's dark, one-way windows to catch a glimpse of whomever the celebrity might be in the backseat. What would they say if they knew it was only me?

Interestingly, Oprah doesn't see herself as a celebrity. "There's a difference," she once said, "between being a celebrity for seventeen minutes and being a legend."[2]

Oprah's the legend. I'm the seventeen-minute type.

I spend the night in a palatial five-star hotel, in the suite where comedian Eddie Murphy stayed the previous night.

In one of my favorite Eddie Murphy skits on *Saturday Night Live*, Murphy goes undercover as a white person and discovers "when white people are alone, they give things to each other for free." A newsstand operator gives him a newspaper because nobody's around. After the only other black man gets off at his bus stop, a public bus suddenly turns into a cocktail party on wheels. A bank manager hands Murphy $50,000 in cash, saying he doesn't have to pay it back, and when Murphy seems to hesitate, the banker urges him, "Take it, take it."

That's how I felt that night in the elegant suite. There was a minibar stocked with choice delicacies and a wet bar loaded with expensive liqueurs and wines—all for me, all for free. Don't be afraid. Don't hold back. Just "take it, take it."

As I settled comfortably into my room, sitting in a plush armchair and sipping a fine glass of bordeaux, it struck me how empty my life would be if this were all I had in it, and I wondered how well Erin and Dustin did on their entrance exams today and whether Walter had any luck locating a house for us to rent. It was an adventure to be here, preparing to go on *Oprah* tomorrow. I felt a thrill of excitement. I won't deny that. But I also saw how wretchedly lonely all my career success would be if I had no one who cared how well I did on the show, and no one with whom I could share the adventure once I got home.

It occurred to me that by focusing almost exclusively on money, power, and career while denying women's deeper longings for love and a family, the modern women's movement got its priorities upside down and backward. I thought, *As strong, independent women, we need to be speaking out loudly and clearly about the truth that "success" in life isn't just about careers, sex, power, and money. All these trappings are nothing without love. In fact, they're just that: loveless traps that don't set you free, but only enslave you by getting you to chase after transitory pleasures that will never fulfill the deepest desires of your heart.*

Just before I drifted off to sleep on a perfect mattress with a perfect pillow beneath my head, I thought that tomorrow, when I went on the show to discuss my latest *Cosmo* article, "Don't Be Afraid to Marry Down," I needed to try to get this point across to Oprah's millions of viewers.

The next morning, the phone rings. It's my wake-up call from the front desk. The warm, soft, comforting recorded voice on the other end of the line gently nudges me into consciousness by giving me a "positive affirmation" about myself—something like, "You were born with potential. You were born with goodness and trust. You were born with ideals and dreams. Turn them into what you want— today." Those aren't the exact words. But the underlying gist of the message is: You are gorgeous, you are wonderful, you will look great on TV. *Wow!* I think to myself. *If this is the way famous, rich people wake up every morning, no wonder they act so confident and seem to feel so good about themselves.* The Dog-Slobber Journey seems a million miles away.

My limo driver meets me in the hotel lobby. When we arrive at the studio, I'm hustled off to a brightly lit room where a makeup artist/hairstylist makes me look better than I have ever looked in my entire life. Once I have my television "glamour mask" on and in place, I realize I've become like one of those models I met in the

Cosmo lobby, a plain Jane turned into a glamour symbol for someone else's profit.

The detailed backstage preparations for the show fascinate me. The couples chosen to appear today (those ordinary people Helen Gurley Brown called *civilians*) have been carefully prepped by the producers. Everything they'll say on the show is, if not prerehearsed, at least well worked out. Although the studio and viewing audiences will be surprised by their confessions, the producers know ahead of time exactly what those confessions will be, and so does Oprah. To me the goal seems to be that she just has to pry their secrets out of her guests when the right time comes for the most dramatic effect.

My *Cosmo* article will provide the psychoanalytic backdrop for these couples' real-life stories. I'm to act as if all the information in the article belongs to me. The interviews I did with psychologists and other experts are now history. Although I'm just a journalist, I'm to act onstage as if I'm an expert on the topic of women marrying down. I'm told Oprah is especially interested in the subject, because she's dating Stedman Graham, and of course, no man can top Oprah in terms of fame, glamour, or financial status.

As I gather with the other guests backstage before the show begins, one producer tut-tuts at the three couples about to go onstage. She warns them they'd better not clam up when they get out there. They'd better tell Oprah all the dirty little secrets they told her. (*Otherwise*, I think to myself, *Oprah won't have a show.*) It occurs to me the stage is like a public confessional, and Oprah is the all-forgiving priestess, listening to and absolving these couples from their sins.

The three couples are seated onstage when the show begins. I'm brought on for the third segment. Oprah seems to agree with me that now "thanks to women's liberation ... women don't need men to support them and to define their social status, and that superachievers who still insist on a superior mate may have only a handful of men in their city to choose from."

One exchange goes like this:

ME: Women are beginning to look for more in a man than just a meal ticket. We don't need a meal ticket anymore. We've got our own meal tickets.
OPRAH: That's right. We can buy the restaurant ...

ME: We need new definitions of "up" and "down".... We can't just see a man in terms of success symbols anymore and say he's "up." The stockbroker who makes you cry is far more "down" than the taxi driver who makes you laugh.

OPRAH: *Pleeeeeze* say that again! [Long applause from the audience.]

Overall, the show seems to be moving along well, and I'm feeling great. Kay, the woman to my left, is blonde and pink with a porcelain-doll complexion, very pretty although quite overweight. She says she comes from a rich family. Her husband Paul was a used-car salesman when they met. Thinly built with dark hair, a Charlie Chaplin mustache, and a firm set to his mouth, Paul now works in an auto-parts factory in Michigan City. In school, Kay was used to dating boys who went on to become chiropractors, attorneys, and art dealers. Paul drove a beat-up old Plymouth with a spare tire in the back to hold up his front seat. Kay listened to Tchaikovsky. Paul was a Merle Haggard fan. She suggests she married him because she was rebelling against her mom and because she saw him as a "Tom Selleck type." All this causes great laughter from the audience. Despite their problems, Kay adds they've been married for seventeen years, "so it's not too bad." (Applause.)

When Oprah asks if she's tried to change Paul, Kay replies, "Oh, yeah. You have to ... to keep your sanity." Kay admits she enjoys feeling superior to Paul, and says if she had to do it all over again, she wouldn't marry him.

Paul says he *would* marry Kay again (which again gets applause), but Oprah is now ready to go for the jugular. Pretending she doesn't know the secret she's digging for, Oprah says: "I would think, I would just think now, I'm not accusin' anybody of anything, but I would think that if there are times in your relationship during this seventeen years when you felt somewhat emasculated or inferior that that would cause you to have a wandering eye and try to find somebody who made you feel more manly or made you feel more superior. Has that ever happened to you?"

As Oprah asks the question, Paul gulps nervously and his Adam's apple bobs up and down.

Then he musters up his courage and replies, "Seven times."

The audience goes nuts. *Ooooooooooohhhhhh!*

Beside me, Kay emits a deep sigh, as if a knife has just been stabbed through her heart. She likes to feel one-up in the relationship? Well, I guess he fixed her, didn't he? The suffering emanating from Kay is so raw it's palpable. With this dark turn, the goal of the show suddenly seems to me to be, not to explore the central importance of love in marriage, but to create as much drama as possible out of human betrayal and suffering.

Oprah remains the calm eye in the middle of the storm.

"Seven times?"

"Yes'm."

"So you've cheated seven times."

"Yes."

"And is that the reason why?" (She's referring back to her previous question about his possible feelings of emasculation and inferiority.)

"No, no."

The audience is laughing, giggling, and tittering a lot now. They're getting a great kick out of this man's betrayal and his wife's anguish.

Oprah looks somewhat puzzled. "I thought I was onto something here, but ... we'll be back. We'll find out *why* he's cheated seven times ..." And we cut to a commercial.

Oprah now uses Paul's last secret (*why did he do it?*) to hold the home-viewing audience in their seats until the end of the show. In the final segment, she at lasts asks Paul her final provocative question, thereby allowing him to twist the knife one more time.

"We never found out why you cheated seven times. It wasn't because she was making you feel inferior?"

Paul shrugs. His tone is indifferent. "That plus variety."

Kay's mouth flies open in shocked outrage. The audience explodes with raucous delight. They can't get enough of it.

So much for the seventeen-year marriage Kay described, just a few short minutes ago, as "not too bad."

In the Rexall Drug Store in New Hampton, I longed to be part of the world of fashion, beauty, and charm behind those glossy magazine covers on the newsstands. I worked hard to escape from what I perceived to be my small-town mindset and to climb what I believed to be the ladder to the wider world of truth, happiness, and freedom. And this is what it leads to—sitting on this tiny stage next to this devastated overweight woman while her husband tells the world he's had seven affairs? My career reaches its culmination in this wretched place?

This is The Dream?

Kay says she loves feeling superior. Paul cheats on her. Oprah helps an adulterous husband throw his wife under the bus, and the crowds eat it up? And what about me? I wrote an article for *Cosmo* laced with lies, and now I've perpetuated the charade by masquerading on TV as an expert on a subject I know almost nothing about. Is anyone innocent here?

By the time the show ends, the limo driver delivers me to the airport, and I buckle up my seatbelt for the flight back to L.A. I'm so happy to be going home to Walter and the kids, I don't even care that *Oprah*'s big-time producers (now that I've done the show) have sent me back economy class. Scrunched in a narrow plane seat with no leg room, I now see the whole Celebrity Treatment Routine in a new light. It seems to me it was all just part of a scam to make me feel like a celebrity for a few minutes so I'd perform well and look as good as I possibly could on TV—anything to beef up those Nielsen ratings. *No more free champagne for you, little Sue*, I thought to myself.

Suddenly, it was all I could do not to burst out laughing. One of Oprah's seventeen-minute celebrities had just been set free from yet another of her small-town illusions.

When I later watched my VHS tape of the show, I was surprised to discover Oprah had over-delivered. I was onstage before the eyes of the world (minus commercial time) for precisely 22 minutes and 42 seconds.

Chapter 15

Our Nightmare in Cerritos

Thus says the LORD, your redeemer, the Holy One of Israel: I, the LORD, your God, teach you what is for your good, and lead you on the way you should go.

—Isaiah 48:17

My experience on the *Oprah Show* turned my stomach and left a sour taste in my mouth. I had performed well as a "relationship expert" on the show, so much so an *Oprah* producer would phone me a few months later and ask me to appear again, this time to expound on a subject I hadn't even written an article about (I forget what it was). I politely declined, suggesting the name of a psychologist who'd written a book on the subject and might know more about it than I did. If I'd only played the game, if I'd kept pushing the fame bar like a laboratory rat frantically pushing a bar for food, I might have become a star. Or, then again, I might not have. In any case, I didn't want to be famous, anymore. Fame, like glamour, had become for me just another sick illusion.

While I was doing my *Oprah* shtick in Chicago, Walter had productively spent his time getting Dustin and Erin enrolled in school and locating a rental he wanted to show me. It was a yellow-stucco, three-bedroom house with no refrigerator and, of course, no furniture, not even a chair. It had a covered patio out back and a dismal little cinder-block-surrounded backyard, which we thought might look prettier if we planted some flowers. We had no time to spare or to be picky. We decided to take it.

Before we could sign the lease, however, the woman who owned the place said she had to check our credit.

Yikes! I'd forgotten that in the sprawling City of Angels, where everyone's a stranger and no one knows you well enough to judge your character, you're measured only by how well you can pay your bills.

Our credit was atrocious.

We had no credit cards, and while waiting for long-overdue payments from various publishers, we'd bounced umpteen checks in Roxbury. Whenever we'd had to choose between bouncing a check and not feeding the kids for a week, we made the first choice.

There was one thing I knew for certain: *we would never pass a credit check.* However would we be able to rent a house in this town? I was in a panic.

But Roxbury was a small town, and Doris, the banker there, did something unbelievably kind, something I'll never forget.

The following day, our new potential landlady phoned us and happily chirped, "I just talked to Doris at your bank, and she said your credit is perfect. You've never even bounced a check."

I was stunned. A banker had lied for us to help us get a fresh start in life. Praise God! (And thank you, Doris, wherever you are.)

The next day we moved into the little yellow-stucco house.

Longing to Be "Just a Housewife"

Starting over again in Cerritos was a nightmare. It's one thing to understand you're on the wrong train in life. It's quite another to switch trains when you're barreling pell-mell down the tracks. Walter got a little temp job working at McDonnell Douglas, and I was stuck home alone all day with no air conditioning and no furniture in the house. No beds, either. I think we had brought Erin's bed with us. But the rest of us slept on the floor. The furniture I missed most was the chairs. It's amazing how many armchairs, sofas, recliners, and other seats humans need just to have a place to rest our derrieres. Look around you: chairs *everywhere*.

When he was a young man, Walter frequently said he never wanted to own anything he had to lock up. Well, he certainly had achieved his goal. What I now saw as Walter's self-glorifying pursuit of truth, beauty, and freedom at all costs—his pursuit of what we had once called "the dream"—was wearing thin on me. Why couldn't we just go to work every day and live a peaceful life in the suburbs like other people? Sitting home taking care of a house and family while your husband went to work began to sound to me like bliss. I found myself passionately longing for the life Betty Friedan had excoriated and rejected in her *Feminine Mystique*.

Slowly, we began to add furniture to the place. One day we bought a refrigerator. The next month we bought a bed. I wrote mostly for *New Woman*, but I was also working more regularly for *Reader's Digest* and *Woman's Day*. *New Woman* made me a contributing editor, which netted us a monthly stipend. Royalties from *The New Age Baby Name Book* continued to arrive twice a year. With Walter working at Douglas and me freelancing at home, our finances again began to stabilize.

Cerritos with its endless rows of tract houses and streets resembling parking lots didn't begin to compare with the idyllic pastoral beauty of Roxbury. I missed New England terribly. Sometimes I felt so homesick for the rolling Litchfield Hills I'd break down and cry. Without God at the center of my life, I felt depressed, lonely, and empty.

It didn't help any of us that Walter had come to California to write screenplays and he was now stuck working a forty-hour-a-week job with a group of aerospace engineers. Walter had been studying to be a chemical engineer when I met him, and he had turned his back on that career path long ago. Now here he was, working essentially as a glorified secretary for a group of men who shared none of his poetic sensibilities and few of his values. The worst part of working at Douglas was that it broke his concentration and writing rhythm. He'd just get something going on the page, and he'd have to abandon it to go for eight hours to Douglas. By the time he got home again and back to his desk, the inspiration had vanished.

Although Walter was never afraid of hard work, he had a huge, insurmountable problem when he came to Hollywood, and this problem would be his downfall: he was incapable of selling out. The man was literally incapable of it. He steadfastly wrote stories not for the glands but for the heart. Producers didn't just reject his screenplays. They called him up personally by phone to scream at him as they rejected them. The pages mounted. Thousands upon thousands of pages of scenes and dialogue poured from his typewriter and later from his computer. They were bound tightly in neat little binders:

red, blue, yellow, green. They were romances, comedies, serious dramas. It was painful just to watch him. None of them sold.

A Sad, Dark Time

In our cross-country move, we had lost our beautiful little Roxbury church community, and we had not found another. We attended a large Episcopal church in Long Beach a few times, but Walter didn't like the sermons, and we quit going. Demons from Walter's horror-filled childhood were coming up too. It was a sad, dark time for Walter, and he fell into a hardworking state of despair. I remember nights when he sat outside on the back patio, writing, writing, writing. I'd wake up to find his place beside me in bed empty, and I'd wander through the house looking for him. I vividly recall one night as I stood in the kitchen and looked through the sliding glass door outside to the patio. There he was at 3:30 A.M., seated at our round white-metal patio table, hunched over his typewriter in his pajamas, type, type, typing away, with only one lamp lighting his page and his face shadowed in darkness.

"The writer must believe that what he is doing is the most important thing in the world," Steinbeck said. "And he must hold to this illusion even when he knows it is not true."[1] Walter was a writer to the marrow of his bones. At the same time, Walter knew the story-telling craft can become so all-consuming that a foolish person can turn his own writing into an idol. When Erin first began to get interested in becoming a writer, he sternly cautioned her, "Never turn your writing into your god."

As Walter continued to struggle, I began to think of the tall, black building that housed McDonnell Douglas as the evil Dark Tower in J.R.R. Tolkien's *Lord of the Rings*. It was, after all, a place where war machines were made. As Walter continued to work there, he began to lose his poetic vocabulary. One day, in despair, almost with tears in his eyes, he confessed to me when he was at work he would sometimes try to voice a deep thought to one of the engineers, and he could no longer recall the words he needed to express the idea. It was as if the Walter I knew was being erased and replaced by somebody else.

In the midst of all this, he began to blame me.

Nothing I could do was right. Everything I did or had ever done was wrong. It was all my fault. Every sin I'd ever committed against him came up, and there were many. He thought I had abandoned him, that I was turning against everything we had worked for together, and in some ways he was right.

I said we always went too far. He said we always stopped too soon.

We fought—and fought.

I became even more deeply depressed. There were long, black days when Walter was at McDonnell Douglas, and I spent hours contemplating suicide. I also considered divorce. One night we had a huge screaming fight in the backyard, and Walter hurled and smashed a glass into a cinderblock wall.

We were both a spiritual mess.

To top it all off, my menstrual periods were getting heavy, and a tumor had appeared in my uterus. When I lay down, my formerly flat stomach would sort of "sit up" at attention, almost as if I was pregnant. That's the only way I can explain it. There was something growing in there that wasn't there before. Was it cancer?

Another Demon from the Past

We'd never had medical insurance. Now we needed it desperately. In his great capacity for suffering without complaint, Walter had not let his loathing for his job show at work. On the contrary, he was so popular with the engineers that McDonnell Douglas now offered him a permanent position with medical benefits. Although he shuddered at the thought of staying in the Dark Tower for the rest of his life, he took the job for the perks—and for me.

A visit to a doctor revealed what was wrong. "You have a large mass," the gynecologist told me. The good news: it wasn't cancer. It was a benign tumor known as a fibroid. The bad news: the doctor said I needed a hysterectomy.

I had frequently been writing medical articles for women's magazines, and I knew many hysterectomies were unnecessary. "A hysterectomy?" I asked. "Are you sure? Aren't those controversial? Don't I have any other choice?"

With strained patience, the doctor explained that if I were younger or wanted to get pregnant, my uterus might be worth saving. But at *my* age (I was 42), the uterus was useless. "You can keep your ovaries if you like," he added, trying to be reassuring. I knew that mounting evidence suggested the uterus may serve more functions beyond reproduction, including releasing a hormone that may guard a woman against heart problems. After a hysterectomy, my mother suffered terrible adhesions, which later led to her having part of her large intestine removed. I left his office so anxious my knees were shaking.

Seeking a second opinion, a third, and a fourth, I finally found myself at the University of Southern California in the office of one of the best fibroid surgeons in the nation. The silver-haired doctor assured me he could shrink the fibroid and remove it with laparoscopic surgery, which would require only a tiny incision.

The surgeon had a proud tilt to his head and spoke with an arrogant tone. (He knew how good he was.) But he was also thorough, and he seemed willing to answer my questions. As I sat across from him, a broad mahogany desk marking the distance between us, I suddenly asked a question that surprised even me.

In a small voice, I asked, "Can I keep it?"

The doctor looked at me strangely. A puzzled look of concern started in his eyes and moved slowly over his face, stopping at his mouth.

"Well, sure," he replied more gently. "It's not an emergency. We just need to monitor the tumor to make sure it doesn't grow too big. Come back again in a year."

I never returned to that surgeon or to any other. Instead, I "kept" the fibroid, even when it grew to be the size of a cantaloupe and people began asking me when the "baby" was due. Some fibroids feed on estrogen, and this was that kind. When I went through menopause in my fifties, the tumor shrank. But I kept and carried that "piece of tissue" around inside me for another fifteen years.

The Devil Strikes Again

Although I told myself I'd left *Cosmo* for good, I didn't leave it far enough. My associations with the magazine came back once again to haunt and attack me. A sex therapist I'd frequently interviewed while writing for *Cosmo* phoned me one day with a "hot idea" for a book. She wanted me to be her collaborator. She'd found a small subset of women who, during lovemaking, were having what sounded to me (in my spiritual ignorance) like mystical experiences. During sex, these women were having out-of-body experiences, seeing fireworks, and floating up into the clouds to meet God. These women were real. I talked to them. She wasn't making this up. During lovemaking, the women she'd found seemed to be dancing with the universe. The sex therapist said they were experiencing "supersex," and it was hard to deny it.

I had a literary agent; the therapist had no agent. I had New York publishing connections; she had none. Her flattering words to me were sweet as butter. Anything I wanted to do with the book would be more than wonderful with her.

In my vanity and desire for money, I took the bait.

The supersex book garnered a $150,000 advance in New York and another $100,000 in Germany. This gave our family enough money to allow Walter to quit his McDonnell Douglas job and to begin writing full-time again. The money was good. We could even afford to send Erin to Johns Hopkins University, her dream school.

Despite the good that came from it, the book project blew up in my face. I was trying to write about mystical experiences, my coauthor was trying to become famous, the publisher wanted a book on how to have a fantastic orgasm, and my agent just wanted us all to stop fighting and get rich. When the Sinclair Institute (affiliated with the Playboy Foundation) wanted to turn the book into a soft-porn "educational" videotape series, and my agent suggested I could make a cool $1 million on the deal if I'd just go along with the program, I washed my hands of the whole ugly business and walked away in disgust, telling everyone as I slammed the door they could do whatever they wanted to do with the book. I was through with it. (They turned it into a porn series.)

It felt to me in Cerritos as if everything I had worked so hard for in my life had blown up in my face. Why did the modern women's movement invest so much energy into glamorizing and idealizing what it was like to have money, fame, power, sex, and success? Why did so many of the movement's founders downplay traditionally feminine values like compassion, empathy, and caring? The world had once been my oyster. It now felt more like a poisonous octopus squeezing me to death.

About now, some readers may suspect my only problem was I hadn't become successful *enough*. The Dog-Slobber Journey wasn't exactly the peak of a wealthy, glamorous lifestyle. If I had made it really Big, with a capital B, some may protest, then at last I would have found happiness and true freedom. I beg to differ. Certainly no one was higher on the Fashion-Power-Money-Sex-Glamour-Status Ladder than Helen Gurley Brown. Coming from an unprivileged childhood in the Ozarks, skinny, unpretty, little Helen (who called herself a "mouseburger") was the queen of worldly ambition fulfilled. Yet in 1994, the very year the Sinclair Institute was clamoring to buy the supersex book, Helen candidly admitted she still didn't know how to be happy.

At age seventy-two, even as she prided herself on *Cosmo*'s success and tallied up everything she *had*, Helen confessed to *Psychology Today*, "My biggest failure is that I really can't assimilate all this [success] and be as grateful for it as I should be. All I can do is be very fearful that it's going to disappear pretty soon, which it will because of how old I am. Isn't it a shame that I can't just be thrilled and happy that I have had this wonderful magazine and a terrific husband? We're both healthy; we've done okay financially. [An understatement: they were multimillionaires.] Why can't I be happy about that? I really can't." Poor Helen, who boasted all her life of "having it all," complained at age seventy-two of "waking up scared every morning."[2]

At age eighty-five, Brown claimed to be happier, but still exhibited little understanding of the interior life. When *Vanity Fair* asked, "If you could change one thing about yourself, what would it be?" Helen replied, "I'd get my tummy to be flat again."[3]

Of O.J. and Roses

I wasn't waking up scared every morning or fretting over the shape of my tummy. At least I had that much in my favor. But I certainly wasn't waking up happy. To find some escape from my interior chaos, I watched a lot of television. Starting on January 24, 1995, the

O.J. Simpson murder trial (for allegedly killing his wife Nicole and waiter Ronald Goldman) was on nearly every channel. The televised courtroom testimony lasted 133 days, and as the circus wore on, I became increasingly agitated over what I perceived to be a travesty of our criminal justice system.

One day, as I got out of my car and walked across the parking lot to Ralph's Supermarket to buy groceries, I was spitting angry at the whole O.J. affair when a voice came to me. Was it my voice or someone else's? I don't know. But the voice, or thought, said: "Sue, this is not your life. Why are you letting this trial upset you so much? You don't know whether he did it or not. Just let it go."

Since my appearance on *Oprah*, I had come to think of television as the propaganda box in my living room. On the one hand, I was almost addicted to watching it. On the other hand, I wanted nothing more to do with it. Most of what I saw on TV now seemed to me to be just a pack of lies. Walter had always despised the boob tube. When I returned home from Ralph's, I clicked off the television and, except for a few dramatic moments (such as September 11, 2001), we never turned it on again.

Even before he left McDonnell Douglas, Walter began to return to himself. He'd been reading Saint Augustine's *Confessions*, and the book deeply touched his heart. Like Saint Augustine in his youth, Walter had been intellectually infected with a form of dualism known as Manichaeism, a gnostic religion that originated during the first half of the third century. Just as I had picked up on the Watchmaker God idea, without knowing where the notion came from, Walter had picked up on some of the Manichaean notions in the sea of ideas all around us. Mani, the founder of this religion, taught that the world is dominated by two eternal, opposing principles, one benevolent ("light," equated with God), and one malevolent ("darkness," equated with matter). "As with all gnosticism," the *Encyclopedia of Religion* explains, "Manichaeism is permeated by a deep and radical pessimism about the world, which is seen as dominated by evil powers, and by a strong desire to break the chains holding the divine and luminous principle inside the prison of matter and the body."[4] One fragment of Manichean text read, "Liberate me from this deep nothingness, from this dark abyss of waste, which is naught but torture, wounds unto death, and where there is no rescuer, no friend."[5] Saint

Augustine, who brilliantly defended orthodox Christianity against
Manichaeism, banished the roots of this false pessimism from Walter's
faith. Before long, he was once again feeling hopeful.

I remained a mess. Suffering from empty-nest syndrome, I felt as if
our whole family was disintegrating. Dustin was at UCLA, majoring
first in theatre and then in English literature. Erin was at Johns Hopkins, where she planned to major in music (she later switched her
major to English). My children had been almost everything to me,
the joys of my life. And now they, too, were gone. All three of them.

Erin and Walter were much alike—intense, intellectual, passionate, creative. As a result, they argued ferociously when she was in
high school, and the war escalated when she came home from college
for holidays. I cared little or nothing for the controversial philosophical questions that could set either of them off and trigger a heated
quarrel. During one Christmas vacation, the day before Erin was due
to fly out of LAX and return to Johns Hopkins in Baltimore, they
both became so angry over some philosophical issue or other that
Walter stormed out of the house and stayed overnight in a motel
room rather than prolong the fight.

The next morning, after the airport shuttle van arrived to pick her
up and Erin left with all her baggage, I was home alone. Searching
your interior life for motivations lurking deep in your unconscious
past is an uncertain business. I cannot guarantee you I'm telling you
the whole truth about this. But if I were to guess the reason for what
happened next, I would say it came at least in part from my unre-
solved grief over the abortion. I was intensely attached to Erin (my
baby), so much so I would call my clinging unnatural. When the
cobalt-blue-and-white shuttle arrived that day and drove away with
Erin inside, I knew deep in my heart she was leaving home in a way
she had not left before.

Archbishop Fulton Sheen once said, "Sometimes the only way the
good Lord can get into hearts is to break them."[6]

I was heartbroken with the suffering grief one feels only at the
death of a loved one. In a frustrated rage, I took every plate out of
the dishwasher, one by one, and smashed them onto the black-tile
kitchen floor. With each swing of my right arm, a plate would hit the
hard floor, crash, and explode. Shards of broken pottery flew everywhere. It was cathartic. I understood for the first time why Walter

hurled objects when he was angry. It felt really, really, *really* good. I smashed those plates into smithereens until I destroyed every last one of them and the kitchen resembled a bombed-out war zone. Then I left piles of smashed pottery all over the black-tile floor, went back into my study, and sat down at my desk.

When Walter came home, he could see this wasn't the right time for an intimate, heart-to-heart chat. Standing in the doorway of my study, regarding me with concern, he said tenderly, with a slight touch of cheer in his voice, "Have a little accident, did we?"

I said nothing.

He went into the kitchen, swept up the broken plates, and discarded them in the trash.

About six weeks later, on Valentine's Day, I was again home alone and in a brooding, cynical mood. Curled up on the sofa, staring blackly into space, I was counting up all the people in my life who'd "done me wrong." I'd accumulated a long list.

Suddenly, Walter came sweeping through the front door carrying a stunning bouquet of long-stemmed red roses, two dozen of them.

"Happy Valentine's Day!" he said merrily, handing me the flowers.

I burst into tears. I told him I didn't have anything left to live for anymore. The only things I knew that I loved were flowers and music and sunshine.

Walter took no offense at this.

He didn't defensively retort, "Well, you've got *me*. What about *me*?"

Instead, he replied gently, "Well, if you've got flowers and music and sunshine, I think you're doing pretty well."

I smiled up at him through my tears and buried my face in the roses. He truly was a treasure.

Shortly after that, we moved again—this time to a town on the edge of the city, a place called Corona.

Chapter 16

Two Monks in Corona

It is Jesus that you seek when you dream of happiness; He is waiting for you when nothing else you find satisfies you; He is the beauty to which you are so attracted; it is He who provoked you with that thirst for fullness that will not let you settle for compromise; it is He who urges you to shed the masks of a false life.

—Pope Saint John Paul II, World Youth Day 2000

The two-story, four-bedroom house Walter had located for us in Corona was elegantly pristine: cathedral ceilings, white carpets, white walls, a glassed-in fireplace before which we could sip our morning coffee and relish long, intimate chats. A high circular window facing east let in the sun's morning rays, bathing the front room at dawn with peach-and-golden light. My upstairs study overlooked pastel rooftops of homes resembling two-story versions of the fantasy suburban houses in the film *Edward Scissorhands*. During the days, as we wrote, we turned on the stereo and listened to Gregorian chant.

Clicking off the propaganda box and becoming detached from the news was perhaps the most essential step for a news-obsessed journalist like me to take before I could begin to live a more authentic life. It is said God writes straight with crooked lines, and I'm living proof it's true. In the serenity of Corona, far from the shattered rhythms and incessant babbling of modern life, we went back to church.

The people at Saint John's Episcopal Church in Corona were friendly and welcoming. We soon felt at home, much as we had in our little church in Roxbury.

Although we loved our new parish, Walter wasn't entirely content in the Episcopal Church. One day we invited the pastor, Father John, to our home for lunch. In the middle of a delightful and pleasant meal, Walter (who abhorred overly polite table talk) piped up that he thought "Martin Luther made a mistake" when he broke away from the Catholic Church. Father John, a gentle soul with an open, boyish face, who reminded me of my dad, accepted the observation with good humor and even calmly nodded, as if he partially agreed with Walter. But he said nothing, and what could have developed into a lively discussion fell flat.

After services, Saint John parishioners routinely gathered outside in front of the church to chat. One day a visitor told me the service we'd just celebrated was "more Catholic" than the Mass he'd attended last week at the Catholic church up the street. I found his comment perplexing. Never having been to a Catholic Mass, I had no idea what he meant.

Our Fear Culture vs. Raphael

Walter frequently declared we live in a Fear Culture, which he said began during the French Enlightenment when men turned their backs on God and thereby "closed off the sky." He believed many evils in the world are committed, not through outright malice, but because people are afraid, and that much of the evil done in the 1960s and '70s was done out of a naked fear of the bomb.

I tended to agree with Walter. His theory of the Fear Culture went along with my conviction that *fearlessness* was the path to freedom.

Saint John's had a ritual of sorts for people celebrating their birthdays. You'd stand in front of the congregation and tell everyone how old you were (if you wanted to—it wasn't required). Then you'd reveal what you would do differently in your life if you could do it all over again. On my birthday, I stood up and said, "If I had to do it all over again, I would be fearless."

"It isn't too late," Father John cheerfully observed.

Everyone laughed, including me. But it wasn't meant to be funny, and, of course, he was right.

With no television, few outside distractions, and plenty of time to contemplate the direction of our lives, Walter and I jokingly began

to call ourselves "the two monks." In fact, of course, neither of us
had ever met a monk, and we were nothing of the sort.

By now I was earning a good living writing medical articles for
Reader's Digest, *New Choices*, and *Woman's Day*. I also wrote parenting articles for the *Digest* with titles like "When Your Child Hates
School," "How to Raise a G-Rated Child in an X-Rated World,"
and "Mom, I Want to Live with My Boyfriend." This last article
(written under the pseudonym Kimberly Scott) detailed all the latest
scientific research revealing how harmful cohabitation is for women.
The marriage of the sexual revolution with the women's movement
had been a disaster for women, and the cohabitation trend was just
one of the many ways women had been betrayed.

While researching that story, I'd acquired a dear phone friend, a
Catholic named Margot Sheehan. Margot lived in Phoenix and ran a
Twelve-Step program called Unwed Parents Anonymous for young
single parents who felt lonely, dispirited, and overwhelmed by all the
challenges they had to face.

One day, during one of our typical hour-long phone conversations,
Margot (who loved angels) brought up a story in the Bible involving
the angel Raphael. Interested to read more, I asked, "Where is that
story in the Bible? I want to read it."

Margot replied it was in the Book of Tobit, but "that book isn't
in your Bible."

What did she mean it wasn't in "my" Bible?

She explained the Catholic Bible contains seven more Old Testament books than the Protestant Bible does.

I was flabbergasted. "Who took the books out of the Bible?" I
demanded.

I don't recall what Margot said in reply. I think she just giggled.
But I was astounded later to learn that Luther did it—fifteen hundred
years after Christ's crucifixion and Resurrection.

The year Margot told me about the Book of Tobit (1996), Walter
gave me two leather-bound Bibles for Christmas: a brown, gold-
embossed, large-print Protestant Bible (King James Version) and a
white, gold-embossed Catholic Bible (New American, Saint Joseph
edition). Setting the brown book aside, I eagerly immersed myself in
the Catholic Bible and avidly read the missing books.

I was particularly fond of the Book of Wisdom. One passage,
"Court not death by your erring way of life, nor draw to yourselves

destruction by the works of your hands. Because ~~God did not make death~~" ~~(1:12–13),~~ struck me like a thunderbolt. *God did not make death?* On some level, since that night when I was eight years old and saw *The Glenn Miller Story*, I had believed God *did* make death. Why would anyone in his right mind remove such a beautiful book from the Bible?

Not long after this, I received a package in the mail ~~from Margot. It contained a gift: the book *Rome Sweet Home*, by Scott and Kimberly Hahn. The opening line of the preface read: "The late Archbishop Fulton Sheen once wrote: 'There are not over a hundred people in the United States who hate the Roman Catholic Church; there are millions, however, who hate what they wrongly believe to be~~ the Catholic Church.'"

This quote from Archbishop Sheen didn't resonate with me at all.

It has been said the opposite of love isn't hate—it's indifference. If this is true, then Larry Lader (who hated the Catholic Church with a passion) and Helen Gurley Brown (who considered Catholics "the enemy") may have been closer to converting to Catholicism than I was. ~~I didn't "hate" the Catholic Church. I didn't even care about it.~~

Helen Dances with the Archbishop

Just as a brief aside, when I suggest Helen may have been closer to converting to Catholicism than I was, this isn't hyperbole. Helen's ability to spread her "sex-without-the-kids" philosophy throughout the world justifiably earned her a chapter in Donald De Marco and Benjamin Wiker's *Architects of the Cultural of Death*. At a luncheon in Washington, D.C., the two authors report, Helen "found herself seated next to the editor of an orthodox Catholic magazine." When she learned of his occupation, "she glowered at him and said, 'So, you're the enemy.'"[1]

And yet ... after her husband of fifty-one years (producer David Brown) died, Helen donated $1 million of her money to the foundation for the Cardinal Hayes High School, a prominent Catholic boys' school in the Bronx. The *New York Times* reported Helen decided to donate after a senior attorney at the Hearst Corporation, which owns *Cosmo*, told her about a donation he had made to the school.

On October 20, 2010, we find Helen at age eighty-eight in her black fur, drop-waist dress, and lace-topped stockings attending a special Mass and ceremony held at the high school in honor of popular TV host Regis Philbin, one of Cardinal Hayes' best-known alumni. According to the *Times*, Helen was standing on the school steps "leaning on a cane and being supported by an aide when Archbishop [now Cardinal] Timothy M. Dolan pulled up in his car.... Ms. Brown tried to walk forward to greet him, but she started tottering. Archbishop Dolan spotted her and jogged up the steps to help. Meanwhile, the school's marching band burst into the Cardinal Hayes marching song, inspiring the archbishop to take Ms. Brown in his arms and twirl her around."

The *Times* ran a photo of "the burly, six-foot-three archbishop, clad in his clerical robe, embracing the five-foot-four editor of Cosmopolitan magazine in a tender waltz."[2] The archbishop gazes down upon Helen with love, and the expression on her face is one of joyful peace.

Which just goes to prove the adage that truth is, indeed, stranger than fiction—and more interesting.

Seeking the Will of God

Although the New American Bible was the only one I now read, I placed *Rome Sweet Home* on the floor beside my bed stand, where it lay, gathering dust.

I was also reading another book: Thomas Merton's *Life and Holiness*. Now that I was actually trying to practice my Christian faith, I was deeply concerned about how to do God's will in my life. In a chapter on "What Is the Will of God?" Merton was asking the same tortuous questions that tormented me: "How am I going to be faithful to that mysterious and holy will? How do I know when a sacrifice is pleasing to the heavenly Father, and when it is only an illusion of my own will?"

Merton said the will of God is "manifested in the Christian above all in the commandment to love."

Of course, I agreed with that. But what did it mean? What was this mysterious "will of God," and precisely how was I to fulfill it?

Morning-coffee conversations with Walter began to center more frequently on philosophical and spiritual questions. One morning we were seated side by side on our blue-and-white floral sofa, looking out to the west of the house through the sliding glass door toward the patio and the yellow roses in the backyard. As our conversation deepened, we began talking about how so many people today seem to think reality is just whatever they happen to say it is, that many people just seem to be making up some fake reality in their heads and then trying to live by it.

Suddenly, Walter firmly declared, "I want to know *God's Reality*."
The phrase *God's Reality* struck a deep chord in me. Exactly! I agreed with him 100 percent. I didn't want to know and live by Helen Gurley Brown's reality, or Betty Friedan's reality, or Larry Lader's reality, or Oprah's reality, or any other human person's utopian fantasy of reality.

God's Reality. That's the true ticket to freedom, I thought to myself. *That's what I want to know too*. After all, God's Reality is the only Reality with a capital R that actually exists. All those other phony-baloney realities are wisps in the wind, mere human illusions.

Not long after that, Walter read the passage in the Bible where Christ says, "Where your treasure is, there your heart will be also." He had recently finished yet another novel, which had taken him nearly two years to write. It was a thriller he'd tentatively entitled "The Donor." In it, a dying billionaire who needs a heart transplant plots to prolong his own wretched life by spending a small fortune to hire a man (our hero) whose heart is a perfect match for a transplant. As our hero ambitiously climbs the corporate ladder to what he perceives to be success and freedom, the villain is secretly plotting to kill him and harvest his heart.

I'm not sure why he did it. Perhaps Walter decided the thriller was just a potboiler, an attempt to earn money with no greater and lasting value. Perhaps he saw the book as an idol. I don't know. In any case, the day he read the "where your treasure is" passage, he set "The Donor" aside and never submitted it again to another publisher.

Instead, he went to work on a book about a self-absorbed millionaire who falls in love with a woman. She dies. He has an encounter with an angel in a redwood grove, experiences a conversion of heart, and becomes a beggar on the streets of San Francisco (and after his death is declared a saint). When the story opens, a cynical journalist has just been assigned to a write an article on this newly declared

saint, and the tale is told through the journalist's jaded eyes. Originally titled "Angel in the Grove" and later "The Beggar and the
Rose," that novel didn't sell either.

Of Big Sur and Amazing Grace

Now that both Erin and Dustin had graduated from college, Walter
and I had more money to spend on travel. One day, we decided to
take a "let's-go-and-do-nothing" trip by driving up California Highway 1 to Big Sur along the spectacular Pacific coast. We stayed for
several nights in a cabin at the Big Sur Lodge in Julia Pfeiffer Burns
Big Sur State Park. One morning when we woke up and stepped
outside, it had just stopped raining. The giant redwoods outside our
cabin door were dripping with raindrops. Mists of fog hovered over
the rooftops. The cool air was fresh and alive with the pungent aroma
of redwood needles.

Walter was mesmerized by the beauty of it all. In awe, he said, "I
want to live in a place like this."

That morning we ate breakfast in the lodge, with wooden beams and
skylights over our heads and a log fire crackling in the woodstove in
the far corner. After breakfast, we took a bracing hike through majestic
redwoods. Walking along a creek-side path winding through patches
of clover-like redwood sorrel, we reached a waterfall dropping from a
sixty-foot cliff and plummeting in a cool spray into a pool below. After
our hike, we lunched outside in a little café at a table situated beside a
giant redwood tree growing through the deck.

When we returned to Corona, our house by comparison looked
cheap and ugly to Walter, and he had a new dream: it was Big Sur,
or bust. He wanted to live in redwood country.

This time I thought he really had lost his mind.

"Walter, do you know how *expensive* it is to live in Big Sur?"

I tried to make him see reason. We were doing well enough financially, but this new dream of his was way beyond our means. Even a
treehouse in Big Sur cost $1 million! There was no way we'd be able
to afford a house there.

Walter was not deterred. He began praying for a house in the
redwood country. He was like an innocent little kid praying for a
red tricycle for Christmas. Unshakably certain God would give him

the gift he asked for, he started spending his free hours searching the Internet for houses in Big Sur.

As far as I knew, this was the first time in his life Walter had ever prayed for any "thing" for himself. He may have prayed for courage, love, guidance, or a host of other intangible gifts. But he was no materialist, and praying to God for "things" wasn't his style. In Corona, his faith seemed to be blossoming in a new way. If this crazy prayer of his went unanswered, would his faith become shaken?

I prayed, "Please, God, don't let him be disappointed."

There was a little oceanside restaurant in Laguna Beach where we loved to eat. It was called Las Brisas. We even had our favorite table on the outside patio, where we liked to drink margaritas. Undaunted by failure, Walter had started a new book. This one was about talking show cats who unite together in an unbreakable bond of friendship to rescue one of the cat's human "moms," who's been kidnapped by evil bad guys. I did not believe for an instant a book about talking cats, written for adults no less, would sell. I spent three hours under the stars one evening over margaritas at Las Brisas, trying to persuade him to give up this fantastic new project of his and work on something more sensible. (My attempts were, of course, futile. He would work on the untitled novel we would simply call "The Cat Book," off and on again, for the next ten years.)

Just a few steps from Las Brisas, a brown-shingled gazebo topped by a dolphin weathervane overlooked the ocean. One day we were standing in the gazebo, admiring the spectacular view. A harpist was in the gazebo playing music. As waves gently lapped the sun-drenched, sand beach below and the strains of "Amazing Grace" filled the cool salt air, tourists gathered in the gazebo to look and listen.

Suddenly, one tourist turned to another and said, "This is the most beautiful view in the world."

The second tourist replied, "Yes, it is beautiful. But you have to remember, I'm from Willits."

He said, "I'm from Willits," the way Connecticut Yankees used to say, "I'm from Roxbury," as if Willits were a secret little hideaway, a treasure off the beaten path where anyone who knew about it would live if he could.

Walter hadn't overheard the exchange between the two tourists in the gazebo. So as we drove home, I told him about it. In unison, we both asked, *"Where's Willits?"*

When we arrived home, I googled "Willits" on the Internet, and was astonished at what I found. Willits was a small town of about five thousand people two hours or so by car north of San Francisco. "Walter!" I called out. "There are redwoods in Willits, and it's not that expensive to live there."

The next time we drove north along Route 1 to Big Sur, we spontaneously decided to drive on up the coast another 280 miles to check out Willits.

Journey to Redwood Country

The town itself was no tourist destination. Willits had been an old lumber-mill town. The lumber mills had closed, and it had become a rundown center for a lot of marijuana dealing. The land in the surrounding area, however, was spectacularly beautiful, with huge green mountainous hills and towering redwood forests.

While exploring Willits, we learned that giant redwood trees, in their majestic serenity, have an invisible secret. Strong and invincible as they appear, they are actually quite fragile and have remarkably shallow root systems. Without the anchor of a deep tap root, a single tree can easily be blown over in a storm by a strong wind. What typically prevents this from happening is that most of these trees grow in communion with one another. Beneath the surface of the soil, redwood-tree roots spread out like long fingers and intertwine with the roots of neighboring trees to form a giant web. This interconnected web helps to anchor each individual trunk. The tallest of trees and among the oldest living things on earth, redwoods have managed to survive for centuries because they are stronger together than any one of them would be if standing alone. A redwood grove is not made up of isolated individuals. A redwood grove is an interconnected *system*.

Mesmerized by the glory of the redwoods, Walter thought living in Willits was a definite possibility.

I wasn't so sure. The closest decent medical library was more than two hours away by car—at the University of California in Davis. By now I was writing mostly medical articles, and I needed good, up-to-date medical research at my fingertips if I was to stay current. I know the Internet has lots of great stuff, but for me nothing beats a library. I had been using the University of California at Irvine and also the UCLA medical library for research. Whatever would happen to my writing career if I moved to a hole-in-the-wall place like Willits? My career would just die.

Well, it was just a thought, and we let it pass and drove home.

The woman who owned our house in Corona was an excitable little lady from Taiwan. She barely spoke English, and she was unfamiliar with American customs. One day she had a medium-sized tree cut down and dismembered in our backyard, and she left it for us, the tenants, to dispose of.

Walter had been picking up limbs and branches and stashing them in our green bin for the trash collectors. He'd done this for several weeks without complaint.

But early one Friday morning, as we sat together outside on the patio, Walter glowered at the huge pile of leaves and branches still left in the yard and groused, "You know, for ten bucks I'd move to Willits."

Since I was the phone researcher of the team, he added, "Why don't you go call the Willits newspaper and see if there are any rentals available up there?"

So, without fully thinking through what this might mean, I did it. I called the *Willits News*.

There was one rental available on forty acres of land just outside of Willits, and it was within our price range. We called the owner, who lived in San Francisco. He said another tenant lived in a second house on the property, but we could see the place on Monday.

We left immediately with the idea of getting to Willits (555 miles away) late Friday night so we could have the weekend to scout around and locate other possible rentals. As we drove north on U.S. 5, it suddenly struck me that this might mean we were leaving Corona forever and we were moving to a place where I would no longer have a career. We were earning enough money from our books by this point that I didn't actually *need* to write medical articles for magazines for us to survive. Together Walter and I had written a little gift book, *101 Secrets a Good Dad Knows* (how to: feed a horse, hammer a nail, skip a rock), which was selling quite well. But, still, *give up my career*? I didn't want to leave Dustin and his new wife Jen, who also lived in southern California. And what of our little church community? Whatever would I do without Saint John's?

I began groaning and whining and complaining. There was no way I was going to move to Willits. I was furious with Walter. What was he thinking? Had he gone *nuts*?

As we left U.S. 5, turned west toward Willits, and followed Route 20 down along Upper Lake, we passed through a little lakeside town called Nice. I was having a genuine hissy fit. We had just passed a small road angling up the hill to our right. The street sign read Floyd Way. I remember the place distinctly, because Floyd was my dad's name.

And then a voice came to me out of the silence. I did not hear the voice with my ears. No audible voice shook the sound waves of the world. I can only say I heard with the ears of my heart. The voice said: "Do not worry. I will take care of you."

The message so startled and astonished me, I inwardly replied, "*What?*"

The voice came to me again, simple and reassuring: "Do not worry. I will take care of you."

Until this moment, I had been flooded with fear. Suddenly, all my fears evaporated. A warm peace flowed like water through my whole being.

I turned to Walter.

Continuing to speak in the same hissy fit tone I'd been using up until that moment, I said, "This house is going to have to be awfully ..."

He thought I was going to finish the sentence " ... awfully *good* for me to take it."

Instead, I said, "This house is going to have to be awfully *bad* for me to turn it down."

Walter did a double take. He looked at me with surprise.

I gave him a big grin. We both laughed out loud.

Then we continued happily on our journey.

Chapter 17

Lessons under the Redwoods

Faith and love are like the blind man's guides. They will lead you along a path unknown to you, to the place where God is hidden.

—Saint John of the Cross, *The Spiritual Canticle*

We took a room that night in Willits at the Baechtel Creek Inn and Spa, a quiet creekside motel tucked down a hill away from Highway 101. The next morning we picked up a copy of the *Willits News* and read the classified ads. Sure enough, there was another house available for rent—a log cabin up a hill in a forested area called Brooktrails.

When we saw the log cabin, I couldn't believe my eyes. It was almost the spitting image of the Big Sur Lodge. It had a giant redwood tree growing through the front deck, beams and skylights overhead, a woodstove in the corner, and thirteen redwood trees in the yard. It even had a little breakfast deck off the bedroom, where we could sit outside and sip our morning coffee. It was Walter's house!

I took one amazed look at that log cabin with the redwood growing through the deck, and I thought, *Oh, no! I'm going to have to move to Willits!*

We signed a lease that Sunday and moved six weeks later. Walter was overjoyed. He was like a giddy little kid.

After we moved to Willits, we discovered the Episcopal church in town appeared to us to be falling apart. There's no more polite way to say it. The small congregation met in an old Pacific Gas and Electric Company office, and one Sunday a lay woman gave the sermon. It was clear to me this well-meaning parishioner had gotten the Gospel almost entirely wrong. After the service, I went home and read

the Bible for an hour (not a bad thing), in a futile attempt to figure
out where she'd gone astray.

Walter's declaration of independence—"I want to know *God's
Reality*"—kept echoing in my head. I had only begun to learn my
Christian faith. I certainly didn't want some woman I'd never met
making up my religion for me. It didn't help that the female pastor
of the church later phoned and urged us to return, saying (in what
I took to be an attempt to reassure me) that I didn't have to believe
Christ walked on water—I didn't have to believe in any of those
miracles in the Bible—just please come back; they needed people. I
thought to myself, *If He wasn't able to perform miracles, how is He going
to raise me from the dead?*

Searching for someone who could preach the truth, we began
driving seventy miles roundtrip along narrow, twisty Route 20
through the redwood forests to the Episcopal church in Fort Bragg,
along the Pacific coast. The pastor of the church, a sweet man, often
seemed confused about Scripture readings. He suggested the story
about Jonah and the whale was just a joke (not to be taken seriously),
and he would often begin his sermons by looking down at his toes
and then up at the sky, as if he was confused about what to say. That
Christmas Eve, Route 20 with its many hairpin curves was so slick
with black ice that we had to miss Christmas services. Finding a parish to replace Saint John's was tough.

Ever the problem solver, Walter suggested, "Why don't we try the
Catholic Church?"

"I'm not going to join that patriarchal old Church!" I snapped.
Apparently, I was more hostile toward Catholicism than I thought.

Still, we seemed to be stuck between a hard place and a rock.

Luther and Henry VIII

Walter was an avid history buff. I'd taken only one history course in
college. To gather ammunition so I could explain to Walter why we
shouldn't become Catholics, I decided to read up on the Protestant
Reformation to see why my forebears had broken away from the
Catholic Church. Since we'd accumulated a book collection the size
of a small library, help was close at hand. I picked up Volume 6 of

The Story of Civilization: The Reformation by Will Durant. I opened it to Chapter XIX, "Luther and Erasmus, 1517–36," and began to read.

Luther didn't exactly endear himself to me. I read that Luther "had the traditional and German conception of woman as divinely designed for childbearing, cooking, praying, and not much else." Luther was quoted as saying, "Take women from their housewifery, and they are good for nothing," and, "If women get tired and die of bearing, there is no harm in that; let them die so long as they bear; they are made for that." He despised educated women, saying of his wife, "I wish that women would repeat the Lord's Prayer before opening their mouths." *This* was the guy who broke away from the Catholic Church to give Protestant women our "freedom"? Wow! Not only did Luther seem to despise women, but his rants and ravings—calling the Pope "the Devil's sow," the bishops "larvae," and unbelievers "ignorant apes"—didn't sound like love to me.

What about the Episcopal Church we belonged to, the church founded by Henry VIII when the Catholic Church wouldn't give him a divorce? If anything, Henry VIII was even worse than Luther. He was divorcing and killing wives right and left because he wanted a male heir. Walter put this in more modern terms when he told me, "Henry VIII broke away from the Catholic Church because he didn't want a woman to rule England." This unsettling insight brought me up short.

My brief foray into church history plainly showed me Protestantism at its roots was hardly the place to seek women's liberation. I told myself *Christ* (not Luther or Henry VIII) was the founder of Christianity. Plainly, the Church founded by Christ and His apostles in the first century was the Catholic Church. It was this Church who wrote the Gospels and other books of the New Testament, this Church who chose which books were inspired and belonged in the Bible. Therefore, it seemed to me if we wanted to find the Church that began with Christ as its foundation, we had go to Catholicism. After this realization, I agreed to check out the Catholic Church with Walter to see what was up.

I phoned Saint Anthony of Padua Catholic Church in Willits at 9:30 one Friday night, thinking that at that hour I'd get an answering machine telling me the Mass schedule. Instead, Father Bruce Lamb answered the phone. He told me the English-speaking weekend Mass was at 5:30 Saturday evening and 9:00 A.M. Sunday and added that if, after attending Mass, we wanted to talk further, he was available.

Getting Catechized

We went on Saturday night and sat in a back pew. The Mass was beautiful, surprisingly similar to the service at Saint John's. The Old Testament reading was about Jonah. Father Bruce, a convert from Judaism with a firm voice and an even firmer faith, didn't seem at all confused. After the service, we made an appointment to meet with him the following week in the rectory.

Father Bruce asked us a series of questions: What was our spiritual background? Had we been baptized? (He seemed disturbed to learn we'd both been baptized twice and brusquely declared, "The first one is the one that counts.") When we told him we'd been married thirty-six years and this was our first and only marriage, he visibly breathed a sigh of relief.

Suddenly, Walter blurted out, "We've had an abortion!" Until that moment, I thought of the abortion as a burden I was carrying alone. I had no idea Walter considered the abortion "ours." It had never occurred to me that all these years he had been silently grieving right along with me.

Although Walter did not express this idea at that moment, I think he believed the real error of *Roe v. Wade* was not all the propagandistic legal and historic errors the opinion contained, egregious as those were. The deeper and much more fundamental error of the opinion, in his view, was that it enshrined into U.S. law the egoistic Fear Culture mindset bequeathed to us by the Enlightenment—the belief that a woman is alone in the universe, cut off from God and man, locked away in the prison of her own body, with no hope that anyone will ever love her enough to set her free. Christian feminist Frederica Mathewes-Green, who listened carefully to expectant mothers who'd had abortions for her book *Real Choices*, articulated the woman's fear mindset when she wrote, "No one wants an abortion as she wants an ice-cream cone or a Porsche. She wants an abortion as an animal, caught in a trap, wants to gnaw off its own leg."[1]

When Walter confessed to Father Bruce that *we'd* had an abortion, I suspect he thought this was the unforgivable sin of all sins that would prevent us from entering the Catholic Church.

Instead, Father Bruce simply nodded his bald head. He said matter-of-factly that several parishioners at Saint Anthony's had had abortions. He explained that all sins, including abortion, can be forgiven—except one: blasphemy against the Holy Spirit, which is calling good evil and evil good, not out of ignorance, but out of malice.

Father Bruce's primary concern during our first meeting seemed to be that we understand and believe in the Real Presence of Christ's Body and Blood in the Eucharist. He suggested that before we met with him again the following week, we buy a copy of the *Catechism of the Catholic Church* and read the section on the Eucharist. We bought two, one for Walter, one for me.

The *Catechism* amazed me. This wasn't the "stuffy, old, patriarchal church" I'd heard about. The Church's teachings were all about love, joy, and forgiveness. The Virgin Mary, Mother of God—a woman!—was revered as the first true human being and the model of authentic *personhood* and joy, not only for women, but also for men.* This was a complete system of philosophical thought and mystical faith with answers the entire world needed to hear. The Church talked about man and the universe in a systemic way, much as the new physicists talked. I was stunned: the Catholic Church understood systemic, holistic thinking two thousand years before scientists began talking about systems. The Catholic Church wasn't so old and out-of-date that she was obsolete. *She was so fresh and new it was hard for anyone trapped in the old mechanistic Cartesian-Newtonian worldview to understand what she was saying.* The Church contained within herself the wholeness and unity I had sought all my life!

I suddenly saw that to live in the fullness and joy of the Catholic faith, to follow *Christ's way*, is to be united in love with all of mankind: friends and enemies, rich and poor, saints and sinners—from the most powerful billionaire to the weakest one-celled boy or girl in the womb. Did anyone ever tell Betty Friedan that in the Church we are called to participate *in the very life of God*? Did she ever hear

---

* Christ our Lord is, of course, *uncreated* and both fully human *and* fully divine.

the liberating news that Mary, the Mother of God, a woman, is the model of sanctity for all humanity, men and women alike? If Betty had ever heard what the Church actually teaches, I wonder: What would she have said? The Mere Fifty-Seven's overly narrow community of love extended mostly to other women, primarily to well-educated, power-seeking women like themselves. The Church's much broader community of love extends to all mankind, even to the tiniest "little guy," who's so weak that he's a nonentity in the world's eyes. I saw that the fight over abortion in our culture today is not really one of "yes" or "no." Rather it's a conflict over "bigger" and "smaller" communities of love. Though often accused of rigid, overly narrow thinking, Catholics are, in fact, seeing the *bigger* picture!

Plainly, when the media frame the abortion war as part of a larger culture war between secularists and Christians, they have the story wrong. The abortion war is not a conflict of Christians vs. non-Christians, blue states vs. red states, or even Democrats vs. Republicans. Love is beyond politics. Love transcends politics.

"The line dividing good and evil cuts through the heart of every human being," Aleksandr Solzhenitsyn wrote from his experiences in a Soviet labor camp. "During the life of any heart this line keeps changing place; sometimes it is squeezed one way by exuberant evil and sometimes it shifts to allow enough space for good to flourish. One and the same human being is, at various ages, under various circumstances, a totally different human being. At times he is close to being a devil, at times to sainthood."[2]

If every Christian in America had stood firmly with the smallest, weakest, and poorest in our society—that is, if each and every Christian had stood firmly with the innocent preborn child nailed to the cross—we would have far fewer abortions than we do in the United States and the world today. I say this not as one of the righteous, but one of the guilty. For I was, for most of my life, on the abortion-supporting side of the lifeline.

With a flash, I saw that the Catholic understanding of mankind, God, and the universe does not just embrace pieces of reality (half truth, selected truth, or truth out of context). This was *the whole truth*. This was *God's Reality*. The unity I had previously experienced by reason through systemic thinking I now experienced by faith through revelation. I was filled with wonder. The Catholic Church was the last place on earth I would have thought to look for all this. It was the last place I *did* look.

I couldn't put the *Catechism* down. I read it for three days and nights. It felt to me as if I'd been a Catholic for years and just didn't know it.

One day, as we stood in the bedroom of our log cabin, Walter remarked, "Don't you think it's odd that the only church available for us up here is the Catholic Church?"

I stared at him, as a flashbulb exploded in my head: *Margot Sheehan!* I immediately called my Catholic phone friend in Phoenix, the one who'd pointed to the missing books in my Protestant Bible.

"Margot," I asked in a tone of mock accusation, "have you been praying that I'll become a Catholic?"

In a tone of mock innocence, Margot replied, "Only for seven years."

We both laughed.

That night, I picked up *Rome Sweet Home*, the gift Margot had given me seven years before, and began to read it seriously for the first time.

Chapter 18

Finding Our Way to Freedom

Jesus then said to the Jews who believed in him, "If you remain in my word, you will truly be my disciples, and you will know the truth, and the truth will set you free."

—John 8:31–32

What happened next was very strange and only explained to me years later when I read a quote by Archbishop Fulton Sheen. "The nearer Christ comes to a heart," Sheen wrote, "the more it becomes conscious of its own guilt; it will then either ask for His mercy and find peace, or else it will turn against Him because it is not yet ready to give up its sinfulness. Thus He will separate the good from the bad, the wheat from the chaff. Man's reaction to this Divine Presence will be the test: either it will call out all the opposition of egotistic natures, or else galvanize them into a regeneration and a resurrection."[1] This was to be my test: Was I ready to give up my self-centered egotism and return to Him? Or was I determined to keep doing everything my own way?

Before you're received into the Catholic Church, you must receive the sacrament of reconciliation, also known as confession. Walter and I both went to confession for the first time on the evening of April 14, 2003. A reconciliation service was held at Saint Anthony's, and four or five priests came to hear confessions. I confessed to a priest I'd never met. If I'd told him everything I'd done wrong *in detail*, we'd still be sitting there to this day. I ran through my worst sins, hitting the lowlights as quickly as possible. The priest nodded (almost indifferently, it seemed to me) and forgave me everything, including, he said, the sins I hadn't confessed.

Deeply conscious of my personal guilt for the first time in my life, I was mortified. When I returned to a pew and knelt to say the Our Father (the prayer the priest gave me as a penance), my face burned red-hot with shame to the tips of my ears.

When Walter and I returned to the cabin, he was upbeat and at peace. I was an emotional wreck. But we were too tired to talk about it. Instead, we just went to bed.

Around 4:00 A.M., I awoke. Unable to fall back to sleep, I went into the living room. As I sat on our loveseat, God recalled to my mind the promise I'd made to Him as a child—that I knew right from wrong, and I wouldn't do anything wrong. I realized I had broken every one of the Commandments, even "Thou shall not kill." An image of Christ hanging bloodied on the Cross flooded my mind, and I saw, with horror, that *I* was the one who had put Him there. He died for *me*. Alone in the dark, I wept bitter tears of unconsoled grief.

Three Days in Hades

My personal encounter that night with Christ on the Cross was as factual—indeed, more factual—than any truth I had previously encountered. I saw that Christ is Truth, with a capital T. Truth is a Person—the Person of Jesus Christ—and the Bible is not just a book of arbitrary rules but the greatest love story ever told.

Reflecting back on it now, I suspect all that time I was attending the Episcopal Church, I was only using the church as my own personal therapy. I went mostly because it made me feel good about myself. (All about *me* again.)

The Catholic Church was a whole different matter. For three days after my Monday-night confession, I was in torment. When Walter invited me on a drive through the countryside on Thursday to admire the spring wildflowers, I went with him but ruined the trip by righteously demanding, "How can you look at wildflowers when *Christ died for your sins?*"

Poor Walter. He truly was a saint to put up with me. But he didn't just put up with me. He loved me sincerely, without romantic illusions. A character in one of his screenplays observed that when you love someone, "God has bound your fates with a silken chain—silk, because love is sweet, but a chain, because it is servitude."

Back in the cabin under the redwoods, as I sat slumped on our loveseat, Walter knelt before me, his two hands grasping mine. In anguish, I told him, "You can become a Catholic if you want to, but I can't."

Then I added, choking back tears, "God doesn't want me."

I'll never forget the look in Walter's eyes, a mix of worry, pain, and helplessness. He had no idea what to say.

Maybe I should call Father Bruce and tell him I'm in trouble here, I thought. *Maybe I did the confession all wrong, and I need to do it again.* I was so convinced Christianity was supposed to make me *feel good* about myself, it never occurred to me this suffering could be a precious gift from God.

Reluctant to call Father Bruce, I picked up the *Catechism* to read up on confession and see if I could figure out where I'd gone wrong. That's when I found the passage on "conversion of heart." The *Catechism*, in the section on interior penance, states: "This conversion of heart is accompanied by a salutary pain and sadness which the Fathers called *animi cruciatus* (affliction of spirit) and *compunctio cordis* (repentance of heart).... The human heart is converted by looking upon him whom our sins have pierced."[2]

Salutary pain? *Healthy* pain? Affliction of spirit? Repentance of heart? The two-thousand-year-old Church, in her wisdom, knew more about what was happening inside me than I did—and she even had *names* for it.

I had plunged into the sea of faith before I found out I didn't know how to swim. But Christ reached out, took my hand, and gently lifted my head above water. With a sigh, I let go. God was in charge here. I wasn't. He had everything under control. He told me at Floyd Way not to worry: He would take care of me. And God never goes back on a promise. With that, my fears vanished.

***

We are received into the Catholic Church on Easter Vigil, 2003.

Father Bruce signs the Cross on my forehead with holy oil with such exuberance that the oil drips off the end of my nose.

About one hundred or so individuals have been called out of the world to gather for the service. As we rhythmically chant hymns together in unison, in the darkened church lit only by the uncreated light of Christ represented by the candles we each hold in our hands, I silently ask, *Are our hearts all beating in unison? Is everyone in this church community around me truly one Body, one Heart, one Mind? On the level of the electron, in the dimension of the invisibly small as well as in the dimension of the invisibly immense, are we all a unity of one in the great dance of the universe with the Father, the Son, and the Holy Spirit?*

The Church, through God's self-revelation, knows the universe is unified not by a great thought but by a word, and the Word is Love.

Before such mysteries, my mind grows still and falls silent. When Walter and I receive God on our lips for the first time, I only know in the depths of my heart that, after all my searching, I have at last found the Truth who promises to make me free, if I will trust only in Him.

Perhaps one day, with God's grace, I think with rising hope, *I might even become fearless.* For the Holy Spirit through Saint John the Apostle says, "There is no fear in love, but perfect love drives out fear" (1 Jn 4:18).[3]

Back home that night in the cabin, I can almost hear the angels singing.

My Second Confession

Our entering the Church, of course, was not the end of our journey to God. It was a new beginning. It is said the Church is both a hospital for sinners and an army barracks. So it's hardly surprising the first stage in this new beginning involved healing.

Although Walter had gone to Father Bruce and found healing for traumas he had endured during his childhood, I still had my own post-abortion demons, which I'd never honestly faced. I feared if I ever started talking about the abortion, I would never stop crying. Although I'd confessed the abortion during my first confession and I knew God had forgiven me, guilt continued to haunt me. Not constantly. I wasn't obsessed by it. But I couldn't stop blaming myself. So at last I took my post-abortion trauma in confession to Father Bruce.

In the confessional, Father Bruce tells me something that on one level of my being I do *not* want to hear: in Christ, the baby we aborted is not dead, but alive.

This revelation sends a chilling ripple of shock through my entire body, from the hairs on the back of my neck to the tips of my toes. Do I really one day want to meet the little person I killed—*face-to-face*? I shudder at the thought. My shock is intense.

But Father Bruce calmly and patiently reasons with me. Would I rather have our child dead than alive?

No, of course not!

Suddenly, I let out a deep sigh of relief. Although Father Bruce doesn't tell me this now, I will later learn that in the hymns sung by the Church in honor of the Holy Innocents, the boy babies the tyrant Herod killed in his hatred for Christ, are spoken of as adorned with palms and flowers and rejoicing in the presence of the Lord for whom, unknown to themselves, they had given their lives. From the vantage point of this world, the abortion holocaust which America, in her fears, has embraced for herself and exported to poor women around the globe is a scene of defeat and slaughter. But from God's viewpoint, the vantage point of eternity, the scene is one of triumph, victory, and joy.

At this very hour, after a quarter century of unspoken grief over the abortion, I at last begin to be healed. The Church, in her all-forgiving love, is so beautiful that I feel as if I'm living inside a two-thousand-year-old poem.

As my penance, Father Bruce tells me to go home and contemplate how much God loves me.

Unharnessed, I leave the confessional and walk through the church door out into a new day filled with the light of a freedom from fear I have never known before.

Joy under the Redwoods

Back home on the deck of the log cabin under the giant redwoods, I stretch out in a lounge chair, close my eyes, and contemplate how much God loves me.

Suddenly, I am filled with serenity and peace. There is no way to express the experience in words. I can only say that for a moment in time, it seems to me as if I enter into the timeless joy of the Love that holds the universe together, the eternal dance of the Father, the Son, and the Holy Spirit.

As I reflect back over all that has happened, I see with deeper clarity that the God of all genuine love did not wind up the universe like a clock and walk away. Even when I turned my face away from Him, He has been with me through it all, with our family, and with our whole nation.

He was there leading me by the hand and giving me His truth at the University of Missouri when I first detected the lies on the pages of *Cosmo*, and I told my fellow journalists-in-training the anecdotes were so pat they appeared to be fabricated. He was there in a big way when Dr. Bernard Nathanson saw a baby's image on a fetal ultrasound, quit doing abortions, and spilled the beans about the propaganda he and Larry Lader had manufactured to sell abortion to women and the American public. He was there in truth in the Mayflower Hotel when Pauli Murray walked out in protest and withdrew her name from nomination to NOW's national board on the grounds that human rights are "indivisible." He was there nagging at the back of the troubled mind of Justice Harry Blackmun when he told the *Washington Post* the *Roe v. Wade* decision could one day be regarded as "one of the worst mistakes in the court's history." He was there in the truth Betty Friedan spoke when she said the women's movement had come to an end, and she told a reporter "our blind spot was the family." He was there in the suffering sigh of the woman sitting beside me onstage at the *Oprah Show*, as her husband told the world he'd had seven affairs. He was there at Hartford Hospital when I gave birth during a race riot, and He was there again in the concerned eyes of the black intake nurse who tried to get us to consider our abortion decision more carefully. He was there in the deeply conflicted heart of the abortion doctor who couldn't stop himself from blurting out the truth when he said, "I usually deliver them alive."

God is not only here with me now under the redwoods, but He has been, is, and always will be with each and every one of us through it all.

Despite all the suffering in the world, we cling not in vain to hope. For hope is not ours to invent, but His to give. All my efforts to direct and control my own life have come to nothing. For every good thing is His. Only the God who is Love can give us the wholeness and fullness of being we seek. Only God can fill the human heart with joy. With Saint Augustine, I cry, "O, how late have I loved You!"

And now as I rest gently under the redwood trees, the tears freely fall, no longer hot, mortified, and burning, but refreshing, forgiven, and cool. I surrender my suffering mind, heart, and soul into the arms of Christ on the Cross, and He carries them into the tomb, buries them under the earth, and rises bodily from the grave, transfiguring all fear, sorrow, and death into His eternal love.

Such sweet grief.

Epilogue: Christmas in the ICU

[The hospital] is a microcosm a thousand times more real than the normal and healthy world surrounding it. Here everybody is busy with the essential, and the essential is now, in the light of the end, of eternity. That's why everything, every detail is important: there are no cheap emotions, no rhetoric, no idle talk. Each word is important.

—Father Alexander Schmemann,
The Journals of Father Alexander Schmemann, 1973–1983[1]

On Friday, June 15, 2007—two days before our fortieth wedding anniversary—Walter was diagnosed with lymphoma. A normal white-blood-cell count is 5,000 to 10,000. Walter's blood contained more than 500,000 white cells, the highest count his doctor had ever seen. White cells, of course, are critical to the body's defense system. The horror hit me: *How can he beat cancer if the very immune cells he needs to fight the disease are cancerous?*

As we leave the doctor's office, being by far the less courageous member of the team, I ask, "Oh, Walter, what are we going to do?"

Walter surprises me with his serenity. For months, due to his doctor's nagging, he's been on a weight-loss diet to lower his blood pressure. Through ascetic self-discipline, he's lost twenty-two pounds. Turning to me, he cheerfully replies, "Well, if I'm going to have cancer, I'm going to enjoy it. Let's go get some ice cream."

He'd once heard of a man whose last words on his deathbed were, "I wish I'd eaten more ice cream."

Walter said, "I don't want to be that guy."

So we go straight to the local Thrifty Drug in Willits and order two giant waffle cones with pecan praline. Walter has three scoops.

From that hour forward, I could barely keep him in ice cream. He ate gallons in a multitude of flavors and regained twenty pounds. Walter courageously endured countless hours of poisonous chemotherapy infusions, and his white blood-cell count plunged from 580,000 to 4,000. Delighted with this surprising response, his oncologist and nurses fondly called him their "Miracle Boy."

But one Saturday night, just a few days before Christmas, Walter suddenly had a seizure and wound up in the ICU at Howard Hospital in Willits.

Walter's fever was high, and he was so sick that I called Saint Anthony's to tell Ed, who runs the church office, that I want him anointed.

The priest is out of town. When Father Larry returns around 6:00 P.M. on Tuesday, December 18, he comes almost immediately to Walter's bedside. Walter cannot make his confession, because he's been unconscious for most of the day. But as the priest and I softly pray the Our Father together, Walter suddenly stirs awake long enough to repeat the prayer with us.

"Thy kingdom come. Thy will be done ..."

Walter has been so out of it for most of the day that I'm amazed he woke up to pray and receive Christ in the Eucharist.

Father Larry nods. He says he's seen that happen with a lot of people in situations like this.

The doctor in charge isn't sure what is wrong with Walter. It could be an infection; it could be the cancer.

"I think it's the cancer," I say.

The doctor nods. "So do I." He explains that Howard Hospital lacks the expertise to treat this condition, and transferring Walter to a major medical center in San Francisco will give him "the best possible chance" to recover.

Okay, great. That's what we want. The best possible chance.

I drive to the log cabin through pouring rain to pack for a trip to San Francisco. Walter will be flown to San Francisco in a helicopter. I will follow in a car. Dustin is flying up from Los Angeles. He will rent a car and drive me to San Francisco. Erin and her husband will come to see us later at the hospital.

While I'm in the bedroom, packing my bags for the trip, the phone rings. It's Dr. Bruce Andich, Walter's doctor at the hospital. "We had an incident," Dr. Andich says. "Walter stopped breathing. We didn't have a 'do not resuscitate' order, so we put him on a breathing machine. If we hadn't, he would have died. I hope that's what you wanted."

"Yes!" I reply. *Of course that's what I wanted. What sort of a world do we live in where a doctor has to ask a woman if it's all right that he saved her beloved husband's life?*

Altogether, between the two hospitals, we spend seventeen days in the ICU together. He is hooked up to a respirator and sedated to the point of unconsciousness most of the time. I sit by his bedside. On our little wing of the ICU at the California Pacific Medical Center, there are seven little rooms. Only four are occupied. We are in Room 302. As far as I can tell, Walter is the only patient who's been here four days. People come and go rapidly here. The diagnosis has been confirmed: the cancer has gone to his brain.

On Christmas Eve at 3:30 P.M., I am in the room alone. Walter and his bed are gone. The orderlies have wheeled him away to get an MRI on his brain. The room is empty except for a few machines, three pillows piled on a trash can, a tray table, and a tree of Walter's IV bags. The only bag I recognize is a clear upside-down bottle of brown muck that passes for food. A respirator machine with blue and white tubes hisses quietly in the corner.

In the next room, a woman is groaning. The walls here are those collapsible walls that open and close like an accordion. From various rooms come the sounds of machines measuring people's vital sounds. *Beep, beep, bing! bing! bing!*

I look down at my hands and observe Walter's gold wedding ring on my right middle finger. When we arrived here, the nurses asked my permission to remove his ring to keep it from cutting off Walter's circulation should his fingers swell. Since our wedding day forty years ago, this is the first time the ring has been off his finger. The gold is covered with little dings, nicks, and scratches from a lifetime of hard work. I envision Walter always busy on some new project: hammering nails to build a giant tree house for Dustin and Erin when they were kids, sawing boards to build me a little room of my own as a study, replacing the motor in our old Datsun when we were too broke to buy a new car or get it fixed by a mechanic. All the big and little sacrifices Walter made out of love for our children and for me are etched into this gold band.

When Walter is wheeled back into Room 302, he's still sedated and unconscious, although the nurses tell me he can hear me when I talk to him. I pray continuously at his bedside from 4:30 to 10:30 P.M. I pray for his complete healing from brain cancer, or for God's mercy on his soul if this is his time to pass on. As I pray, a "shock of peace" runs through me. There's no other way to explain it. Peace of mind in this dark hour so startles me, it comes as a sweet shock. Gratitude mysteriously fills my heart with reverent wonder and a strange new sort of joy. I do not see death winning here, but death being defeated.

I know Walter agrees. In late June, a week or so after he'd been diagnosed with cancer, we were sitting on the deck of our log cabin under the giant redwoods, sipping cappuccino. Walter hadn't spoken to me at all about his cancer, and I feared he was in denial and he might need to talk. "You know, Sweetheart," I said gently, "you do have cancer. What if you die?"

Walter gave me that quirky little half-smile of his, as if we were sharing a secret, and replied, "Aren't you looking forward to dying—just a little?"

It took me a second to grasp the full significance of what he'd said. Then it hit me: his faith in Christ's Resurrection was so strong that for him death was just another new adventure in *life*.

I smiled. "Well . . . maybe just *a little*."

That said, we fell silent and went on sipping our cappuccinos.

Now as we sit here in the ICU awaiting the cry of a newborn Baby who will make all things new, the mystery of His virgin birth speaks to my heart more deeply than it ever has when I was home surrounded by candies, tinsel, and presents under the tree. I realize we await, not the gift of a cell phone or a new computer, but the gift of Christ Himself, who comes to us on this Bethlehem night not as a powerful tyrant with a thousand armies at His command but as a sweet little baby you can hold in your arms and love.

As I take Walter's hand, a song rises in my heart, and to my surprise, I suddenly find myself singing:

> Joy to the world,
> The Lord is come,
> Let earth receive her King!

Love for God and others, including love for the little person in the womb, is what gives meaning to life, even in the midst of pain and suffering. This is the unseen dimension of women's lives that the

Mere Fifty-Seven overlooked when they created an anti-relationship, pro-abortion political agenda that overfocused on work, economic status, and power while severing sex from love.

On Christmas morning, I attend an early Mass at Saint Dominic's Catholic Church on Bush Street. Inside the beautiful neo-Gothic structure, graced with stained-glass windows and statuary, the liturgy with its prayers and Christmas carols gives me some sacred time away from the ICU to regain my bearings. In his homily, a fat, joyful, red-haired priest who could pass for Saint Nick tells us to look for unexpected gifts—gifts of wonder from God that always come to us in surprising new ways.

Saint Dominic's is situated within easy walking distance of the med center. As I walk along the streets of San Francisco under a bright blue Christmas sky, I ask myself what new and wondrous gift God might be giving me right now, and it strikes me: He's giving me His peace! The deep calm I felt last night and now again today can only be explained as *His* peace, the peace that passes all understanding.

Back in the ICU, our nurse Mandy tells me the doctors' worst fears—that Walter's kidneys might fail—haven't materialized. His kidneys are working just fine. Another wondrous gift! I love Mandy and all the other nurses we've met. Here in the ICU, we belong to each other. No one here is alone. This place is absolutely brimming with Good Samaritans: nurses, doctors, priests, ministers, brothers, sisters, parents, children, and friends. People have filled this place with compassion and mercy. I pray that Walter lives. But should he die, in this blessed ICU, it will not be because nobody cared. As all creation celebrates a tiny Infant's birth from timelessness into time, we are surrounded by an army of love.

I sing, "O Come All Ye Faithful" and "God Rest Ye Merry Gentlemen" to Walter. Even through the sedation meds, he tries to open his eyes. More good news!

Mandy has worked two twelve-hour shifts: one on Christmas Eve and this one on Christmas Day. Like me, she is exhausted. Toward the end of her shift, I give her a hug.

"It's sort of like sharing a foxhole together, isn't it?" I say.

We have an encounter of the eyes that speaks deeper than words. "Yes," she replies.

Time passes differently here in the ICU than it does in ordinary life. You waste days, weeks, even years, of your life. Then when it comes to this moment, you don't have ten minutes left. No matter what you did or didn't do in your life, there's nothing more you can fix. Years of waste, followed by not ten minutes to spare. I wouldn't say the ICU is timeless. Rather, it's a place beyond time, where all the hustling and bustling busyness of life has no meaning. As you try to cling to every second, time slips through your fingers, and you suddenly discover a whole day has passed. In the ICU, there is no yesterday or today. There is only now.

On the fourth day of Christmas (December 28), Walter is moved to a new room. At dawn, I open the window blinds in Walter's new room, and we watch the sunrise together. The sunrise in San Francisco turns the tall buildings across the street all peachy and pink. As the dawn explodes into a bright new day, Walter closes his eyes.

On the same day, toward dusk, he again opens his eyes. They are perfectly calm. For all the suffering he has endured, his face looks peaceful and radiant, as if lit by an interior light.

In this ICU, good news and bad news always come side by side. One minute Walter seems to take a turn for the better, and I'm certain he'll make it, and we'll one day walk out of this place. The next minute, he seems to take a turn for the worse. Walter is a novelist, artist, and poet, who has always said love is the glue that holds the universe together. Leaning over the bed rail, I softly whisper in his ear, "You were right, Walter. At last I understand what you meant when you said love is the glue that holds the universe together. If we paid attention to what's said by every doctor and nurse who walks into this room, we'd go crazy. The only thing that never changes is love. Anchored in love, we can handle anything."

I stop talking and sit silently at his side as we watch the sunset together. On the buildings across the way, fiery splashes of red, gold, and rose change like a kaleidoscope, shifting into lavender. Right before it dies, the sunlight explodes in a burst of flame, like the splash of brilliant fall foliage on the trees in New England. Then all the colors slowly fade into gray and are gone. There is something about this particular sunset that is beyond time, as if all the sunsets we've ever watched together are rolled into one. As night falls over San Francisco, Walter once again closes his eyes. I tenderly give him a kiss. He woke up today for both the sunrise and the sunset. What a precious day this has been. I fall joyfully asleep at 5:15 P.M., no dinner needed.

For the next three days, Walter doesn't open his eyes. I witness not even a flutter. On the seventh day of Christmas, on New Year's Eve, I decide I will try to wake him up. Early in our marriage, we created a secret signal: three hand squeezes. Squeeze-*I*, squeeze-*love*, squeeze-*you*. It's a private signal we have used everywhere—at boring dinner parties, on crowded subways, in bed at night before drifting off to sleep. I frequently thought this silent hand signal of ours would come in handy at a moment like this, if one of us ever wanted to communicate but could no longer speak.

Over and over, I send our private signal, repeatedly squeezing Walter's hand three times:

I-love-you.

I-love-you.

I-love-you.

I receive no hand squeezes in return. This tells me only one thing: on some deep, wordless level, Walter is unable to respond.

So I sing to him. Since it's New Year's Eve, I try a rendition of *"Auld Lang Syne."*

I am no great singer. I tell Walter, "Sorry, Sweetie, you've got the poor man's choir here. But this is the best I can do."

As midnight nears, I switch to prayers and hymns.

> *Tantum ergo, Sacramentum.*
> *Veneremur cernui.*
> *Et antiquum documentum*
> *Novo cedat ritui.*
> *Praestet fides supplementum,*
> *Sensuum defectui.**

I watch the clock on the wall as the second hand clicks to midnight. As the rest of the nation shoots off fireworks, pops champagne corks, and watches the ball drop in Times Square, the ICU remains silent.

---

*Down in adoration falling / This great Sacrament we hail. / Over ancient forms of worship / Newer rites of grace prevail. / Faith will tell us Christ is present / When our human senses fail.

A few minutes pass. Suddenly, the monitor measuring Walter's blood pressure begins to go wild. The numbers on the monitor shoot up to 224 over 98, then plunge to 120 over 50. Up-down, up-down, every minute or so like a roller coaster. He's breathing heavily. I rush from the room to tell our nurse what's happening, and she calls the respiratory therapist on the phone.

Minutes drag by. No one comes. Walter's blood pressure is soaring and plunging. I become frantic.

Up until now, I have been Little Miss Patience in the ICU. I have quietly left the ICU when the nurses asked me to leave. I have gone to stand patiently in the corner of the hospital room when the doctors come in, making their rounds. These medical specialists know what they're doing. I have worked diligently to stay out of everyone's way and not be a pest.

This is serious. I can no longer sit still. I rush out onto the ICU floor and grab the nearest doctor on duty, a man in a white coat who towers over me by more than a foot. "You must come. You must come and look at this—right now!" I demand.

As I lead him back into the room, I hastily explain, "I don't know what's going on. He's not breathing right."

The respiratory therapist arrives. Walter's breathing is spiking higher and higher.

I stand helplessly in a corner of the room to get out of everyone's way.

The doctor towers at the foot of Walter's bed, intently watching what's going on.

"Is he dying?" I ask softly.

All the doctor's confident self-assurance vanishes, and he visibly slumps. He humbly replies, "I don't know."

I love him for his integrity. We have reached the end of medical science and are on the precipice of mystery, and this man in white is wise enough to know it.

Several more doctors rush in. They say Walter appears to be bleeding in the stomach and possibly in the brain. I am asked to leave the room. I obey. Seemingly out of nowhere, an entire emergency team appears. They take Walter off his breathing machine and rush him past me on a gurney out of the ICU. I don't know where they're going.

I sink to the floor in a corner of the hall of the ICU. In wordless grief, tears stream down my cheeks.

Within seconds, the whole team reappears in the ICU with Walter on the gurney and rush him past me back to his room. Someone informs me Walter stopped breathing, and they need to get him back on the respiratory machine right away.

I stand alone outside his room as everyone frantically works on him.

"Are you his wife?" The question comes from a kindly ICU doctor I've never seen before.

"Yes."

"You know," he says gently, "we could take him down and x-ray his stomach and try to stop the bleeding. We could do a lot of procedures. But we reach a point when we're not doing anyone any favors."

"I know."

"I want you to remember something very important. When you go home, I don't want you looking back on this, thinking you made a life-or-death decision here. Because you didn't." They are words spoken to me by a stranger. And yet they are perhaps the kindest words ever spoken to me in my life.

I nod. "I know," I say softly. "Because even if we could get all his vital signs stabilized again, he still has brain cancer, and it already stopped him from breathing once, and now twice."

"Right," the doctor replies. He hands me his card. He is no longer a stranger. "We will take him off all his medications (he's referring to the blood thinner, the insulin, and any others—not life support). Then we will close off the room with a curtain, so you can be alone with him."

"Thank you."

I go into Walter's room and sit by his side. I hold his hand. A technician is standing there, turning off the machines. One stupid machine just won't stop bleeping. *Bleep-bleep-bleep-bleep.* I feel a deep loathing for these irritating, noisy machines. I wish it would stop. Finally, the technician manages to get it turned off.

Walter's eyes are open and clear. All this excitement has jolted him awake. He looks directly at me. His eyes are filled with light and peace.

"I love you so dearly, Walter. You know that. You know how much I love you." I kiss him. "You are my treasure, my sweetheart, the joy of my life."

He can't answer, of course, because he still has the breathing tube in his throat. I pray, "Our Father, who art in heaven . . ."

Walter peacefully closes his eyes.

The technician is still in the room, standing quietly by the machines. I ask, "Is he dead?"

"No," he says, showing me a blue line of life—his heartbeat on a machine.

One last thin ray of hope for a miracle healing rises within me. I lean over and whisper in Walter's ear, "Wouldn't it be funny if they took you off all the machines, and you just kept going? Five years from now, we would laugh and laugh about this."

But, of course, he doesn't keep on going. Within seconds, he departs and goes to God. I give him one last, tender kiss.

Then I rise from the chair and walk out of the room. Many people are standing there: doctors, nurses, technicians. One nurse is crying. I think someone hugged me. I don't really remember. I only remember waiting for some person to come and verify the time of death, being handed some forms to sign, and being given Walter's belongings: his watch, his trench coat, and his house slippers.

A security guard offers to drive me back to the Cathedral Hill Hotel, where I took a room in which I have seldom stayed. I gratefully accept his kind offer. I am astonishingly calm. The peace I feel is the peace that passes all understanding. It is God's grace. He has been with us through it all, even to this moment.

As I leave, the doctor who gave me his card compassionately asks, "How are you doing?

"Okay," I calmly reply. "We were married forty joyous, beautiful years. I'm not going to diminish them now by complaining and moaning because it's over."

Walter died shortly after midnight on the Eighth Day of Christmas. The Eighth Day is that day without an evening, that mystical day of the week, which doesn't appear on the calendar, when Christ rises from the tomb and makes all things new. The Eighth Day is that day beyond time of fresh new beginnings—for Walter, for me, and for us all.

Acknowledgments

With warmest gratitude to Dustin, Jen, Father David Anderson, and all the beautiful people at St. Peter Eastern Catholic Mission. Without your love and your prayers, this book could not have been written.

* * * * *

Grateful acknowledgment is hereby made for the use of the following copyrighted materials:

Passages from *The Feminine Mystique* by Betty Friedan. Copyright © 1983, 1974, 1973, 1963 by Betty Friedan. Used by permission of W. W. Norton & Company, Inc.

Passages from *Propaganda* by Edward Bernays © 1928, 2005. Used by permission of Anne Bernays.

Passages from *The Paradox of Choice* by Barry Schwartz © 2004. Used by permission of Barry Schwartz.

Passages from William Faulkner's speech at the Nobel Banquet at the City Hall in Stockholm, December 10, 1950. Used by permission of The Nobel Foundation.

Passages from *Poustinia: Encountering God in Silence, Solitude and Prayer* by Catherine Doherty © 1993, 2000. Used by permission of Madonna House Publications.

Lyrics from "On the Road Again", words and music by Willie Nelson. © 1980 Full Nelson Music, Inc. All rights controlled and administered by EMI Longitude Music. All rights reserved international copyright secured. Used by permission. Reprinted by permission of Hal Leonard Corporation.

Endnotes

Chapter 1: The Inside Witness

[1] DeNeen L. Brown, "First Person Singular: Sometimes, It Is About You," *Telling True Stories*, eds. Mark Kramer and Wendy Call (New York: Plume, 2007), 83.

[2] Chris Welles, "Helen Gurley Brown Turns Editor—Soaring Success of the Iron Butterfly," *Life*, November 19, 1965, 72.

[3] Lawrence Lader, *Abortion II: Making the Revolution* (Boston: Beacon, 1973), vii.

[4] Ibid., viii.

[5] Mark Crispin Miller, introduction to *Propaganda*, by Edward Bernays (originally published in 1928; Brooklyn: Ig Publishing, 2005), 26. Miller writes, "In all such cases, the investigative journalist is the propagandist's natural enemy, as the former serves the public interest, while the latter tends to work against it."

[6] Sue Ellen Browder, "Kinsey's Secret: The Phony Science of the Sexual Revolution," *Crisis Magazine*, May 28, 2012, www.crisismagazine.com/2012/kinseys-secret-the -phony-science-of-the-sexual-revolution (accessed July 22, 2014).

[7] Konrad Kellen, introduction to *Propaganda: The Formation of Men's Attitudes*, by Jacques Ellul (New York: Vintage, 1965), v.

[8] Ibid.

[9] Janann Sherman, ed., *Interviews with Betty Friedan* (Jackson, Miss.: University Press of Mississippi, 2002), xiii.

Chapter 2: The Problem That Had No Name

[1] Betty Friedan, *The Feminine Mystique* (originally published in 1963; New York: Norton, 2001), 15.

[2] Ibid., 20.

[3] Ibid., 22.

[4] Ibid., 21.

[5] Ibid., 31.

[6] Ibid., 20–21.

[7] Ibid., 31.

[8] Ibid., 33.

[9] Dick West, "Poor Stein—Alone at a Hen Luncheon," *Oakland Tribune*, June 3, 1963, 19. Stein, in return, agreed that "it's wrong to try to convince every woman that she will find fulfillment in having babies and baking bread." But he said, "It's equally

wrong to try to convince every woman that she will find fulfillment in practicing a profession or pursuing a career."

[10] *Cosmopolitan* in the 1950s and early 1960s was a general-interest magazine, not all that popular, and Mother didn't subscribe to it.

[11] Friedan, *Feminine Mystique*, 344.

[12] Ibid., 364.

[13] Caroline Bird, *Born Female: The High Cost of Keeping Women Down* (New York: Pocket Books, 1969), 82.

[14] Lader, *Abortion II*, 39.

[15] Daly, a lesbian, later argued against equality, believing that women should govern men. She also wrote and published *Beyond God the Father: Toward a Philosophy of Women's Liberation* (1973).

[16] This quote from Thomas Merton appears on many editions of Daly's book.

[17] Later to be called the National Assembly of Religious Women. In *Ungodly Rage* (San Francisco: Ignatius, 1991), journalist Donna Steichen reports the "characteristic temper" of this group "was exemplified at the 1983 convention in Chicago, where members boosted their spirits by singing, 'I have a fury deep inside my very soul. I will not live forever on my knees. Waves of hate wash over me and wash me clean of fear'" (314).

[18] These words are taken from the book *Hidden and Triumphant: The Underground Struggle to Save Russian Iconography*. In that book, the author, Irina Yazykova, was not referring to the United States in 1968. She was referring to Russia in the year 1917.

[19] Paul Johnson, *Modern Times Revised Edition: The World from the Twenties to the Nineties* (New York: HarperCollins, 2001), 613.

[20] J. Francis Cardinal Stafford, "The Year of the Peirasmòs—1968," *Catholic News Agency*, http://www.catholicnewsagency.com/resources/life-and-family/humanae-vitae/the-year-of-the-peirasms-1968/ (accessed March 1, 2013).

[21] After college, my former roommate must have thought twice about rejecting the teachings of the faith, because I later heard by way of the grapevine that she and her husband had six children.

[22] Unfortunately, in suffering side effects from the original high-dose Pill, I was hardly alone. Women's magazine freelance writer Barbara Seaman launched the women's health revolution when, in her book *The Doctors' Case Against the Pill*, she revealed over fifty potential side effects of the Pill, ranging from blood clots, infertility, and breast cancer to irritability and depression. In early 1970, Seaman's revelations sparked a U.S. Senate hearing—the Nelson Pill Hearings. Angry young women repeatedly disrupted the hearings, demanding to know why female patients weren't testifying and why there was no pill for men. As a result of the Nelson Pill Hearings, drug companies were forced to place a health warning to patients on oral contraceptives, the first informational insert on any prescription drug. But Seaman, who earned her living as a magazine writer, would pay a steep career price for this victory. In the 1980s, she would be blacklisted from magazines by powerful pharmaceutical companies who refused to advertise in publications that carried her stories. Magazines that would no longer publish her articles included *Ladies' Home Journal, Family Circle, Omni*, and *Hadassah*. See http://en.wikipedia.org/wiki/Barbara_Seaman.

[23] G. S. Perry, "Los Angeles," *Saturday Evening Post*, December 15, 1945, 14.

[24] Bill Kovach and Tom Rosenstiel, *The Elements of Journalism: What Newspeople Should Know and the Public Should Expect* (New York: Crown, 2001), 11.

[25] Betty Friedan, *Life So Far* (originally published in 2000; paperback edition, New York: Simon & Schuster, 2006), 79.

[26] Betty Friedan, *It Changed My Life* (New York: Random House, 1976), 94.

[27] Sherman, *Interviews with Betty Friedan*, 108.

[28] Ibid., 92.

[29] Michael Shelden, "Behind the Feminine Mystique," *London Daily Telegraph*, August 9, 1999; available in Sherman, *Interviews with Betty Friedan*, 191.

[30] Ibid.

[31] Friedan, *Life So Far*, 77–78.

[32] Daniel Horowitz, *Betty Friedan and the Making of the Feminine Mystique* (Amherst: University of Massachusetts Press, 1998), 46, see also footnote 15 on 273.

[33] Friedan, *It Changed My Life*, 83.

[34] Friedan, *Feminine Mystique*, 338.

[35] Betty Friedan, *The Second Stage* (originally published in 1981; paperback edition, New York: Dell, 1991), 305.

Chapter 3: Making Up a Revolution

[1] Helen Gurley Brown, *Sex and the Single Girl* (originally published in 1962; paperback edition, New York: Pocket Books, 1963), 3.

[2] Ruth Rosen, *The World Split Open: How the Modern Women's Movement Changed America* (New York: Penguin, 2000), 319.

[3] Jennifer Scanlon, *Bad Girls Go Everywhere: The Life of Helen Gurley Brown* (Oxford: Oxford University Press, 2009), 184.

[4] Ibid., 185. Originally from text of television show, July 24, 1991, from the Helen Gurley Brown Papers, housed in the Sophia Smith Collection at Smith College, Northampton, Mass.

[5] Scanlon, *Bad Girls Go Everywhere*, 185.

[6] Brown, *Sex and the Single Girl*, 3–4.

[7] Ibid., 20.

[8] Tom Smith, "American Sexual Behavior: Trends, Socio-Demographic Differences, and Risk Behavior," National Opinion Research Center, General Social Survey Report, March 2006, 5.

[9] Margaret Sanger, *The Pivot of Civilization* (originally published in 1922; Amherst, N.Y.: Humanity Books, 2003), 251.

[10] Ibid., 254.

[11] "When He Doesn't Want Sex" was just one of the first of many articles published in women's magazines that pointed to the unspoken reality that when sex is too self-focused, passion—and interest—fades.

[12] *Cosmopolitan*, March 1976.

[13] *Cosmopolitan*, June 1984.

[14] We could argue about how "creative" it was.

[15] James Landers, *The Improbable First Century of Cosmopolitan Magazine* (Columbia, Mo.: University of Missouri Press, 2010), 225, 271–72. Helen's first issue was July 1965.

[16] Scanlon, *Bad Girls Go Everywhere*, 220.

[17] Kurt Vonnegut Jr., *Mother Night* (New York: Avon, 1967), v.

[18] Welles, "Helen Gurley Brown Turns Editor," 72.

[19] Ibid.

Chapter 4: The Deceiver Becomes the Deceived

[1] Bernard Nathanson, *The Hand of God: A Journey from Death to Life by the Abortion Doctor Who Changed His Mind* (Washington, D.C.: Regnery, 1996), 86.

[2] Lawrence Lader, *Ideas Triumphant: Strategies for Social Change and Progress* (Santa Ana, Calif.: Seven Locks Press, 2003), 99.

[3] Ibid., 102.

[4] Ibid., 103.

[5] Lader, *Abortion II*, viii.

[6] See http://americanhumanist.org/Humanism/Humanist_Manifesto_II (accessed July 24, 2014).

[7] Friedan, *Life So Far*, 233.

[8] Nathanson, *The Hand of God*, 87.

[9] Moore had picked up the Malthusian idea from a book, *The Road to Survival* (1948), by William Vogt, a director of Planned Parenthood Federation. Vogt's doomsday predictions so alarmed Moore he decided to make population control the sole concern of his life. As Steven Mosher of the Population Research Institute reports in *Population Control: Real Costs, Illusory Benefits* (New Bruswick, N.J.: Transaction, 2008), Moore was warned that Vogt wasn't a population expert—"'There is just enough truth in [Vogt's] book to make it dangerous,' Frank G. Boudreau of the Milbank Memorial Fund told him." Still, "Moore found Vogt's warning of imminent catastrophe credible anyway" (64).

Over a decade and a half, Mosher reports, Moore mailed one and a half million copies of his pamphlet "to every group of politicians, educators, officials, journalists and people of influence he could think of" (*Population Control*, 38).

Moore also took out full-page advertisements in the *New York Times*, *Washington Post*, *Wall Street Journal*, and *Time* magazine, running copy deliberately intended to shock. One ad, an open letter directed to President Richard Nixon, pictured a newborn baby and was headlined: *"Dear President Nixon: We can't lick the environment problem without considering this little fellow."* The caption beneath the baby's photo read: "Every 7½ seconds a new American is born. He is a disarming little thing, but he begins to scream loudly in a voice that can be heard for seventy years. He is screaming for 26,000,000 tons of water, 21,000 gallons of gasoline, 10,150 pounds of meat, 28,000 pounds of milk and cream, 9,000 pounds of wheat, and great storehouses of all other foods, drinks, and tobacco. These are his lifetime demands of his country and his economy." Therefore (the unspoken message), *don't let him be born.* There was nothing in this pessimistic advertisement about what a newborn baby might one day contribute positively to his country. In Moore's way of thinking, a fetus was as disposable as a paper cup.

In 1966, when the Catholic bishops called upon the faithful "to oppose, vigorously and by every democratic means, those campaigns already underway in some states and at the national level toward the active promotion, by tax-supported agencies, of birth prevention programs as a public policy, above all in connection with welfare benefit programs," Moore ran a full-page ad in the *New York Times*, lambasting the Church and headlining in huge bold type: "Catholic Bishops assail birth control as millions face starvation." For a detailed report of the highly successful Hugh Moore population-control campaign, see *Breeding Ourselves to Death: 30th Anniversary Edition*, by Lawrence Lader (Santa Ana, Calif.: Seven Locks Press, special edition printing, 2002).

[10] Hugh Moore, *The Population Bomb* (New York: Hugh Moore Fund, 1954.)

[11] Steven Mosher, *Population Control*, 37.

[12] Lader, *Breeding Ourselves to Death*, 1.

[13] Friedan, *Life So Far*, 200–201.

[14] Lader, *Ideas Triumphant*, 91.

[15] Bernard Nathanson with Richard Ostling, *Aborting America* (Toronto: Life Cycle Books, 1979), 32.

[16] Ibid.

[17] Ibid., 32–33.

[18] Ibid., 33.

[19] Ibid., 51.

[20] Ibid., 33.

[21] Ibid., 52.

[22] Ibid., 33.

[23] Ibid.

[24] Ibid.

[25] Ibid., 52.

[26] Ibid., 53.

[27] Noam Chomsky, *Media Control: The Spectacular Achievements of Propaganda*, 2nd ed. (New York: Seven Stories Press, 2002), 26.

[28] Lader, *Abortion II*, 20. Larry wrote, "Ironically, I would eventually split with Margaret over abortion—only in a theoretical sense since, by 1963, she was too ill to carry on our old discussions. Margaret had always opposed abortion. In her work as a nurse on Manhattan's Lower East Side around 1910, she would watch in horror the long lines of immigrant women, worn out by poverty and constant childbearing, waiting outside the offices of nonlicensed abortionists with five dollars clutched in their hands. The rate of injury, and even death, from this crude, underground surgery was frighteningly high. Margaret detested the waste and degradation of human life, and pleaded for contraception as a rational and humanitarian alternative."

[29] John T. Noonan Jr., *A Private Choice: Abortion in America in the Seventies* (New York: Free Press, 1979), 37.

[30] Lawrence Lader, *Abortion: The first authoritative and documented report on the laws and practices governing abortion in the U.S. and around the world, and how—for the sake of women everywhere—they can and must be reformed* (Indianapolis, Ind.: Bobbs-Merrill, 1966), 169.

[31] Pilpel was an attorney for Planned Parenthood of New York City and Planned Parenthood Federation of America. Ephraim London, a specialist in constitutional law, argued nine cases before the U.S. Supreme Court and won them all. His 1956 defense of the film version of D. H. Lawrence's *Lady Chatterley's Lover* struck down an essential

aspect of New York State's thirty-six-year-old film censorship system. The third legal
powerhouse in the trio, Cyril Means, was a NARAL attorney. In 1968, Means was
appointed by Governor Nelson Rockefeller to a commission to study New York State's
abortion laws and make recommendations for changes. New York was the first state to
legalize abortion.

   [32] Lader made much of the theological "ensoulment" debate that occurred among
some theologians during the Middle Ages. Since the medieval "ensoulment debate"
was the kernel of partial truth around which Lader wrapped his modern propagandistic
retelling of Catholicism, let's examine this question more closely.

   Some early Church Fathers argued "that if Jesus acquired a rational soul at the
moment of conception, and Jesus shares the same human nature as all other human
beings, then everyone acquires a rational soul at conception." This was the position of
Saint Maximus the Confessor (ca. 580–662), who said that although Jesus was conceived
miraculously in the womb of a Virgin, in his humanity he was no different from those
of us conceived in the ordinary way. Saint Gregory of Nyssa (335–395) and Saint John
of Damascus (645–749) also held to this early Church doctrine that all humans have souls
at conception.

   Other theologians, however, began to argue that since Jesus' conception was mirac-
ulous, it didn't necessarily follow that all human beings receive their souls at conception. The most influential theologian to believe the soul was "infused" into the human
embryo at some time later than conception was Saint Thomas Aquinas. He was probably
influenced by Aristotle's theory, popular in universities during the Middle Ages, which
held that the soul developed in "stages" (vegetable, animal, human) and that the fetus
was not fully "formed" until forty days after conception for a male and eighty or ninety
days for a female. Aquinas made what David Albert Jones calls "a coherent and powerful argument for delayed ensoulment," which became dominant among theologians
during the Middle Ages. Aquinas also believed that the Lord was never an embryo, was
conceived as a fetus, and attained human perfection "not by making progress but by
possessing it from the first" (David Albert Jones, *The Soul of the Embryo* [London: Con-
tinuum, 2004], 124, 140).

   Lader claimed Saint Augustine also believed the fetus was "ensouled" only when fully
"formed," but this claim was only partly true. Saint Augustine expressed different views
in different writings. "Augustine remained uncertain," Jones observed, "and kept open
the possibility that the soul might be present from conception" (ibid., 123).

   In the argument that so influenced the Supreme Court, Lader ignored the early
Church Fathers and made much of Aquinas. But Jones states that Aquinas' idea that Jesus
was exceptional at receiving his soul at conception is plausible "only to the extent that
other claims about [Jesus'] humanity are plausible" (that Christ was never an embryo,
was conceived as a fetus, and possessed human perfection from the first). "From a
modern perspective," Jones observes, "the account of Jesus in the womb outlined by
Maximus the Confessor is far more satisfactory than that given by Thomas Aquinas and
other medievals" (ibid., 140).

   The essential problem with the "ensoulment" concept is that it implies a soul-body
dualism, in which the human body and soul are separate. As Father John Breck writes
in *The Sacred Gift of Life* (Crestwood, N.Y.: Saint Vladimir's Seminary Press, 1998),
Eastern Christianity would "take issue with the ... doctrine of ensoulment, at least as

it has been expressed in Aristotelian and Thomistic terms" (140). "Language such as 'ensoulment,' 'infusion of an immaterial rational soul,' or simply 'a principle of immaterial individuality or selfhood,' sounds dualistic to Orthodox ears.... From an Eastern patristic (and biblical) perspective, the soul or *nephesh* constitutes the very personhood of the individual. Accordingly one may properly affirm, 'I *am* a soul,' rather than 'I *have* a soul'" (ibid., 140).

The age-old ensoulment debate, Breck observes, "appears to be grounded [not in a defective theology but] in a defective anthropology, one which views the material body as animated by a rational soul created separately from it and infused into it at fertilization, at implantation, or at some subsequent stage in its development" (ibid., 140).

33 Johannes Quasten and Joseph Plumpe, eds., *The Didache*, no. 6 in *Ancient Christian Writers* series (New York: Newman Press, 1948), 16.

34 Joseph Dellapenna, *Dispelling the Myths of Abortion History* (Durham, N.C.: Carolina Academic Press, 2006), 13.

35 Ibid., ix.

36 Ibid., 14.

37 Ibid., 14–15.

38 Bernard Nathanson, "Confessions of an Ex-Abortionist"; pamphlet obtained personally at the Path to Rome Conference held at the Hilton Phoenix East/Mesa in Phoenix, Arizona, November 5–7, 2004. Nathanson was a speaker at the conference.

39 Ibid.

40 Ibid.

41 Even today, forty years later, historians, journalists, and politicians continue to point to Lader's false statistics as solid reasons why current abortion laws should remain on the books and abortion should in no way be restricted. For instance, in a work published in 2007, Harvard-educated legal scholar Cass Sunstein wrote, "Studies suggest that in the 1960s, there were 1.0 to 1.5 million abortions in the United States each year" (*What Roe v. Wade Should Have Said: The Nation's Top Legal Experts Rewrite America's Most Controversial Decision*, ed. Jack M. Balkin [New York and London: New York University Press, 2005], 150). Once a fabricated statistic works its way into reliable sources, it's almost impossible to weed it out. Sunstein cited the same figure in *California Law Review* (May 1991): 766.

42 Friedan, *Life So Far*, 200.

Chapter 5: A Fly on the Wall of the Chinese Room

1 Friedan, *Life So Far*, 204.

2 Originally from an article in *McCalls*, May 1971; quoted in Lader, *Abortion II*, 37.

3 Lader, *Abortion II*, 37.

4 Judith Paterson, *Be Somebody: A Biography of Marguerite Rawalt* (Austin, Tex.: Eakin, 1986), 71. Paterson personally interviewed Marguerite Rawalt, Betty Boyer, and a number of other women who attended the NOW Conference in the Chinese Room in the Mayflower Hotel on November 18, 1967.

5 Lader, *Abortion II*, 37–38.

[6] Paterson, *Be Somebody*, xvi.

[7] Ibid., 62.

[8] Ibid., 160.

[9] Lader, *Abortion II*, 38.

[10] Judith Hennessee, *Betty Friedan: Her Life* (New York: Random House, 1999), 111.

[11] Ibid., 93.

[12] Paterson, *Be Somebody*, 70.

[13] Ibid., 146.

[14] Ibid., 132.

[15] Ibid., 68.

[16] Author's interview with attorney Mary Eastwood (January 24, 2014), who along with Catherine East was largely responsible for encouraging Betty Friedan to start NOW.

[17] Paterson, *Be Somebody*, 180.

[18] Pauli Murray, resignation letter to Kathryn Clarenbach, November 21, 1967, Schlesinger Library, Catherine East papers, series IX, folder 26.52.

[19] Ibid.

[20] Paterson, *Be Somebody*, 177.

[21] Ibid., 181.

[22] Lader, *Abortion II*, 37.

[23] For the minutes of the meeting and a more complete transcription of the controversy, go to: http://350fem.blogs.brynmawr.edu/1967/11/19/national-conference-of-now-minutes (accessed September 3, 2014).

[24] Paterson, *Be Somebody*, 182.

[25] Ibid., 179.

[26] Ti-Grace Atkinson, "Resignation from N.O.W." and "Catholic University," in *Amazon Odyssey: The First Collection of the Writings by the Political Pioneer of the Women's Movement* (New York: Links Books, 1974), 9–11 and 190–97.

[27] Eastwood interview.

[28] All quotations come from the transcribed minutes of the meeting, http://350fem.blogs.brynmawr.edu/1967/11/19/national-conference-of-now-minutes.

[29] Friedan, *Life So Far*, 206.

[30] Paterson, *Be Somebody*, 181.

[31] Ibid., 186.

[32] Ibid., 182.

[33] Ibid., 181. This and other information about the founder of WEAL come from Paterson's personal interviews with Betty Boyer in Marguerite Rawalt's apartment in Arlington, Virginia, on April 30, 1983.

[34] Ibid., 185–86.

[35] Judith Hole and Ellen Levine, *Rebirth of Feminism* (New York: Quadrangle, a New York Times company, 1971), 95–98; also author's interview with Patricia Bliss-Egan, Betty Boyer's niece and head of the WEAL Foundation in Rocky River, Ohio.

[36] Marguerite Rawalt papers, Schlesinger Library, series V, folder 25.26.

[37] Friedan, *Life So Far*, 206.

[38] Betty Friedan, November 20, 1967, NOW press release regarding second annual national conference, Feminist Majority Foundation, accessed October 19, 2014, http://www.feminist.org/research/chronicles/early4.html.

[39] "NOW Is Out of Kitchen—Stresses Abortion Reform," *Washington Post*, November 21, 1967, C1–C2.

[40] Lader, *Abortion II*, xi.

[41] Ibid., 88–89.

[42] For a detailed, eye-opening description of this conference, see *Aborting America*, by Bernard Nathanson with Richard Ostling (Toronto: Life Cycle Books, 1979), 34ff.

[43] Lader, *Ideas Triumphant*, 106.

[44] Ibid., 107.

[45] Linda Charlton, "Women Seeking Equality March on 5th Ave. Today," *New York Times*, August 26, 1970, 44.

[46] Ibid.

[47] Friedan, *Life So Far*, 215.

[48] Friedan, *Beyond Gender* (Washington, D.C.: Woodrow Wilson Center Press, 1997), 7.

[49] Paula Gribetz Gottlieb, "My Side: Betty Friedan," *Working Woman*, February 1982, 130–32; quoted in Sherman, *Interviews with Betty Friedan*, 55.

[50] Pamela Marsh, "Betty Friedan Calls for Less Abrasiveness, More Emphasis on the Family," *Christian Science Monitor*, October 28, 1981, article on Friedan's *The Second Stage* (New York: Summit Books, 1981).

Chapter 6: Good-bye to Glamour

[1] When Helen was editor, Scavullo shot 95 percent of the cover photographs for *Cosmopolitan*.

[2] The "New Age" would soon become associated with astrology, tarot cards, pyramidology, numerology, and other such forms of superstition. As the writing progressed, Workman urged me to insert astrology and numerology charts into the book, which I dutifully did. The "new age" to me at that time vaguely meant an age when prejudice and fear would at last melt away and people of all races, nationalities, and creeds would live side by side in mutual respect, understanding, and peace. Thus, "The Third-World Baby Name Book" slowly morphed into *The New Age Baby Name Book* (and I even claimed at one point that I—and not the publisher—had given it that title). I thereby claimed "ownership" of the idea for the book when it was not my idea, and I was never truly what became popularly known as a "new ager." This is the sort of thing that can happen in publishing when one writes someone else's ideas on demand just for the money.

Chapter 7: Philosophy of a Little Gray Man

[1] Hennessee, *Betty Friedan*, 81.

[2] Paul Vitz, *Psychology as Religion: The Cult of Self-Worship* (Grand Rapids, Mich.: Eerdmans, 1995).

[3] A. H. Maslow, *The Farther Reaches of Human Nature* (New York: Viking Compass Edition, 1971), 10.

[4] Edward Hoffman, *The Right to Be Human: A Biography of Abraham Maslow* (Los Angeles: Tarcher, 1988), 304.

[5] Ibid., 276.

[6] Ibid., 331.

[7] Maslow, *Farther Reaches*, 10.

[8] Ibid. These are themes that run throughout *Farther Reaches* and other books Maslow wrote.

[9] Ibid., 36.

[10] Thomas Dubay, *The Evidential Power of Beauty: Science and Theology Meet* (San Francisco: Ignatius, 1999), 241.

[11] Maslow, *Farther Reaches*, 7.

[12] Germaine Greer, *The Female Eunuch* (New York: Bantam, 1971), 254–55, 258.

Chapter 8: Harry's Dilemma

[1] Linda Greenhouse, *Becoming Justice Blackmun* (New York: Times Books, paperback edition, 2006), 3, 5–7, 14–15.

[2] Ibid., 8.

[3] Library of Congress, Blackmun Papers, box 1376, folder 11, from "A Eulogy for My Father's Memorial Service," by Nancy Blackmun, given at the Metropolitan Memorial United Methodist Church, Washington D.C., March 9, 1999.

[4] Bob Woodward and Scott Armstrong, *The Brethren: Inside the Supreme Court* (1979; New York: Simon & Schuster, paperback edition, 2005), 206.

[5] Ibid.

[6] Greenhouse, *Becoming Justice Blackmun*, 83. Greenhouse reports that Susan described this episode "in her father's presence, while addressing a dinner in his honor."

[7] Woodward and Armstrong, *The Brethren*, 220.

[8] Ibid.

[9] Ibid., 221–23.

[10] Meehan's well-researched article "Justice Blackmun and the Little People" is available at www.meehanreports.com/blackmun.html (accessed February 15, 2013).

[11] "Memorandum to the Conference," dated May 18, 1972. Blackmun Papers, box 151, folder 4.

[12] Blackmun Papers, box 1557, folder 10.

[13] Woodward and Armstrong, *The Brethren*, 275.

[14] Blackmun Papers, box 152, folder 8.

[15] Lader, *Abortion*, 1966.

[16] Blackmun Papers, "Footnotes: *Doe v. Bolton*, No. 70-40," box 152, folder 4.

[17] Blackmun Papers, box 152, folder 5.

[18] David J. Garrow, "The Brains Behind Blackmun," *Legal Affairs*, May/June 2005; available online at http://www.legalaffairs.org/issues/May-June-2005/feature_garrow_mayjun05.msp (accessed March 6, 2013).

[19] James Tunstead Burtchaell, *Rachel Weeping: The Case Against Abortion* (San Francisco: Harper & Row, 1982), 252.

[20] Ellul, *Propaganda*, 111.

[21] Ibid., vi.

[22] Greenhouse, *Becoming Justice Blackmun*, 135.

[23] Laurence Tribe, "The Supreme Court, 1972 Term—Foreword: Toward a Model of Roles in the Due Process of Life and Law," *Harvard Law Review* 87, no. 1 (1973): 7.

[24] Dennis Horan, Edward Grant, Paige Cunningham, eds., *Abortion and the Constitution: Reversing Roe v. Wade through the Courts* (Washington, D.C.: Georgetown University Press, 1987), 58.

[25] *The Washington Post*, February 6, 1974; Blackmun Papers, box 151, folder 9.

Chapter 9: Just Broke—Again

[1] Frank Herbert, *Dune* (Radnor, Penn.: Chilton, 1965), 8.

[2] Burtchaell, *Rachel Weeping*, 230.

Chapter 10: Two Roads Diverge

[1] Helen Gurley Brown, *The Writer's Rules* (New York: William Morrow, 1998), 84.

[2] Helen Gurley Brown, *I'm Wild Again* (New York: St. Martin's Press, 2000), 198.

[3] De Marco and Wiker, "Helen Gurley Brown," in *Architects of the Culture of Death*, 234–46.

[4] Cindy Osborne, "Pat Goltz, Catherine Callaghan, and the Founding of Feminists for Life," in Rachel MacNair, Mary Krane Derr, and Linda Naranjo-Huebl, eds., *ProLife Feminism: Yesterday and Today* (New York: Sulzburger & Graham, 1995), 151–52.

[5] Ibid., 152.

[6] Ann Crittenden, "A Colloquy on the Sanger Spirit," *New York Times*, September 18, 1979.

[7] Ibid.

[8] Gail Collins, *When Everything Changed: The Amazing Journey of American Women from 1960 to the Present* (New York: Little Brown, 2009), 234.

[9] "Feminist Chronicles—1979," Feminist Majority Foundation, accessed December 10, 2014, http://www.feminist.org/research/chronicles/fc1979.html.

[10] Nathanson, *The Hand of God*, 196.

Chapter 11: The New Woman Asks New Questions

[1] Mary Anne Dolan, "When Feminism Failed," *New York Times Magazine*, June 26, 1988.

[2] Kay Ebeling, "The Failure of Feminism," *Newsweek*, November 18, 1990.

[3] William Faulkner, Nobel Prize Banquet Speech (Stockholm, December 10, 1950), http://www.nobelprize.org/nobel_prizes/literature/laureates/1949/faulkner-speech .html.

[4] Ibid.

[5] M. Scott Peck, *People of the Lie: The Hope for Healing Human Evil* (New York: Touchstone, 1983), 222.

Chapter 12: From *Cosmo* to Cosmos (and Back Again)

[1] For a good review of the new physics, see *Quantum Enigma: Physics Encounters Consciousness*, by University of California at Santa Cruz physicists Bruce Rosenblum and Fred Kuttner (Oxford: Oxford University Press, 2011).

[2] Sir James Jeans, *The Mysterious Universe* (New York: Pelican Books, 1937 edition), 137.

[3] Fritjof Capra, *The Tao of Physics* (New York: Bantam, 1977), 228–29.

Chapter 14: Seventeen Minutes of Fame

[1] "Geraldo Rivera's Nose Broken in Scuffle on His Talk Show," *New York Times*, November 4, 1988.

[2] See http://grantland.com/hollywood-prospectus/remember-that-time-oprah-winfrey -leaked-old-footage-of-oprah-winfrey-on-the-oprah-winfrey-show/.

Chapter 15: Our Nightmare in Cerritos

[1] Henry Raymont, "Steinbeck's Letters Will Be a Book," *New York Times*, June 2, 1969, 52.

[2] Virginia Rutter, "Bad Girl," *Psychology Today*, March–April 1994, 22.

[3] "Helen Gurley Brown," *Vanity Fair*, August 2007.

[4] "Manichaeism," in *The Encyclopedia of Religion*, ed. Mircea Eliade, volume 9 (New York: Macmillan, 1987), 161–63.

[5] Ibid.

[6] Henry Dieterich, *Through the Year with Fulton Sheen* (San Francisco: Ignatius, 2003).

Chapter 16: Two Monks in Corona

[1] De Marco and Wiker, *Architects of the Culture of Death*, 246.

[2] Vivian Yee, "When Prince of Church Hugged Queen of Cosmopolitan," *New York Times*, August 15, 2012.

Chapter 17: Lessons under the Redwoods

[1] Frederica Mathewes-Green, *Real Choices: Listening to Women; Looking for Alternatives to Abortion* (Ben Lomond, Calif.: Conciliar Press, 1997), 11.

[2] Aleksandr Solzhenitsyn, *The Gulag Archipelago* (New York: Harper & Row, 1973), 168.

Chapter 18: Finding Our Way to Freedom

[1] Fulton J. Sheen, *Life of Christ* (New York: Doubleday Religious, 2008), 36.

[2] *Catechism of the Catholic Church* (New York: Image, Doubleday, 1995), nos. 1431–32.

[3] Fear *per se*, of course, is not wrong. Father Reginald Garrigou-Lagrange writes: "It is not unfitting to tremble at times in the presence of God, but love must predominate. We must fear God filially through love, and not love Him through fear; therefore filial fear, that of sin, grows with charity, whereas servile fear, that of punishment, diminishes" (*The Three Ages of the Interior Life*, vol. 2 [Rockford, Ill.: TAN, 1989], 196).

Epilogue: Christmas in the ICU

[1] Alexander Schmemann writing of his experience at Johns Hopkins Medical Center as his wife underwent brain surgery, in *The Journals of Father Alexander Schmemann, 1973–1983* (Crestwood, New York: St. Vladimir's Seminary Press, 2000), 205.

INDEX